Divine Destiny

DIVINE DESTINY

Gender and Race in
Nineteenth-Century Protestantism

Carolyn A. Haynes

University Press of Mississippi *Jackson*

Library of Congress Cataloging-in-Publication Data

Haynes, Carolyn A.
Divine destiny : gender and race in nineteenth-century
Protestantism / Carolyn A. Haynes.
p.   cm.
Includes bibliographical references and index.
ISBN 1-57806-018-4 (hardcover : alk. paper)
1. Protestant churches — United States — History — 19th century.
2. Sex role — Religious aspects — Christianity — History — 19th century.
3. Race relations — Religious aspects — Christianity — History — 19th
century.   4. United States — Church history — 19th century.
5. Protestantism — History — 19th century.   I. Title.
BR515.H38   1998
280'.4'097309034 — dc21   97-29364
CIP

British Library Cataloging-in-Publication data available

For Martha F. Haynes and Nicole Tonkovich, two women who have interacted with Christianity and have helped to shape my identity in wonderfully different ways.

Contents

Acknowledgments

As the women and men examined in this book read, heard, contested, modified, and utilized one another's ideas, I too have benefited from the diverse and helpful thoughts, criticisms, and advice of many intelligent and supportive people. In particular, I would like to thank members of my two writing groups: Sheila Croucher, Lori Varlotta, Shawn Smith, and Molly Rhodes. Their longstanding friendships and their generous readings of and astute comments on various chapters of the book were invaluable. These pages also owe much to fruitful discussions with and the careful criticism of Robert Haynes, Peter Williams, Mark Pedelty, Curtis Ellison, Benjamin Bertram, Michael Davidson, Barbara Tomlinson, Kathryn Shevelow, and Rachel Klein. Moreover, without the unfailing enthusiasm of Catherine Haynes, Martha Haynes, Bo Platt, Karen Evans, Elyane Laussade, Claire Legas, Karen Miksch, Gail Della Piana, and Muriel Blaisdell, this project could never have been completed. Each of them has helped to foster the varying religious, feminist, and historical sides of myself. My editor, Seetha A-Srinivasan, has been supportive and patient throughout the project. Finally, to Wai Dimock and Nicole Tonkovich, whose critical care and warmth have immeasurably enhanced this book as well as many other aspects of my academic life, go my deepest gratitude.

Introduction

Many momentous social and political changes in the nineteenth-century United States — the expansion of the nation, the usurpation of native territory, the defense and abolition of slavery, and the ascendancy of the middle class — were undergirded by two separate but interrelated rhetorics: manifest destiny and domesticity. The rhetoric of manifest destiny predicted and celebrated a divinely ordained spread of democracy, individualism, capitalism, and civilization throughout the North American continent, while the rhetoric of domesticity codified "natural" differences and duties of American men and women. In this scheme, while a variety of activist and public roles were promoted for men, women were to exist within the private realm of domesticity, piety, and purity and to remain isolated from the tumultuous world of men, politics, and the marketplace. If women fulfilled their godly roles as devoted daughters, wives, and mothers, then men could devote their energies to a divinely sanctioned appropriation and control of the continent.

While the two rhetorics were touted as "universal" in their application and appeal, in actuality, both were firmly undergirded by a belief in masculine Anglo-Saxon American superiority. The triumph of the nation could only be accomplished through the concomitant removal, acculturation, or elimination of nonwhite peoples and through a careful circumscription of white women.

Not only were the rhetorics linked through a virulent ethnocentrism and misogyny, they also were connected through their reliance on the Protestant belief system and the Church itself.

This relationship between Protestantism and the rhetorics of manifest destiny and domesticity has posed a vexing problem for interpretation. On the one hand, nineteenth-century politicians, educators, historians, and ministers unabashedly called upon the Bible and some tenets of Protestantism to justify expansionist and separate-spheres notions. When arguing for the acquisition of the Oregon Territory, for example, John Quincy Adams described the U.S. mission: "To make the wilderness blossom as the rose, to establish laws, to increase, multiply and subdue the earth, which we are commanded to do by the first behest of God Almighty."[1] In 1822, a special committee advised the Board of the American Baptist Foreign Mission Society "to carry the gospel and the blessings of civilized life to the dark and distant regions of the west, until the rocky mountains shall resound with harmony and praise and the shores of the Pacific shall be the only boundary of this wide sweep of human civilization and Christian benevolence."[2] In 1893, Congregationalist minister Josiah Strong wondered if it were not reasonable to believe "that this race is destined to dispossess many weaker ones, assimilate others, and mould the remainder, until in a very true and important sense, it has Anglo-Saxonized mankind."[3] Using similar references to the Christian God, popular ministers such as George Burnap boldly invested their pronouncements on the proper behavior of women: "The God who made them knew the sphere in which each of them was designed to act, and he fitted them for it by their physical frames, by their intellectual susceptibilities, by their tastes and affections. . . . Woman despises in man every thing like herself except a tender heart. It is enough that she is effeminate and weak; and she does not want another like herself. Just so with man" (46–47). Not only was the land itself destined to a providential outcome, but each person in it was assigned to a set role that depended, among other factors, upon religion, race, and gender.

Despite the exclusionism of the Protestant rhetorics of manifest destiny and domesticity, the nineteenth century featured a remarkable growth in the conversion of nonwhite people and white women to the Protestant faith. Indeed, by 1860, not only did white women comprise 75 percent of congregational memberships and 60 percent of the active missionary force, but they also served as Sunday School teachers; deaconesses; auxiliary and charity organizers; elected assembly and conference members; prayer leaders; evangelists; and lay, itinerant, and ordained ministers. Although the majority of American blacks did not regularly attend church, a burgeoning of Protestant conversions among African Americans did occur immediately before and after the Civil War.[4] What had been an "invisible" or in many cases a nonexistent Protestant Church of the southern plantations during slavery became visible following emancipation; both northern and southern African Americans succeeded in expanding the size and number of independent Protestant churches. For example, while the African Methodist Episcopal Church had only 20,000 members in 1856, and 75,000 by 1866, it boasted more than 200,000 members just ten years later; and in 1880 the organization claimed a membership of some 400,000, most of whom were freedmen in the rural South (Banks, *Black Church*, 35). While the Protestant mission to Native Americans was certainly less voluntary and successful than that to white women and African Americans, it nevertheless carried a lasting impact. Robert F. Berkhofer reports that during the first half of the nineteenth century Protestant missionaries ministered to at least one-eighth of the total indigenous population and enjoyed particular success with the Cherokee, Choctaw, Seneca, and Tuscarora tribes. Indeed, for better or for worse, the Christian Church, perhaps more than any other institution in the nineteenth century, sought humanitarian assistance for Indians and African Americans and strove to do what they felt was necessary to save them from extinction and slavery, which included augmenting literacy rates among those populations. Consequently, many Native Americans and African Americans who published their work during the nineteenth century were members of a Protestant church, and as a result, they typically infused their writing with Christian rhetoric and Protestant ideals. These facts have caused contemporary scholars to face a nettlesome challenge: how to address, explain, and analyze the prevalent and at times clearly willing use of Protestant rhetoric and ideology during the nineteenth century by the very people who may have been the most victimized by it.

One important consequence of this challenge has been to spark a reconsideration of the traditional understanding of the rhetorics of manifest destiny and domesticity. Reginald Horsman and Thomas R. Hietala have shown that the nineteenth-century view of the United States as a white man's country came in a variety of mutations and from an array of sources, each vying for hegemonic control. Horsman notes that after 1815, the term "Anglo-Saxon" was ethnically but not ideologically shorn from its roots in pre-1066 Britain and was used increasingly to represent virtually any person of European descent who was willing to identify with that label (*Race and Manifest Destiny*, 94). Manifest destiny rhetoric changed in tone and content from the early to the midcentury, taking on a distinct racialism as the century progressed and as new challenges from non-"Anglo-Saxon" peoples arose. Like the scholars of manifest destiny, historians dealing with the rhetoric of domesticity have eschewed the notion that it represented an accurate or "natural" depiction of truth and have argued that it functioned as a self-serving trope for the dominant group (Kerber). In other words, the public-private and savage-civilized assignations were artificial and mutable rhetorical constructions that attempted but were unable to circumscribe individuals' actions or to represent historical truth completely. Thus, while the Church may have officially exhorted women to remain in their "private" sphere and nonwhite persons to become "civilized," the intended audience may not have consistently followed those dictates. In addition to questioning the appeal of the rhetorics, other scholars have pointed out the double standard used by the Church when assigning public-private and savage-civilized labels to various forms of behavior. No matter what the nondominant individual did—be it holding outdoor prayer meetings, delivering pamphlets to urban neighborhoods, visiting prisons, asylums, and orphanages, or serving as missionaries and lay ministers—the Protestant Church invariably dubbed those actions as "private" or less civilized than the same actions performed by white men.

The scholarship cited above attests to the inadequacy of the rhetorics of manifest destiny and domesticity as prescriptive, proscriptive, or descriptive codes of behavior. It also exposes the remarkable mobility and fortitude of nineteenth-century white women and nonwhite peoples as they both followed and transgressed dominant constructions of gendered and racialized codes of conduct. Although scholarly treatment of gender and domesticity and race and manifest destiny has been quite variegated, complex, and carefully contextualized, the academic consideration of Protestantism and its relationship to nondominant peoples has been remarkably uniform. Typically, there are two approaches to interpreting this relationship. Either Protestantism is fundamentally at odds with the best interests of white women and nondominant peoples, or while Protestantism may initially provide the catalyst for women's, Native Americans', and African Americans' entry into the public world of politics, it had to be formally shunned or gradually outgrown for nondominant groups to become fully emancipated. By considering Protestantism and the advancement of nondominant people as mutually exclusive, critics have overlooked the interactive and complex connections between these two phenomena and have promoted a false hierarchy of secular over spiritually based activism. Such hierarchizing bolsters a rigid and binary opposition between Protestants and nondominant groups, falsely compartmentalizes Protestantism as a stable and unified constant, and, in the end, unnecessarily attributes more power to conservative or fundamentalist Protestantism than is probable.

This book explores the actual words and rhetorical choices made by selected individual white women, African Americans, and Native Americans. It reexamines the split between nineteenth-century Protestantism and nondominant peoples and argues that identity is comprised of a number of dimensions, including religion, which are not closed, fixed, distinct, or even perpetually in competition with one another but instead are often mutually sustaining, interactive, and dialectic. Perceiving an acceptance of Protestantism as a sign of the disavowal of sex, race, or culture does not account for the complex historical and experimental processes of appropriation, translation, and invention, processes suggesting cultural interaction rather than assimilation or extermination. Such processes reveal persons not merely temporarily utilizing Protestant rhetoric to overturn or escape it but instead positioning themselves within a developing institution and nation. Moreover, the book will contend that even radical thinkers who worked outside the institutional bounds of Protestantism often ended up relying on many of its rhetorical forms, methods, and assumptions.

My intent in pursuing this argument is not to euphemize or endorse nineteenth-century Protestantism and what I see as its integral role in the identity formation of many nondominant writers; nor do I seek to defend uncritically all of the actions of nondominant thinkers. I aim to counter what has become a fashionable trend in scholarship, and particularly in my home discipline of American literature, either to view Protestantism as a purely debilitating or a merely utilitarian force, or, to ignore its presence and effects altogether. Instead, I seek to show its importance in the work of some of the most progressive antiracist and antisexist thinkers of the era: Olaudah Equiano, William Apess, Catharine Beecher, Harriet Beecher Stowe, Sojourner Truth, Amanda Berry Smith, Maria Stewart, Hannah Whitall Smith, Frances Willard, and Elizabeth Cady Stanton.

The individuals considered in this study do not, by any means, represent the only ones of this period who combined Protestantism with a progressive social agenda. With the exception of William Apess, all were, however, among the most well-known and controversial nondominant Protestant and political thinkers during their lifetimes. Moreover, the figures considered here were either women or nonwhite men as well as members of mainline Protestant churches (Presbyterian, Congregationalist, Episcopalian, Methodist, Baptist). While consideration of socially conscious thinkers in other denominations and sects such as the Quakers and Shakers would undoubtedly yield fruitful and intriguing analyses, in the interest of focusing the study, they were not addressed. Instead, the focus was placed on those nondominant Protestant thinkers who made significant strides in arguing for the rights of women and nonwhite peoples, who synthesized in varying ways their spiritual and political beliefs, and who continue to be of interest to literary and women's scholars today. Although the majority of the individuals examined in the book are women (particularly from the latter half of the nineteenth century), that choice is not purely arbitrary. Women constituted the dominant presence in mainline Protestant congregations from the Civil War forward; and because they had few outlets for public discourse, late-nineteenth-century women, to a much greater extent than men, used Protestantism to advance the cause of women and nonwhite groups.

While care is taken to analyze these thinkers within their historical and religious contexts, the theories used to inform these analyses are drawn predominantly from poststructuralist feminism and contemporary theories in women's psychology. My reasons for utilizing late twentieth-century theory to interpret eighteenth- and nineteenth-century texts are multiple. First, all historical analysis is on some level hermeneutical; the attempt to uncover the meaning of the existing literature of the past is always informed by present ways of thinking, and conversely, our understandings of the present then get reinterpreted based on our knowledge of the past. No critic can ever escape her own historical and ideological context, nor be unaffected by her topic of study. Moreover, beyond informing the perspective of the critic, a self-conscious use of twentieth-century theory has the advantage of making historical texts newly interesting, important, and relevant. In this study, however, finding relevance is not difficult. During the course of my research, I was often amazed at the similarities between the ideas voiced in the texts I was studying and those I had heard or felt during my experiences at church on Sunday mornings. For better or for worse, in cases of moral or religious obligation, although the vocabulary may differ, most of the arguments have remained remarkably the same over the course of our nation's history. Thus, while the theories might be advanced by contemporary thinkers, their analyses are appropriate and relevant for a nineteenth-century setting.

This study is founded on several assumptions about Protestantism and its function in nineteenth-century U.S. society. Religion, like gender and race, must be reconsidered as a historically specific organization of power, discourse, subjects, and emotions. Such an understanding is important because perhaps more than any other aspect of nineteenth-century U.S. culture, Protestantism exerted a pervasive and consequential influence. As Winthrop S. Hudson has noted, by 1860, "the ideals, the convictions, the language, the customs, the institutions of society were so shot through with Christian presuppositions that the culture itself nurtured and nourished the Christian faith" (*Great,* 108). Thus, Christianity formed an overwhelming "culture-shaping power" against or with which individuals identified themselves (Howe, "American Victorianism," 9). Unlike their more secular twentieth-century counterparts, late-eighteenth- and nineteenth-century Americans typically defined themselves by their religious faith. As Christine Stansell points out, "Beyond self-interest, . . . evangelical moral reform served as a nexus of social identity, 'an impulse toward self-definition . . .' which led people to seek each other out across a range of incomes and occupations, differentiating themselves from the classes above and below them" (*City,* 67–68).

Such a consideration necessitates another step — making important distinctions not only between various denominations but also between one historical moment and the next. Historians have routinely cited state governments' formal disestablishment of religion in the late eighteenth and early nineteenth century that eliminated officially financed and sanctioned sects and spawned a plethora of Protestant denominations as being the most important religious happening of the era. Because of this legislation, the more established Congregationalist, Episcopal, and Presbyterian churches suddenly had to battle for congregants and money with the formerly minor and dissident groups of Methodists, Baptists, Quakers, and others. While all of the Protestant denominations may have agreed on basic doctrinal tenets (for example, a belief in the existence of Christ and the primacy of the Bible), they also demurred — sometimes vehemently — on the finer points of faith and biblical hermeneutics as well as on larger doctrinal, practical, and political matters. In addition to disagreeing on the issue of disestablishment and the subsequent privatization of religion, the formerly "established" and new, upstart denominations distinguished themselves in their general outlooks, objectives, and styles. Paul

Kleppner has argued that the nineteenth century featured two broad clusters of denominations: the "liturgicals" and the "pietists" (*Third*, 183–85). The former group, comprised of the older churches (Episcopalians, Lutherans, Presbyterians, Congregationalists), were more ecclesiastically and ritualistically oriented. For them, belief was linked directly to one's knowledge, worshiping practice, and upbringing. By contrast, the newer "pietists" (Methodists, Baptists, Quakers) were more evangelical in emphasis; they tended to stress the New Testament, to be active in parachurch organizations, and to be committed to individual conversion and social reform. For them, belief was directly connected to one's experience and emotions rather than to one's education or background.

Consequential doctrinal and practical disputes also occurred intradenominationally and frequently led to significant transformations within various denominations. The conservative Reformed denominations (Presbyterians, Congregationalists), for instance, switched from a reliance on Calvinist principles and abstruse and intricate systems of theology to a dedication to Scottish Common Sense Realism, a literalist and inerrant biblical hermeneutic, and a premillennial notion of history. Many of the more popular evangelical churches (Methodists, Baptists), on the other hand, moved from a modified Calvinist doctrine of salvation to an acceptance of revivalism, a doctrine of Arminian-based perfectionism, and a postmillennial historiography. Furthermore, as such historians as Paul E. Johnson and George M. Thomas have convincingly argued, the transmutations and fissures within the Protestant denominations bore a dialectic relation to the nation's economic and political modifications. Thomas notes, for instance, that nineteenth-century Protestantism "actively used the broad cultural myths of individualism to forge an extremely individualistic Christianity; this 'revival' of 'true' Christianity, however, was not just the revival of the Church, but the reconstituting of the individual and the nation" (11). Thus, to view religion as a uniform, stationary, causal, or autonomous point of origin is problematic at best. The various strands of nineteenth-century Protestantism not only undulated and merged, they also intimately interacted with the social, economic, and political forces of U.S. society.

In addition to jettisoning a stable notion of American religion, this study eschews the idea of a consistent, unitary spiritual interior state that prefigures or precedes an individual's social and political interests. Individuals were at least as (and probably more) mercurial as the religious institutions to which they belonged. As Ann Douglas has pointed out, not only did many ministers in this period publicly alter their religious convictions, but even more laypersons modified their creedal viewpoints (*Feminization,* 94–95). While recognizing all of these shifts and transformations — both individual and institutional — makes the task of this project all the more complicated, it also serves a potentially beneficial function. To adhere to an ever-mutable and irresolute conception of religion and religious subjects is to destabilize the powerful and conservative claim to a single, stable, and essentialized faith or spiritual identity. Furthermore, by seeing Protestantism and its subjects as variegated, not only is the force of orthodox Christianity diffused, but, with such a fragmented perspective, more cultural possibilities are offered for the constructive use of religion and spirituality. Indeed, one of the goals of this book is to encourage scholars not only to talk about religion as a social and dynamic construction but also to resist automatically accepting religious attributes or effects as necessarily expressive of a conservative interior sentiment.

Beyond recasting Christianity as socially and historically constituted, I want to suggest that religion in nineteenth-century U.S. culture cannot be cordoned off from other discursive systems. Because Christianity was embedded thoroughly into the fabric of Protestant men's and women's lives, it comprised part of what Pierre Bourdieu terms one's individual "habitus." For Bourdieu, the habitus is "a system of internalized, embodied schemes which, having been constituted in the course of collective history, function in their *practical* state, for *practice* (and not for the sake of pure knowledge)" (*Distinction,* 467). Protestantism in the nineteenth century formed both a generative and structuring principle; it enabled individuals to recognize possibilities for action, while it also prevented recognition of other potentialities. All of the individuals examined here were both empowered and constrained by Protestantism — and in particular, the shaming practices of its leaders and spokespersons; and none of them were able to extricate themselves fully from its power. They appropriated, utilized, and resisted Protestantism in manifold ways, and, more important, often incorporated it to subvert or reject the dominant rhetorics of manifest destiny and domesticity. The forms of self-identification and empowerment that these thinkers invented through and against Protestant shaming practices were at least as varied and ingenious as the forms of feminine oppression concocted by the purveyors of the rhetorics of manifest destiny and domesticity.

The following five chapters explore the way Protestant rhetoric is ironically overturned and extended through an interplay with various aspects of Protestantism in the work of important writers. The first chapter examines the 1791 narrative of Olaudah Equiano, a seafaring African convert to the Anglican Church who was also a former slave, and compares his construction of masculinity with that of George Whitefield, the most popular Calvinist evangelical of the mid- and late eighteenth century. While Whitefield's combative notion of masculinity worked to enlarge his vision of himself and the world, Equiano's unwillingness or inability to assume that identity exposed the elitism and racism inherent in early evangelical-Calvinism. The following chapter considers the conversion narrative of William Apess, one of the few surviving New England Pequots in the early part of the century who became a licensed Methodist itinerant minister. Drawing from early American Methodism, Apess defined a new, more fluidly gendered self that worked to counter the powerful anti-Indian, expansionist rhetoric and the growing conception of the United States as a homogeneous Anglo-Saxon, Protestant nation-state. In the third chapter, I consider *The Minister's Wooing*, a midcentury novel by Harriet Beecher Stowe, one of the most celebrated Protestant and abolitionist novelists of the century, and compare her definition of self with that of her famous sister, Catharine Beecher. While Catharine (relying on Reformed Protestant and Common Sense philosophy) advanced a notion of the feminine self based on self-abnegation, Harriet (drawing from a more Arminian-based evangelicalism) promoted a more relational, expansive feminine self to combat conservative gender norms. The fourth chapter looks at a number of mid-nineteenth-century white and black Christian feminists, a term I use to describe individuals who believed that Christianity could be used to advance the cause of women's rights. I argue that noted women such as Frances Willard (president of the Woman's Christian Temperance Union), Hannah Whitall Smith (best-selling author and celebrated lay preacher), Amanda Berry Smith (renowned foreign missionary), Sojourner Truth (popular abolitionist activist), and Maria Stewart (respected abolitionist lecturer) drew from a variety of Protestant doctrines and practices — including liberal historical-critical scholarship and perfectionistic strands of evangelicalism — to overturn conservative Christian thinking about women. Finally, chapter 5 investigates the controversial project, *The Woman's Bible*, spearheaded by Elizabeth Cady Stanton, one of the foremost women's rights activists of the century. Although this project has been touted by scholars as representing a critique or even rejection of Protestantism, it ironically relied on various fundamentalist assumptions and methods to advance its prowoman agenda.

The individuals studied here not only drew upon the variegated strands of Protestantism in manifold and creative ways, they also deployed a stunning variety of styles and genres to examine their religio-political positions and identities: spiritual autobiographies, conversion narratives, speeches, advice books, novels, and biblical commentaries. These writers are all intriguing because they disrupted the unitary illusion of gender, race, religion, and identity on which the regimes of patriarchy, nationalism, and racism rest. Yet, rather than reject Protestantism their critiques demonstrate that nineteenth-century feminism and antiracist activism were typically generated not in opposition to but out of differences and contradictions within Protestantism. Despite, or perhaps because of that, they were able to develop a transformative and variegated contribution to evading Protestant-generated exploitation.

Divine Destiny

Chapter One

"From Conquering to Conquer"

Olaudah Equiano, George Whitefield, and a New Christian Masculinity

On a Sunday morning in Philadelphia in 1766, Olaudah Equiano happened upon "a church crowded with people":

> The church-yard was full likewise, and a number of people were even mounted on ladders, looking in at the windows. I thought this a strange sight . . . I therefore made bold to ask some people the meaning of all this, and they told me the Rev. George Whitfield [sic] was preaching. I had often heard of this gentleman, and had wished to see and hear him . . . I now therefore resolved to gratify myself with the sight, and pressed in amidst the multitude. When I got into the church I saw this pious man exhorting the people with the greatest fervour and earnestness, and sweating as much as ever I did while in slavery on Montserrat-beach. I was very much struck and impressed with this; I thought it strange I had never seen divines exert themselves in this manner before; and was no longer at a loss to account for the thin congregations they preached to. ("Narrative," 97)

Equiano's description underscores the immense popularity of George Whitefield, the "Grand Itinerant," who rose from humble origins in England to achieve notoriety on both sides of the Atlantic. It also emphasizes the fact that the narrator, a young enslaved African man, was so enthralled with Whitefield's persona and preaching that he boldly ventured into a confined public setting filled undoubtedly with hundreds of white people. Whitefield's willingness to labor strenuously for his cause was understandably appealing to Equiano, who had witnessed firsthand an enormous disparity between whites' and blacks' labor efforts. But Equiano admired Whitefield for more than his energy; he also ended up subscribing to a form of Christianity that Whitefield espoused.

It is this aspect of Equiano's attraction to Whitefield or more particularly to Protestant evangelicalism that has concerned and even baffled critics. While some have praised Equiano as "a fervent evangelical" (Potkay, "Equiano," 685) and perceived his embrace of Christianity as a positive organizing principle of his narrative and life (Orban, "Dominant"), others have bemoaned his conversion and missionary zeal. Angelo Costanzo, for example, attributes Equiano's acculturation into Christianity in part to a "concentration camp psychology," wherein due to his enslavement he made himself subservient to his white masters' ways of thinking and control (*Surprizing*, 83). Similarly, Chinosole sees it as evidence of Equiano's "mental colonization" ("Tryin'," 45). A third group of critics has interpreted his acculturation as a move of political savvy and expedience, designed to assist him in persuading an audience who could strike major blows to the slave system (Murphy, "Equiano," 561; Samuels, "Disguised," 64). Finally, others have recognized Equiano's Christian identity but have simultaneously underscored that it is only one role among many. Equiano is as much entrepreneur as evangelical (Fichtelberg, "Word"), as much African as Western European (Andrews, *To Tell*), and as much enslaved as free (Marren, "Between Slavery and Freedom").

Perhaps one reason that Equiano's conversion, along with his subsequent missionary efforts, has proved a contestatory site for critics is that Equiano's own actions — even after conversion — did not always follow what one might expect of a devout evangelical. On the one hand, Equiano appears to be the humblest of all believers, calling himself at one point lower than "the meanest worm on the earth" (136) and blaming his own "sin" for his ship hitting a rock and nearly causing the death of numerous slaves on board (110); yet within a few pages, he takes on heroic powers, noting after surviving the same perilous shipwreck: "I could not help looking on myself as the principal instrument in effecting our deliverance" (111). How can the same individual adopt such seemingly antithetical postures, displaying extreme self-abnegation on the one hand and startling self-aggrandizement on the other? Aren't such contradictory attitudes an indication of his lack of devotional sincerity and complete acculturation? Does it suggest that Equiano's first dedication was to personal enfranchisement and abolitionism rather than to Protestantism? Instead of evaluating the authenticity or magnitude of Equiano's religious sentiment (an issue that cannot be answered definitively anyway), I suggest that what appears as religious backsliding or vacillation can be partially illumined by reconsidering Equiano's idolization of George Whitefield.

Equiano's contradictions can be explained in part by his reliance on an emergent notion of masculinity that Whitefield cultivated and personified and that was based on the sometimes differing impulses of Calvinism and evangelicalism. According to Nancy Ruttenberg, this new prescription for masculine selfhood "asserts that the abasement of the self coincides with its exaltation or 'enlargement,' suggesting a humility—and corollary empowerment—independently achieved . . . as the necessary prerequisite to a future exaltation" ("Whitefield," 431). To enhance self-debasement, the individual endures a series of oppositions that, if surmounted successfully, leads to an assurance of salvation and a concomitant feeling of self-exaltation. Such exaltation can only be sustained, however, by reenacting, translating, and transferring this regenerative, humbling process to others. Thus, according to this ideal, the hardships and scrutinizing self-examination inherent in Calvinism can only be mitigated by experiencing one's new birth and evangelizing successfully to others. While this conjunction of self-denigration and self-enlargement offered Equiano a means for attaining an acceptable masculine selfhood and thus a certain self-empowerment, ultimately he was unable to maintain this conjunction as successfully as did Whitefield. Rather than reflect poorly on Equiano's spiritual fortitude and self-worth, his inability to enact this form of masculinity helped to expose the elitist dimensions of early American Protestantism.

Social historian Peter N. Stearns has argued that eighteenth-century Western men based their identity on three major symbols: patriarch within the family, skilled laborer, and warrior (*Be a Man!*, 13–38). Masculine identity depended on the ability to display physical strength, to face and endure risk of physical injury, and to perfect a respected skill or craft. Traditional manhood was tested and established through competition and camaraderie with other men, participation in actual battle, or the endurance of pain, terror, or suffering. Moreover, to maintain their masculinity, men needed to secure a family and land, produce heirs, and hold absolute dominion over wife, children, and servants. Not all men could achieve this tripartite masculine model of warrior, patriarch, and laborer. Enslaved men, like Equiano, were typically shut out of opportunities for land ownership, marriage, family, and the acquisition of a skilled craft. Although Equiano eventually did secure his freedom, marry, and learn several trades, he never was able to attain the other requirements for manhood. Given the prevailing racism and existing slave system of the eighteenth century, enslaved men's inability to become "men" is not surprising, but other free, white men (such as Whitefield) were also excluded from this ideal.

In the highly stratified society of eighteenth-century England, Whitefield's family situation was far from optimum. George's father owned a small inn in Bristol. When he died suddenly at the age of 35, his wife, who had given birth to seven children, remarried a man who eventually deserted her. Thus, George grew up working in an inn with no fortune and little prospect for social advancement, land ownership, or physical prowess. Moreover, to undermine his social status further, he, as a youth, was attracted to the theater and even played lead roles in school performances. Whitefield writes about this passion in his journal: "During the time of my being at school, I was very fond of reading plays, and have kept from school for days together to prepare myself for acting them. My master seeing how mine and my schoolfellows' vein ran, composed something of this kind for us himself, and caused me to dress myself in girls' clothes, which I had often done, to act a part before the corporation. The remembrance of this has often covered me with confusion of face, and I hope will do so, even to the end of my life" (29). Whitefield's confusion stemmed not only from his awareness (gained perhaps in hindsight) that theater was considered immoral by the elite puritanical circles but also from his own uncertainty over his masculine selfhood. Harry S. Stout notes that the most frequent criticism of the theater during this time period was its supposed "effeminacy": "Men in dresses, men in women's roles, men with high voices — all of these came under attack and derision . . . Theatrical effeminacy threatened to impose directionless and chaotic 'feeling' over 'intellect' and 'understanding.'. . . Selves governed by worldly passions were like a raging sea overflowing its banks and disrupting all order. Or, in another metaphor of the time, they were like a woman" (*Divine*, 23–24). As a member of a subordinate class with a personality that exhibited precisely those condemned qualities of passion and timidity, Whitefield needed to locate a new way of salvaging his manhood.

Like Whitefield, Equiano as a young boy may have faced the charge of unmanliness. Early in his narrative, he recalls that "I was so fond of my mother I could not keep from her, or avoid touching her" (20); and because he frequently committed a cultural purification taboo by touching her during her menstrual cycle, he was forced to be quarantined with her for days at a time.

At least one critic has speculated that Equiano's "feminine" qualities may have caused his eventual abduction and enslavement. Basing her views on field-work done in Equiano's probable hometown of Isseke, Catherine Obianju Acholonu surmises:

> Olaudah Equiano was not simply captured, he was sold, according to his kins-men (which is a very shameful thing for a noble family to admit).... People sold their children in those days when they were highly in debt and could find no way out.... A man of large means, an *ogaranya*, was expected to bestow the *ichi* marks on all his sons. It was a very expensive venture, and was the first step in a series of ceremonies that would lead to the *nze* or *ichie* position in the land. Ichie Ekwealuo must have been at a loss for what to do with this boy who even accompanied his mother into seclusion during her menstrual cycle. No man would have risked spending so heavily to bestow the *ichi* marks of manhood on a boy who was ob-viously more of a woman than a man. ("Home," 11)

According to Acholonu, Olaudah's kidnapping must have been planned since wealthy Igbo children were typically never left unguarded. If this possible pa-ternal rejection and social ostracism did not assault Equiano's sense of mas-culine selfhood, his experiences as a slave certainly did. In addition to watching helplessly as his sister was torn from her home and family, Equiano witnessed a host of other atrocities committed against fellow Africans, including lynch-ings, fatal beatings, and rapes of young girls "not ten years old" (74).

Although the attacks on Equiano's sense of self were certainly more brutal than those on Whitefield's, both men at relatively young ages confronted the necessity of forging a new masculine identity or risked the threat of self-anni-hilation. Ironically, however, rather than flee from self-annihilation, both fig-ures ended up embracing it by succumbing to the Calvinist tenet of the total depravity of the self. According to this doctrine, since the time of Adam's fall, all humans have been utterly and inexorably evil, undeserving of grace or for-giveness. The depraved being cannot do good, unless through an unmerited intervention of God (Johnson, "Pursuit," 34). Moreover, individuals can do nothing to incur God's favor or their own salvation. Indeed, the only way to salvation is through an all-powerful, majestic God who possesses the ability to save all beings but chooses to do so only for an elect few. Thus, God's grace, rather than human will or good works, represents the only path to salvation.

Both Equiano and Whitefield proclaimed their own depravity. For exam-ple, after realizing himself incapable of keeping all ten commandments, Equiano "thought that my state was worse than any man's; my mind was unaccountably disturbed; I often wished for death, though at the same time was convinced that I was altogether unprepared for that awful summons...I became a burden to myself" (135). To prove his adherence to this doctrine, Whitefield placed the origins of his sinfulness in the womb: "I can truly say I was froward from my mother's womb. I was so brutish as to hate instruction, and used purposely to shun all opportunities of receiving it. I can date some very early acts of uncleanness. I soon gave pregnant proofs of an impudent temper. Lying, filthy talking, and foolish jesting I was much addicted to, even when very young. Sometimes I used to curse, if not swear. Stealing from my mother I thought no theft at all, and used to make no scruple of taking money out of her pocket before she was up" (*Journals,* 27). Not sufficiently convicted by the realization of his own sinfulness, Whitefield (while a student at Oxford) felt compelled to denigrate himself further by fasting for lengthy periods of time, wearing "woollen gloves, a patched gown and dirty shoes" (*Journals,* 43), praying for hours on end, and walking outside in freezing weather until his hands turned black. Similarly, Equiano chose to forgo several promising opportunities to escape (92), believing that unless he was certain God willed it, he was undeserving of freedom. In fact, when he is suddenly resold back into slavery after harboring some hope for liberty, he assumes this unfortunate twist of fate is a result of his having uttered a swear word: "My conscience smote me for this unguarded expression: I felt that the Lord was able to disappoint me in all things, and immediately considered my present situation as a judgment of Heaven. . . . I considered that trials and disappointments are sometimes for our good; and I thought God might perhaps have permitted this, in order to teach me wisdom and resignation" (66–67).

Rather than blame God for not guaranteeing everyone's salvation or for creating sin in the first place, Equiano and Whitefield revered Him all the more for His awesome power. As Ann Douglas comments, the Calvinist God's capricious use of atonement "operated as a model of majesty; crushing, humiliating as it may appear and often was, it could be a source, almost uniquely so even among Western religions, of energy. It provided its adherent, no matter how it belittled him, with a supreme and commanding object of worship" (123). Equiano experiences a humbling sense of awe when listening to a sermon in Westminster chapel, which "shewed the justice of God in the eternal punishment of the wicked and impenitent. The discourse seemed to me like a two-edged sword cutting all ways. It afforded me much joy, intermingled with many fears about my soul" (140). Beyond locating it in sermons and scripture,

Equiano detected and admired God's fearsome wrath against sin in the forces of nature, especially in the sea. Describing a sea storm, he writes:

> The roaring of the billows increased, and, with one single heave of the swells, the sloop was pierced and transfixed among the rocks! In a moment a scene of horror presented itself to my mind, such as I never had conceived or experienced before. All my sins stared me in the face; and especially I thought that God had hurled his direful vengeance on my guilty head...And in the midst of my distress, while the dreadful surfs were dashing with unremitting fury among the rocks, I remembered the Lord, though fearful that I was undeserving of forgiveness..., and I thought that as he had often delivered, he might yet deliver. (109)

While sailing from London to Gibraltar, Whitefield endures an almost identical harrowing maritime experience:

> I went on deck; but surely a more noble, awful sight my eyes never yet beheld! For the waves rose mountain high, and sometimes came on the quarter-deck. I endeavored all the while to magnify God, for thus making His power to be known. Then, creeping on my knees (for I knew not how to go otherwise), I followed my friend H. between decks, and sang psalms and comforted the poor wet people.... Though things were tumbling, the ship rocking, and persons falling down unable to stand, and sick about me, I never was more cheerful in my life...Praise the Lord, O my soul, and all that is within me praise His Holy Name! (*Journals*, 116–17)

Out of the storm's mighty power and the fear that it engendered in them and in others, both men ironically came to esteem God more fully.

Whitefield's exuberance is more pronounced and understandable than Equiano's, because unlike Equiano, at the occasion of his storm experience, he had already been converted and thus felt certain of his salvation and no longer feared (or was allowed to express fear of) death. Yet, what about Equiano who at the time of his storm was still unregenerate? If he was not sure of God's favor, why was he able—after nearly perishing in a savage storm—to announce to his fellow crew members, " 'Let us again face the winds and seas, and swear not, but trust to God' "? (117). His certainty at a moment of intense uncertainty may be partially explained by turning to Michel Foucault's concept, "subjectification." The Calvinists' God—as well as their preachers and books—used what Foucault calls "dividing practices," in segregating with swift finality the regenerates from the reprobates, the godly behavior from the ungodly, good morals from bad, and in inducing the replication of those divisions within the individual consciousness. At the same time that Equiano was being indoctrinated into the Calvinist system by external forces, he was also participating in his own process of self-formation. As Foucault puts it, "There are two meanings of the word subject, subject to someone else by control and dependence, and tied to his own identity by a conscience or self-knowledge. Both meanings suggest a form of power which subjugates and makes subject to" ("Subject," 208, 212). This binary world was believable because its subjects found verification for it both internally and externally. Moreover, as John Stachniewski notes, the Calvinist subject was able to maintain a strong fear and respect of this vengeful God and of this stern binary form of existence because these feelings often intermingled with a fearful respect for all masculine authority figures: "The sense of divine rejection was often related to feelings about fathers, father-surrogates, or the social hierarchy. Frequent, often discriminatory or arbitrary, beatings; banishment from the father's presence and the threat of being disowned; guilt feelings arising from lack of filial affection or hatred as a reaction to punishment; the desire to escape from paternal anger; the knowledge that paternal power circumvented any infantile plot: in all these experiences God and actual fathers seem to have been imaginatively conflated" (*Persecutory,* 95).

Stachniewski's insights help to illuminate why individuals, like the young Equiano and Whitefield, who did not enjoy positions of authority or elite social standing might nevertheless be attracted to Calvinism. The Calvinist god made sense in a highly hierarchical and patriarchal world comprised of rigid class regulation and a brutal slave system where unilateral autocratic authority was enacted openly and without reproach. Indeed, the Calvinist respect for abject rule and the conflation of divine authority with the father figure help to explain why Equiano could say of his master, Michael Henry Pascal, "I almost loved him with the affection of a son" (64) or why, after being manumitted in the West Indies, he would elect to remain there for an extended period to work for his former master, Mr. King.[1] One of the most insidious consequences of the slave system was that even when freed, black men were still not accorded respect, considered truly free, or assigned a recognizable social role. After he is manumitted, Equiano continually has to confront kidnappers or naysayers unconvinced of his free status. Moreover, the only time he is beaten or faces extreme personal injury comes after he attains freedom. With no master present to protect him (as "property") or to grant him a recognized social role (albeit a subservient one), Equiano was vulnerable to literal and symbolic annihilation. Similarly, having no father figure or fortune to guide him, Whitefield lacked a certain future role. Thus, in a rigidly hierarchical culture that typically erased the possibility of a respectable identity for non-white, enslaved, and lower-class individuals, Calvinism provided those same subordinated individuals two recognizable subject positions: that of the saved or the damned. Although the reprobate position was not ideal, it, along with the saved one, nevertheless lent its subjects an identifiable social and psychological role. Moreover, while far from a loving, all-accepting, and nurturing parent, the Calvinist divinity did recognize everyone, was worthy of respect given its commanding power, and offered its subjects at least some chance for victory—which was better than most could hope for in an unforgiving eighteenth-century Anglo-American world.

For spiritual autobiographers like Whitefield and Equiano, the chances for redemptive victory were certainly better—at least in their eyes—than those for the typical churchgoer. Scholars have noted that the main motive for this form of writing was to affirm one's election—that is, to put "a good construction on a providence that often felt malevolent...The aim was to construct a narrative governed by a teleology of election, love, acceptance which could convincingly subordinate, while accounting for, all the evidence of experience that seemed to document a narrative governed by a teleology of reprobation, hatred, rejection" (Stachniewski, *Persecutory,* 104). Since Calvinists believed that only God determined one's final destination, they continually sought evidence of their elect status; and since this determination was made before an individual was even born, evidence for election could manifest itself prior to the conversion proper. Moreover, given that everyone, including the elect, were ultimately undeserving of God's grace, spiritual autobiographers—without appearing arrogant—could boast of their personal triumphs by chalking them up to providential favor. Hence, even while still an unconverted slave, Equiano could brag that he was treated more kindly than were other slaves and could regard himself "a *particular favourite* of Heaven" precisely because he "acknowledge[d] the mercies of Providence in every occurrence of my life" (12). Likewise, because Whitefield continually stressed that "God was pleased so to assist me in preaching, and so wonderfully to affect the hearers" (*Journals,* 254) and that his own "soul [was] a blank in His hands, to write on it what He pleased" (*Journals,* 76), he could detail in his journals the magnanimous size of the crowds—sometimes numbering over fifty thousand—that gathered to hear him speak.

Even though Equiano and Whitefield as Calvinist subjects were not supposed to perceive triumph as an individual success, it nevertheless allowed them some personal gratification or self-enlargement for several reasons. First, personal success, if couched in humble terms, proved one's elect status to others. Indeed, James German has recently argued that contrary to popular perception, eighteenth-century Calvinist ministers moved away from an open celebration of communitarian or civic virtue and embraced instead a righteous form of self-interest. According to these ministers, regenerates act in the marketplace and elsewhere with "disinterested love to being in general" and thus are ultimately rewarded in this life and hereafter, whereas reprobates act according to wicked self-interest and thus are certainly damned (*Social,* 998). Through his swift judgment and perfect logic, God secures the greatest possible happiness of the universe and thereby rewards the righteous. Thus, financial and personal success can be a sign of God's favor rather than of personal greed and consequently can be discussed more openly than had been done prior to that time.

The second reason that Equiano and Whitefield could enjoy self-enlargement was that predestination or providence did not entirely preclude the possibility of individual agency. In fact, for Calvinists, predestination cannot be fully equated with determinism or fatalism, both of which deny the efficacy of volition. As Ellwood Johnson explains, "Predestination is indeterminate because it denies natural cause-and-effect determination of human events, and it is unfatalistic except insofar as human character fates itself" (*Pursuit,* 32). Calvinists believed that humans are predestined *because* they possess free will; but their free will differs fundamentally from God's will. Prior to conversion, humans' will is fallible and limited by external natural and material forces, while God's will is immutable both externally and internally. Only through the sanctification of the heart does the will become truly free, although paradoxically the free will is joined to God. The elect then are the only ones who possess free volition. However, not all members of the elect realize their freedom to enjoy God's grace and to cultivate their own success. As Whitefield explains, "I really believe one great reason why so many go mourning all their life long, is owing to ignorance of their Christian privileges. They have not assurance, because they ask it not; they ask it not, because they are taught that it does not belong to Christians of these last days; whereas I know numbers whose salvation is written upon their hearts as it were with a sunbeam" (*Journals,* 372).

In this passage, Whitefield suggests that owing to the fallibility of humans' will, select regenerates have the alacrity and sagacity to understand, cultivate, and appreciate their talents or callings. Because both he and Equiano were conscious of their regenerate status, their explications of their personal victories were justified and even necessary to serve as models for other regenerates who were as yet unaware of their freedom and callings.

Perhaps for these two reasons, Equiano's and Whitefield's descriptions at times sound self-promoting. This 1738 entry from Whitefield's journal is typical: "Preached nine times this week, and expounded near eighteen times, with great power and enlargement. I am every moment employed from morning till midnight. There is no end of people coming and sending for me, and they seem more and more desirous, like new-born babes, to be fed with the sincere milk of the Word. What a great work has been wrought in the hearts of many within this twelvemonth! Now know I, that though thousands might come at first out of curiosity, yet God has prevented and quickened them by His free grace. Oh that I could be humble and thankful!" (188). In other entries, he describes how the rooms where he was to preach would be "so exceedingly thronged that I was obliged to go up by a ladder through the window" (232) or how, while giving a sermon in Northampton, Massachusetts, the " 'good Mr [Jonathan] Edwards wept during the whole time of exercise' " (qtd. in Stout, *Divine*, 126). Even more incredible than Whitefield's firsthand reporting of his preaching experiences are his comparisons of himself with Christ. For instance, in summarizing his birth, he highlights the fact that he was born in an inn, thus "follow[ing] the example of my dear Saviour, who was born in a manger belonging to an inn" (27). Similarly, in recounting his conversion experience, he tells of how he melodramatically bellowed, as Christ did on the crucifix, " 'I thirst! I thirst!' " (48).

Such analogies did not go unnoticed by fellow clergymen. Charles Chauncy, a well-known Congregationalist minister in Boston and virulent opponent of revivalistic preaching, condemned Whitefield's arrogance as "prophane" in a public letter: "This is not the only Instance, wherein your *Fancy* has formed a Kind of Resemblance between *your own*, and the Circumstances of Christ Jesus" (*Letter*, 36–37). Whitefield, however, remained undaunted by Chauncy's and others' criticisms, believing that the enormous size of his congregations on both sides of the Atlantic legitimized his enlarged sense of self. As his biographer puts it, "His ubiquitous audience estimates—recorded [in his journals] even when Scripture texts were not — constituted not only evidence of hubris but a badge of legitimacy. If his ministry was unlawful, would God bless it with such numbers and changed lives?" (Stout, *Divine*, 74–75). Visible, exterior signs (such as large crowds or emotionally affected listeners) signified interior sanctification. Thus, Whitefield continually underscored his popularity as an indication of divine favor.

As a black, enslaved, and then formerly enslaved, man, Equiano could not, of course, afford to be as self-promoting as was Whitefield. While white autobiographers could assume their readership would trust their sincerity, black narrators had "to defend or explain away the same literary egoism that in a white autobiographer might be praised as American pride and self-reliance at its best" (Andrews, *To Tell*, 2). Thus, they had to invent strategies to endow their stories with the appearance of authenticity or to make certain that the stories they chose to tell did not surpass their white readers' limited expectations for what constituted the "truth" about slavery. Because Equiano made clear his view that only God, not the individual, created personal success, he could more safely afford to relate his tales of heroism than could other non-Calvinist slave narrators. And indeed, as Angelo Costanzo points out, Equiano at times assumes "a protean character. He can do almost anything and succeed at it" (*Surprizing*, 62). He gains his own freedom through cunning and business savvy. He escapes numerous perils at sea (including naval battles) (48, 52); his business endeavors succeed while those of others around him fail (91), and he becomes the "sable captain" when he safely maneuvers a ship to port after the actual captain dies. In Georgia, he officiates as a parson at a funeral (118). Later, he embarks on a remarkable attempt to discover a northeast passage and travels closer to the North Pole than any other excursion up to that time (131). He becomes proficient at navigation, hairdressing, and French horn-playing; and finally, he devotes himself to antislavery work, petitions the queen for the abolition of slavery, and gains popularity with major abolitionists and luminaries on both sides of the Atlantic (4). The long list of supporters — including Hannah More, Granville Sharp, John Wesley, Adam Clarke, the Prince of Wales, the Countess of Huntington, and the Dukes of Marlborough, Bedford, and Northumberland — printed at the beginning of his narrative highlights his public acclaim. When Equiano married Susanna Cullen in England in 1792, the announcement in the *Gentleman's Magazine* cited him as "the African, well known in England as the champion and advocate for procuring a suppression of the slave-trade" (qtd. in Costanzo, *Surprizing,* 43). Like Whitefield who moved the celebrated theologian Edwards to tears, Equiano apparently deeply affected John Wesley, one of the founders of Methodism. While lying on his deathbed, Wesley reportedly went so far as to request friends to read to him excerpts from Equiano's narrative.[2]

Whitefield's and Equiano's self-proclaimed accomplishments may seem surprising given their humble upbringings and their adherence to the Calvinist faith, a faith known for its harshness and severity. Many scholars would argue, as Judith Jordan does, that "in a culture which idealizes power over others and views competitive hierarchy as a necessary means to concretize power differentials (a decidedly nonmutual system), the subordinate groups come to 'hold' characteristics of 'weakness' and vulnerability which are disavowed and disowned by the dominant group" ("Courage," 2). Through the mechanisms of denial and projection, her argument goes, subordinated people identify with the "weak" position. Yet, what Jordan neglects to add is that within a fiercely binary world, subjects can suddenly reverse their power positions through the incorporation of a new oppositional discourse. As a starkly binary system of thought, Calvinism enabled at least some of its followers (regardless of their social status) to take on the elect role and reign over those they deemed reprobate. Both Equiano and Whitefield seized this opportunity to personal advantage.

Because Calvinists believed that providence signified the unfolding of God's plan and glory, their autobiographers could focus on the self and on their mundane existence without appearing self-centered. Such an ability was particularly key for Equiano, who needed to detail certain facts of his life not only to affirm his own (and by extension all enslaved people's) worth but also to relate the terrors of slavery. In his book, *To Tell A Free Story,* William Andrews argues that it was this need to discuss the harsh reality of life here on earth that separated the slave narrator from the spiritual autobiographer. While both kinds of autobiographers proclaim gospels of freedom (one seeking escape from sin and the other from bondage), they differed in major ways:

> The spiritual autobiographer reviews the past through the eyes of the metamorphosed, empowered self and appropriates from the past a myth of the true self, beneath the accidents of race, gender, and caste. The slave narrator, by contrast, is expected to concentrate on race, gender, and caste, institutionalized in chattel slavery, as ends in themselves. The one justifies the imaginative leap from empiri-

cal to a presumed essence because the real subject of imitation is the "poten-tialised" self. The other restricts such imaginative projection because its priority is to expose an institution's power to destroy, not celebrate an individual's poten-tial to preserve, the essential self. (64–65)

According to Andrews, unlike spiritual autobiographies that centered on the interior struggles of the writer, the most popular and effective slave narratives placed the narrator on the periphery; and this narrator continually looked outside, not within, and transcribed rather than interpreted (6). Equiano was able to reconcile the antithetical aims of the two forms of autobiography, pre-cisely because he relied on the Calvinist belief that the "Self was obnoxious, and good works I had none; for it is God that worketh in us both to will and to do" (143). He could focus on the particularities of his life as a slave and even as a boy in Africa since they represented not his life but that of God. Furthermore, his emphasis on the details of his life and especially on his many struggles as a slave enhanced, rather than undermined, the Calvinist as well as the abolitionist aims of his autobiography.

For Equiano and Whitefield, rather than signal a deleterious fate, opposi-tion actually provided further evidence of divine favor and the subject's spiri-tual strength. Indeed, both Equiano's narrative and Whitefield's journal read as catalogs of every possible opposition—from the spiritual to the psycho-logical, somatic and social. For example, not only was Whitefield challenged cosmically through continual temptations from Satan in the form of sensual desires or extreme self-emasculation and asceticism (*Journals*, 43), but he faced dire health difficulties as well. Mysterious illnesses, seasickness, tempo-rary hoarseness, and frequent fits of vomiting continually threatened to end Whitefield's brilliant preaching career. He describes his constant battle with his ailments in his memoirs: "Fear not your weak body, we are immortal till our work is done. Christ's labourers must live by miracle; if not, I must not love at all; for God only knows what I daily endure. My continual vomitings almost kill me, and yet the pulpit is my cure, so that my friends begin to pity me less, and to leave off that ungrateful caution, 'Spare thyself'" (qtd. in Gillies, *Memoirs*, 180). Or, as he noted in one journal entry, "I was blooded thrice, and blistered and vomited once, and, blessed be God! can say, It is good for me that I have been afflicted; for as afflictions abounded, consolations much more abounded" (143).

Time and time again, Whitefield would lose the power to stand or speak un-til he mounted the pulpit steps or glimpsed the thousands of people standing outside, eager for his words. His account of a hot summer evening in Savannah, Georgia, is typical:

> Last night, through weakness of body, just as I began family prayer, I was struck, as I thought, with death. I put up a few broken accents and breathed out, "Lord Jesus, receive my spirit."... Though exceedingly weak, and I had almost laid aside thoughts of officiating this day, yet, upon Mr. J's intimating that friends came expecting to hear me, I promised, if I could, to preach, and begged him to read prayers.... He refused, urging that God would strengthen me if I began. Before I had prayed long, Mr. B. dropped down, as though shot with a gun.... The influence spread. The greatest part of the congregation was under great concern. Tears trickled down apace, and God manifested Himself much amongst us at the Sacrament. (*Journals,* 447)

Whitefield's self-depiction suggests that without God's intervention, he literally lacked the psychic energy and bodily sustenance to maintain routine day-to-day living. In a similar way, Equiano gives God credit for granting him the ability to survive a military battle (55), a life-endangering fall (60), a serious illness (94), and several shipwrecks (116). In both men's narratives, near-fatal bodily opposition is surmounted only after the body literally is "dissolved" (Whitefield, *Journals,* 288; Equiano, "Narrative," 145) and then revived in a divine form.

For both Equiano and Whitefield, a "new birth," which represents the defining feature of evangelicalism, enabled them to overcome interior or bodily struggles as well as exterior obstacles. In fact, Equiano's and Whitefield's writings seem to resist Andrews's claim that the spiritual autobiographical form restricts the narrator's ability to expose social inequities. Both narrators spend much of their narratives recounting their direct confrontations with and victory over external opposers. "The more I am opposed," Whitefield affirms, "the more God enlightens my understanding" (193). For the Grand Itinerant, no "enemy" was too formidable. On route to Gibraltar, for example, he was "sent for by a sailor, who has been the most remarkable swearer on board, and whom I in an especial manner warned about two days ago telling him, I believed God would remarkably visit him. He laughed, and said he hoped not. But tonight he sent for me trembling and burning with a fever; he told me what grievous sins he had been guilty of, and prayed most fervently for repentance" (*Journals,* 142). This naval soldier's conversion must have been especially gratifying for Whitefield, the man who only a few years earlier had fretted over his own masculinity. For, as Stout notes, sailors were considered the antimony of effeminacy: "In the rough-and-tumble world of eighteenth-century Anglo-America, soldiers and sailors were the ultimate men. The shipboard life of 'Jack Tar' was notorious for its brutality and the harshness of shipboard conditions. Few fates were more dreaded than impressment into the British navy. Renowned for their violence as well as their profanity, they were, in Whitefield's eyes, the supreme challenge" (*Divine*, 54). By encompassing the manly soldier-sailor into his fold, he enlarges his own selfhood and fashions a new, more expanded and triumphant form of masculinity.

Toward this end, Whitefield continually uses military or physically aggressive imagery to describe his own ability to confront and then encapsulate opposers: "Men may scoff for a little while, but there is something in this foolishness of preaching which will make the most stubborn heart to bend or break. 'Is not My Word like fire,' saith the Lord, 'and like a hammer that breaketh the rock in pieces?'" (*Journals*, 229). Or on another occasion, he comments, "Whereever [sic] I go, God causeth me to triumph, knits the hearts of His people most closely to me, and makes me more than conqueror through His love" (*Journals*, 205). Conquering imagery was Whitefield's particular favorite. Following a highly successful sermon, he "rejoiced that God led me on from conquering to conquer" (*Journals*, 292). Thus, although Whitefield may not have been able to fulfill the dictates of the eighteenth-century secular norms for manhood—patriarch within the family, landowner, warrior—he could fulfill a new sacred version of masculinity that he himself personified: religious patriarch, protector of God's souls, and Christian soldier.

His newfound masculinity—developed through his method of incurring reproach and then effecting victory over opposers as divine confirmation—no doubt assisted him in taking on even larger "foes" than soldiers and audience scoffers. Whitefield spent considerable energy combating established clergy of the Church of England and of prominent colonial American churches. In a recent book, Frank Lambert argues that one of the ways Whitefield maintained power over congregations spanning halfway around the world was, upon arrival, to spend considerable energy winning over the audience at hand and, on the way out of town, to manufacture a memorable controversy that would distinguish him from local religious figures (*Pedlar*, 171). For instance, immediately before departing London for Georgia in 1739, he issued a public attack on the bishop of London, who had earlier criticized his preaching style. Similarly, as he prepared to leave the colonies a year and a half later (after achieving considerable fame and success), he accused the Harvard rector and tutors of neglecting their students' spiritual development. His general tack was to excoriate clergy for emphasizing good works over grace and for being themselves unconverted, or "in a dead Sleep of spiritual Indolence and carnal Security" (qtd. in Lambert, *Pedlar,* 195).

While this combative style caused Whitefield to lose clerical support, it ended up being a powerful boon in terms of generating both a large following of lay supporters and a new distinctive preaching style. Angry at his clerical attacks and jealous of his popularity, the established Anglican and American ministers made complaints that "the churches were so crowded that there was no room for the parishioners, and that the pews were spoiled." And, as Whitefield noted, "Some called me a spiritual pickpocket, and others thought I made use of a kind of charm to get the people's money" (*Journals,* 82). While some lambasted his arrogance and melodramatic homiletic style, most attacked the general practice of revivals, which they claimed were more orchestrations of itinerant manipulations than divine outpourings. In particular, they objected to the revivals' tendency to "move the Passions of the Weak and Ignorant than to inform the Understanding" (qtd. in Lambert, *Pedlar,* 186).

Whitefield's preaching did indeed prove to be a threat to clergy and traditional Protestant worshiping practices. As Ruttenberg notes,

> Whitefield used his "wonderful Power" to mobilize people in the name of a new vision of personal, spiritual and community life. This vision entailed the establishment of a radical itinerant ministry in each of the major colonial denominations, and led consequently to a general fragmentation, or separation, of constituted parishes. Separate institutions for training and licensing such ministers soon challenged the hegemony of Harvard and Yale along with the belief that the ability to interpret Scripture depended more on education than on "experiential knowledge of Jesus Christ and Him crucified." ("Whitefield," 430)

Huge crowds and revivalistic forms of preaching upset the silent and orderly sanctity of Puritan churches. As a result of his unorthodox style, ministers on both continents refused to let him preach within their church walls. Some even questioned his authority to preach at all by quibbling with the terms of his clerical license.

While Whitefield's vitriolic, anticlerical stance might seem to indicate a radical bent on the part of the itinerant, historians argue that it served more as an advertising ploy than as a political statement:

> Whitefield was no social radical bent on overturning society, nor was he in the habit of challenging civil authority — indeed, the crown always elicited his highest praise. But bishops were another matter. Whitefield could challenge them on religious grounds without calling the establishment itself into question. And in

> so doing, he could demonstrate his pulpit power. . . . Invariably, Whitefield set his successes alongside the perceived failures of the established church. With controversy and the press in mind, he was learning to stage preaching events in ways that vaulted him to the forefront of public attention. (Stout, *Divine,* 46)

Whitefield learned quickly that whether he was being praised or damned mattered little so long as his name and image were set before the public eye. Moreover, controversy always yields more attention than conformity.

In addition to creating more attention from the press, clerical attacks pushed Whitefield to be more "experimental" in his religious practices. His ban from churches, as well as the vast numbers of his followers, prompted him to preach in large, open fields and attract (by virtue of this novelty) even larger crowds. To capture and maintain his audience's attention (many of whom may have been positioned far away from the evangelist), Whitefield learned to speak in a booming voice and with considerable emotion. Throughout his sermons, he interspersed dramatic phrases such as "Alas!" or "Hark!"; gesticulated, stomped, and kneeled for added emphasis; and frequently burst into tears. At other times he would act out biblical stories, taking on the tone and persona of various biblical characters. As one listener recalled of his performances: "I hardly ever knew him [to] go through a sermon without weeping, more or less, and I truly believe his were the tears of sincerity. . . . I could hardly bear such unreserved use of tears, and the scope he gave to his feelings, for sometimes he exceedingly wept, stamped loudly and passionately, and was frequently so overcome, that, for a few seconds, you would suspect he never could recover; and when he did, nature required some little time to compose himself" (qtd. in Stout, *Divine,* 41). Opposition, then, was an effective strategy for Whitefield. Not only did it assist him in amassing a large public relations campaign and huge crowds, it also prompted him to create a new style of preaching and to fashion a new, nonaristocratic form of potent masculinity. Whitefield could be a man without having the proper bloodlines, siring children, or owning vast amounts of land. Furthermore, his new form of combative manhood was especially appealing to Americans who, fresh from a war with France and heading into a revolt from England, were self-confidently hostile to external authority.

Like Whitefield, Equiano, in the course of his relatively brief account, constructed a notion of masculinity based on embattlements with numerous opposers: kidnappers, slave traders, enemy fire from French naval forces, unfair masters, cheating traders, incompetent and unstable captains, a drunken and unruly Indian governor, a well-meaning but recalcitrant priest, and finally a racist London bishop who considers his application for missionary duty. Despite his amazing success in surmounting these "foes," Equiano was not as triumphant as Whitefield. Unlike the Grand Itinerant who was able to "melt" the hearts of a large spectrum of society, including fellow ministers (484), African-Americans and Native Americans (150), Equiano's missionary efforts were generally unsuccessful. In 1775, on route to Jamaica, he attempted to convert George, a Musquito prince, and "was in full hope of seeing daily every appearance of that change which I could wish" (153). However, after other natives "laughed and made their jest at him," the prince renounced Equiano and even proceeded to express a wish to "go to hell" (154). When Equiano tried to convince a Spanish Roman Catholic priest of the rightness of Protestantism, not only did the priest fail to accept Equiano's argument, he nearly convinced the African to convert to Catholicism by promising him a free education (151). While Equiano did make headway in the conversion of a Portuguese captain, that success can be attributed more to the fact that the captain had recently been rescued from a near-death situation than to Equiano's persuasive powers (152). Finally, his efforts to be ordained as a missionary to Africa fell through when the Bishop of London declined his application in 1779.

Perhaps more self-defeating than Equiano's failed missionary efforts were some of his other postconversion experiences. In 1776, ten years after gaining his own freedom, he returned to Central America with Dr. Charles Irving — to set up a slave-run plantation. When he decided to return to England and was replaced by a cruel overseer, the slaves were tragically drowned in a failed escape attempt. In an effort to free a wrongly imprisoned friend, Equiano staked out the kidnapper's house, disguised himself in whiteface, hired a lawyer, and appealed to a judge — all to no avail. In fact, his efforts made matters worse, for the man was returned to St. Kitts, staked to the ground, and "cut and flogged most unmercifully" until he perished (135). When confronted with a drunken and unruly Indian governor, Equiano exhibited anything but Christian charity, patience, and good will in handling the situation: "I pointed up to the heavens. I menaced him and the rest: I told them God lived there, and that he was angry with them, and they must not quarrel so: that they were all brothers, and if they did not leave off and go away quietly, I would take the book, (pointing to the Bible), read, and tell God to make them dead. This operated on them like magic. The clamour immediately ceased, and I gave them some rum and a few other things; after which they went away peacably" (157). Rather than feel contrite at this dishonest strategy, Equiano applauded himself, noting that "it succeeded beyond my most sanguine expectations" and that the Doctor marveled at "my success in getting rid of [the] troublesome guest" (157). Ironically, this marked one of the only instances when others raved at his persuasive ability, and he had to resort to blaspheming the Bible and bribing with liquor to gain this acclaim. As Joseph Fichtelberg notes, such experiences expose "the dark counterpart of an intrinsically meaningful Christianity, a sign that [for Equiano] faith only partially restores community" (473).

Equiano's unsuccessful personal and missionary efforts directly contrast those of Whitefield. One possible reason for this disparity may have been the differences in the two narrators' intended readership. Because Whitefield could assume his readers would be supportive of his viewpoint and had a transatlantic, super-regenerate image to uphold, he had no need to include testimony detailing his faults and mishaps. Equiano, on the other hand, could assume from his readers neither respect nor trust. Consequently, in an effort to convey his sincerity and the truth of his story, he may have felt it necessary to include the contradictions, admissions of fault, and accounts of non-Christian behavior that are no doubt part of all religious believers' lives. Moreover, Equiano was not (or was not allowed to be) the professional showman that Whitefield was and therefore may not have had or may not have wanted to display the public relations "savvy" to gloss over his imperfections. While Equiano's narrative certainly gained popularity (running through eight editions in Great Britain and nineteen in the United States and Europe), it was not written with the same self-conscious eye toward commercial success as were Whitefield's journals. Equiano, for example, repeatedly downplayed his literary or commercial prowess and in fact commented in the first few pages that he expected from his book neither "immortality nor literary reputation" (12), while Whitefield consistently touted himself as master of the published word. As one scholar notes, "perhaps Whitefield's greatest legacy was his ability to bend the same powerful market forces that he preached against to his own designs. . . . He was a Jeremiah calling on his followers to adhere to a traditional message while leading them into modern mass evangelism" (Lambert, *Pedlar*, 230–31).

As Nancy Ruttenberg points out, Whitefield's evangelical energy and commercial success derived in part from the conviction that he literally was impersonating God. As opposed to mere imitators who shoddily attempt to duplicate the one they idolize, impersonators empty the self to permit the incorporation of a transcendent Other: "Whereas imitation leads to a depletion of the self, impersonation leads to self-fulfillment as well as to a legitimate sphere of activity, in a word, to a sanctified enlargement of the self" (436). According to Whitefield's testimony of his new birth, God had completely dissolved his old self and subsumed him, only to produce a pure instrument or agent of His will. Repeatedly, in his journals, Whitefield depicts himself as an empty vessel whom God "filled ... with a humble sense of His Infinite mercies" and with the strength of "His mighty arm" (*Journals*, 194). Equiano, by contrast, shies away from the filled vessel image and instead accentuates the mercy of Christ to " 'thus look on me, the vilest of sinners' " (143). Instead of emphasizing his confluence with God after conversion, Equiano persists in highlighting the imbalance of power between him and the deity, a move more typical of would-be converts.

Without the sense of exaltation and righteousness that impersonation offered, Equiano probably could not be as confident or as persuasive a missionary as could Whitefield. Another possible reason for Equiano's missionary difficulties can be found in the recent work of Forrest G. Wood. Wood notes that in his "Narrative," Equiano describes the supreme god of the Ika people in his native region of Benin as the "Creator of all things, [who] lives in the sun, and is girded around with a belt, that he may never eat or drink; but according to some, he smokes a pipe, which is our own favorite luxury" (19). According to Wood, the High God for West Africans "was far too important to be considered a personal god who had the time to notice, or even care about, the trivial and mundane problems of common mortals. Unlike the Christian God ... who presumably filled the believer with his spirit, the African supreme deity was a remote entity whose essence was beyond the reach and comprehension of ordinary human beings" (165). Hence, based on his African upbringing, Equiano may not have felt comfortable achieving complete fusion with Christ. Wood also points out that while many other religions "recognized demons and evil spirits that influenced human behavior and created chaos for mortals," only monotheistic faiths such as Christianity and Judaism "acknowledged an evil being who worked against the interests of God. And early American Protestants saw him connected to Africans and Indians" (35). Whether or not Equiano was conscious of the racist symbolism of the Christian devil, the fact that it existed may have dissuaded him from feeling entitled or even wanting to assume a divine persona. Yet, without this entitlement, Equiano would have had difficulty transcending the good-bad oppositions endemic to Calvinist conversion.

In addition to lacking the entitlement to enjoy a conjunction with God, Equiano, as a result of social constraints, had difficulty transcending oppositions. Whereas Whitefield had to manufacture controversy (which he then overcame) to propel his exalted masculine image, the oppositions Equiano faced were not self-imposed and in fact were often potentially life-threatening. Although Whitefield did at times get pelted with stones or other objects[3] and even faced arrest upon occasion for unlawful worshipping practices, he never endured severe bodily harm or the threat of lifelong imprisonment as did Equiano. Thus, because of his more privileged status, Whitefield could afford to make fairly bold verbal attacks on the traditional Protestant system and derive from his confrontations with authorities "the inward satisfaction that I had now begun to attack the devil in his strongest holds" (*Journals*, 307). Given that evangelical missionizing typically involved controversial critiques on traditional religious belief systems or spiritual authorities, Equiano (understandably fearing for his safety) might have been reticent to proselytize with full force and therefore may not have been able to convert others.

In addition to an explicit rejection of other faiths and spiritual practices, inherent in early American Protestant evangelicalism was the belief in the singular rightness of Christianity. As Wood explains, the British theory of the right of discovery and possession of land and slaves derived from "the tradition of vacuum domicilium, which held that land not 'occupied' or 'settled' was available to any 'civilized' person — that is, Christian — who, of course, had the exclusive right to determine whether or not a land was 'settled'" (*Arrogance*, 217). He further argues that by the mid-eighteenth century, this theory of cultural regeneration that claimed "the power both to transform lives into a new Christian perfection and to uplift backward peoples to the American ideal" was already commonplace among Protestant evangelicals (214). In order to be effective, then, evangelical missionaries had to accept the superiority of Christianity as well as the superiority of Anglo-American ways of living and thinking over all other belief systems and cultural contexts.

As a result of his extensive travels and his early childhood experiences in Africa, Equiano developed a cultural relativism that ran counter to these ethnocentric and hegemonic goals of evangelicalism. Even after experiencing his new birth, Equiano still could not negate the worth of non-Anglo-American beliefs and practices. For example, he confesses in his narrative that at one point he consulted a spiritualist. Despite the fact that he "could not conceive that any mortal could foresee the future disposals of Providence, nor did [he] believe in any other revelation than that of the Holy Scriptures," the woman foretold "many things that had happened with a correctness that astonished" him and prophesied accurately that he would not long be a slave (93). Additionally, rather than buy wholesale into the burgeoning discourse of manifest destiny, Equiano observed the value of non-Christian peoples such as the Turks who were "very honest in their dealings" (126) or the Spanish Catholics who had made a black man pope (151). About the Musquitos, he was even more effusive, commending their simple manners and lifestyle and their lack of swear words or oaths. Although they did not display any recognizable mode of worship, Equiano remarked, "they were not worse than their European brethren or neighbours; for I am sorry to say that there was not one white person in our dwelling, nor any where else, . . . that was better or more pious than those unenlightened Indians" (156). Moreover, he later admired their night of "merry-making," which "ended without the least discord in any person in the company, although it was made up of different nations and complexions" (159). Equiano's "fond[ness] of going to see different modes of worship of the people wherever I went" (126) coupled with his firsthand witnessing of the brutality of self-proclaimed Anglo-Saxon Christians must have prevented him from imbibing the moral absolutism and cultural superiority necessary for successful evangelism.

Undoubtedly even more repugnant for Equiano was the fact that the manifest destiny rhetoric of the seventeenth and eighteenth centuries also typically included a defense of slavery. While some Protestant proponents of manifest destiny believed slavery to be justified since slaves to their mind were not fully human, others accepted slavery as "a convenient and expeditious method of bringing pagans into the Christian 'sphere of influence'" (Wood, *Arrogance*, 115). Historian Alan Gallay argues that it was evangelicals, inspired by the preaching of George Whitefield, who advocated this more paternalistic version of slavery. For them, God created bondage as an unpleasant but necessary means of facilitating the conversion of heathen peoples. Thus, while Whitefield did not oppose slavery per se, he condemned what he considered to be unchristian treatment of bondspeople, called for their religious education, and advocated the idea that they possessed a soul (*Journals*, 380). In early 1740, Whitefield composed an open letter, "To the Inhabitants of Maryland, Virginia, North and South-Carolina, concerning their Negroes," in which he excoriated slaveholders' treatment of slaves: "Your Slaves . . . work as hard if not harder than the Horses" and are treated worse than dogs; "upon the most trifling Provocation, [they are] cut with Knives, and had Forks thrown into their Flesh." While uncertain "whether it be lawful for Christians to buy slaves," Whitefield was sure that "it is sinful, when bought, to use them . . . as though they were Brutes." And he ominously claimed that retribution awaited sinners: "The Blood of them spilt for these many Years in your respective Provinces, will ascend up to Heaven against you." Whitefield prayed that the slaves "may never be permitted to get the upper Hand," but he could not deny that if "such a Thing be permitted by Providence, all good Men must acknowledge the Judgement would be just."[4]

While Whitefield did maintain a lifelong concern for the spiritual well-being of blacks, he also spent considerable time actively promoting the legalization of slavery in Georgia. In fact, in a 1748 letter to the Georgia trustees, he argued that slavery was necessary for the survival of the orphan-house he wanted to found in Savannah: "Georgia never can or will be a flourishing province without negroes are allowed. . . . I am as willing as ever to do all I can for Georgia and the Orphan-house, if either a limited use of negroes is approved of, or some more indented servants sent over. If not, I cannot promise to keep any large family, or cultivate the plantation in any considerable manner" (qtd. in Stout, *Divine*, 198–99). Whitefield, of course, neglected to consider the hypocrisy of his position on slavery. If, as he postulated, divine providence created slavery to convert heathens, then why weren't these same heathens freed at the moment they embraced Christianity? For Whitefield (as for most Christian slaveholders), expedience overcame principle. He was more interested in gaining personal power and the support of southern gentry than in upholding human justice. While Whitefield made a lifelong reputation of confronting traditional figures of authority, slavery constituted one authority he refused to oppose.

Because Whitefield "humanized" slavery by arguing that it was Christian duty "to make [slaves'] lives comfortable and lay a foundation for breeding up their posterity" (qtd. in Gallay, "Origins," 391), he managed to appeal to northerners wary of slavery without cutting off his southern slaveholding constituency. As a formerly enslaved black man, Equiano could not possibly appeal (or desire to appeal) to proslavery and abolitionist audiences alike. Unlike Whitefield, who concluded that God had designed the enslavement of black men and women as a means of christianizing second-generation slaves, Equiano put forth the different view that God uses sin to the advantage of the universe. For him, slavery was designed to separate the saved from the damned and to enhance humanity's appreciation — black and white alike — of liberty, equality, "peace, prosperity and happiness" (81). Slavery is sinful because it not only relegates the enslaved to the "condition of brutes," but it also "hardens [the slaveholders] to every feeling of humanity":

> And, had the pursuits of those men [slaveholders] been different, they might have been as generous, as tender-hearted, and just, as they are unfeeling, rapacious and cruel. Surely this traffic cannot be good, which spreads like a pestilence, and taints what it touches! Which violates that first natural right of mankind, equality, and independency; and gives one man a dominion over his fellows which God could never intend! For it raises the owner to a state as far above man as it depresses the slave below it; and, with all the presumption of human pride, sets distinction between them, immeasurable in extent, and endless in duration! (80)

Unlike Whitefield who saw slavery as the necessary means to greater good, Equiano argued that it impedes rather than serves God's plan for a fully equal, more virtuous world. In other words, only through its abolition could God's intent for "an universal good" be realized (177).

Because late-eighteenth-century Calvinists no longer separated self-interest and economic success from true virtue and universal good and sought evidence of divine providence in economic prosperity, Equiano needed to prove that abolition would not lead to economic ruin.[5] Moreover, he also needed to respond to the evangelical, paternalistic claim that slavery served as a necessary form of African missionization. Equiano answered both the Calvinist and evangelical claims by revisioning Africa as "an endless field of commerce to the British manufacturers and merchant adventurers" rather than as a source of human chattel (176):

> Population, the bowels, and surface of Africa, abound in valuable and useful returns; the hidden treasures of centuries will be brought to light and into circulation.... The manufacturing interest and the general interests are synonimous [sic].... Query — How many millions doth Africa contain? Supposing the Africans, collectively and individually, to expend £5. a head in raiment and furniture yearly, when civilized, &c. an immensity beyond the reach of imagination!... If the blacks were permitted to remain in their own country, they would double themselves every fifteen years. In proportion to such increase will be the demand for manufactures. (176–77)

According to Equiano, for a country to be "civilized" meant it must not only operate successfully in a global market economy but also exude Christian ethics and morals. To realize that vision, Africans living in Africa needed conversion. Thus, Equiano's application to the Bishop of London to become a missionary of Africa countered Whitefield's and other proslavery evangelicals' view that slavery was the only means to Africans' christianization: "My sole motive . . . is the opinion which gentlemen of sense and education, who are acquainted with Africa, entertain of the probability of converting the inhabitants of it to the faith of Jesus Christ" (169).

Equiano's new vision of Africa as a "commercial utopia" (Baker, *Blues*, 38) has been strongly criticized by scholars. Sandiford bemoans his inability to see that this vision was "not a fair exchange for the considerable material profits the Europeans would derive" (*Measuring*, 147), and Fichtelberg views it as "a vision hegemonically European and capitalist": "The biblical gigantism of the language ('endless . . . immense, glorious') and the erotic passivity of the continent as it yields its hidden treasures to the British thrust suggest the worst kind of exploitation" ("Word," 475). While in hindsight Equiano's vision is troubling in terms of both its colonial and ecological implications, placed in a religious context, it is somewhat more understandable. The presence of black Christian missionaries, such as him, in Africa was certainly preferable to forced enslavement of Africans in America. In addition, compared to the more prevailing paternalistic view of slavery held by prominent evangelical spokespersons such as Whitefield (who was considered particularly friendly to blacks and who Equiano himself admired),[6] Equiano's position could be considered personally and politically risky.[7] His view was definitely not a popular one in either evangelical or lay circles. Moreover, as Susan Marren has observed, for Equiano to take a more radical stand would have risked a loss of readership and ironically a loss of his "more subversive narrative feat — the one that amounts to social insurgency" ("Between Slavery and Freedom," 101).

Equiano's nontraditional view of slavery and providence coupled with his cultural relativism and his reluctance or inability to impersonate God not only impeded his ability to gain as popular an appeal as Whitefield enjoyed but also precluded his ability to personify the new Christian man. Confronting the rigid oppositions inherent in Calvinism — between good and evil, the elect and the reprobate — may have served as the first step toward acquiring manliness, but true masculinity could only be achieved if those oppositions could be surmounted and then transcended. While Whitefield could transcend the binaries by incorporating them into his enlarged, exalted self, Equiano had far more difficulty overcoming the oppositions he faced. Yet, rather than indicate personal weakness or spiritual backsliding, Equiano's inability to achieve a fully exalted masculinity ended up exposing some of the more insidious elitism imbedded in Calvinist-based evangelicalism: its mission to annihilate and then incorporate the individual self, its cultural superiority, its propagation of a singular religious truth, and its support of a proslavery view of providence.

On a more abstract scale, his "failure" may have revealed the limitations of a religious system based on hierarchical, binary relational structures where the goal is to augment one's own force, authority, or influence as well as to exercise dominion over others. Rather than promote a cultural order based on greater mutuality and respect for connection between two equal but differing subjects, Calvinism reinforced a subject-object relation, wherein a passive object serves as a vessel for God's and other authorities' projections and transferences. The only escape from the passive object role was through the impersonation of the dominating subject. Equiano's "failure" to fit neatly into either the passive object or dominating subject role may not have been a failure at all but instead a realization of the game's insidious implications. Moreover, because he did not transcend the antinomies inherent in Anglo-American Protestantism, he may have ironically served to inspire other nondominant Christians to adopt different strategies of resistance and empowerment. As will be demonstrated in upcoming chapters, rather than attempt to transcend Protestant binary thinking, some nondominant Christians who lived after Equiano tried, with varying degrees of success, to dismantle it.

Chapter Two

"A Mark For Them All To . . . Hiss At"

The Formation of Methodist and Pequot Identity in the Conversion Narrative of William Apess

Whereas critics have devoted much attention to Olaudah Equiano's narrative and his vexed use of Protestantism to promote antiracism, they have accorded relatively little attention to the conversion narrative of William Apess, a Pequot Indian who led the only successful Indian revolt in New England prior to 1850.[1] One possible reason for the paucity of Apess scholarship is that, unlike Equiano who focused some of his narrative on non-Christian matters, Apess's use of Protestant rhetoric is pervasive and unabashed. Notes Arnold Krupat, one of the few critics to assess his work, "the voice of Protestant rhetoric that sounds everywhere in Apes's[2] text seems to mirror very closely a voice to be heard commonly in the early nineteenth century, the voice of what I call . . . salvationism" (*Voice*, 144). For Krupat, salvationism is "a dialect of aggressive Protestantism" and "the discursive equivalent of a glass trained on Heaven through which all this world must be seen" (142). By inculcating this Euro-American rhetoric so completely, claims Krupat, Apess eliminates any possible inclusion of nonwhite or native voices in his work and in turn "proclaims a sense of self, . . . deriving entirely from Christian culture" (145).

Although his concern with Apess may be unique, Krupat's position on the concepts of ethnicity, culture, and (by extension) nationality is not uncommon. His view falls into a larger, popular trend among cultural critics that Paul Gilroy terms "cultural insiderism." According to Gilroy, cultural insiderism is comprised of a set of rhetorical strategies designed to promote "an absolute sense of ethnic difference... [which] distinguishes people from one another and at the same time acquires an incontestable priority over all other dimensions of their social and historical experience, cultures, and identities" (*Black,* 3). Moreover, cultural insiderism typically constitutes the nation as ethnically homogeneous and invokes ethnicity to undergird the idea of national belonging, the aspiration to nationality or the exclusion from it. In short, for Krupat, Apess's conversion to Protestantism and his eventual ordination as a Methodist minister not only reveals his "wish to be the licensed speaker of a dominant [national] voice" but, more important, propels a tragic silencing of his Pequot ethnicity (*Voice,* 148).

Through the exploration of the conversion narrative of William Apess, this chapter seeks to contest the concept of racial purity or ethnic absolutism and to suggest that identity cannot be conceived in terms of ethnicity or any one category alone. Unlike Equiano and Whitefield, who constructed their identities on the transcendence of oppositions, Apess eschewed the notion of a subjectivity based on hierarchy and binaries altogether. Instead, he based his identity on a variety of dimensions — religious, racial, national, class, gender, and so forth — which are not closed, fixed, distinct, or even perpetually in competition with one another but instead are mutually sustaining, interactive, and dialectic. Perceiving Apess's acceptance of Methodism as a sign of the disavowal of his ethnicity does not account for the complex historical and experimental processes of bifocality that he utilizes, processes that suggest cultural interaction rather than assimilation or extermination. Bifocality, according to Michael M. J. Fischer, is a "shorthand for 'two or more' cultures in juxtaposition and comparison" and involves "seeing others against a background of ourselves, and ourselves against a background of others" (199). Apess repeatedly and in a variety of contexts juxtaposes familiar customs and norms with unfamiliar ones, thereby relativizing, interrogating, and overturning taken-for-granted assumptions about Protestant and Pequot identity.

Apess's ability to engage in cultural criticism would not have been possible, however, with any form of Protestant rhetoric; Methodism, I argue, was uniquely suited to his needs. Like all Protestants, early nineteenth-century Methodists accepted the divinity of Christ, the existence of the holy Trinity and the authority of the Bible. Yet, unlike Calvinist-based evangelicals such as Whitefield and Equiano who followed the doctrines of total depravity, the election of saints, and God as a vengeful, all-powerful figure, these Methodists held that all people (regardless of race, class, or sex) could receive God's grace. Like the Methodism fostered by Whitefield, this early American form of Methodism subverted the traditional culture of honor and patriarchal sovereignty, but it did not do so by cultivating self-exaltation through masculine oppositionality. Instead it tended to promote a more radical egalitarianism in which God and all of His followers operated on a more level footing. Far from being a dominant denomination, Methodism in the early nineteenth century was scorned by the more established and affluent Reformed and Anglican Protestant churches. Thus, Apess's conversion to Methodism did not secure him a ready ticket to power and prestige, but it did provide him a way to gain a wider white audience, to critique the practices of the larger Protestant Church (from within rather than from without it), and to make sense of and turn to his own advantage the opprobrium and discrimination he faced as a Pequot Christian. Methodism helped him not only to define his own dialectic sense of self by enabling a continuously shifting scheme of identification but also to adopt a new, more accepted form of rhetoric that could work to counter the powerful anti-Indian, expansionist rhetoric and the growing conception of the United States as a homogeneous Anglo-Saxon nation-state. Through a complex layering of juxtapositions and comparisons, Apess questions and affirms new gradations of Methodist-Pequot identity and envisions a new American continent.

In order to gain acceptance from the Protestant Church — and, by extension, from the general (and largely Protestant) American public — Apess needed to convey his ideas using a readily recognizable and respected mode of expression. Evangelical Protestants, even those of lower rank, were allowed and even expected on occasion to express themselves through the telling of their personal conversion stories. The conventions of the conversion narrative were strictly defined and therefore relatively unimpeachable. Notes Virginia L. Brereton, the "formula of the conversion narrative has tended to discourage originality of plot or expression, and it is a very stylized language indeed" (*From Sin*, xii). Thus, the conversion narrative offered Apess a straightforward and accepted mode of communication. Yet, while Apess may have followed the typical structure of the conversion narrative, he also used that structure to describe a conversion experience atypical of most Protestant male converts of his era. In other words, the conversion narrative format provided a familiar background upon which to view an unfamiliar style of conversion. By doing so, Apess was able to achieve a form of bifocality within his narrative and, thus, invite his audience to see Protestantism and America in a new perspective.

In an analysis of hundreds of texts spanning almost two centuries, Brereton has identified five distinct stages that virtually all conversion narrators describe: (1) life before the conversion process; (2) the awareness of one's sinfulness (or the conviction); (3) the conversion proper; (4) the immediate rewards of the conversion; and (5) further temptation and subsequent renewal. True to convention, Apess's narrative progresses through these five stages. He was born in 1798 in Colrain, Massachusetts, but was forced to leave there three years later because of his parents' separation and departure. Following his parents' breakup, Apess first lived with his alcoholic and embittered grandparents and then (after a near fatal beating by his grandmother) was sent to reside with one after another white, neglectful, and ostensibly Protestant family. Because he was treated more as a servant than as an adopted son, his white foster families provided him little or no religious training. Despite or perhaps because of their indifference, Apess began on his own accord to frequent Methodist camp meetings held outside of town.

Once enfolded in the Methodist community, Apess entered into the second stage of Christian converts—the realization of his sinful state. He began to experience "fearful visions" and to sense that "my condition was deplorable and awful; and I longed for day to break, as much as the tempest-tossed mariner, who expected every moment to be washed from the wreck he fondly clings to" (*On Our Own Ground,* 128). Frightening visions such as these did not deter Apess from attending meetings and praying, and shortly thereafter, while working in a garden, Apess advanced to the third and fourth stages—those of regeneration and contentment—and underwent a complete change of heart, coupled with a blissful assurance of salvation: "naught could I see but seas of rest and waves of glory before me that I wanted only the wings of angels to waft me to Paradise, that I might dwell around the throne of God forever" (130). But this fulfillment was short-lived (as is typical for new converts), and he soon slipped into the final stage in the conversion process—that of tribulation and eventual rededication—and succumbed to a lengthy period of carousing and drinking provoked by his encounters with white soldiers during the War of 1812. In 1829, however, Apess recommitted himself to the Church, was baptized by immersion, and became an authorized Protestant Methodist minister. During the seven years following his ordination, he wrote and published five books, including his conversion narrative. In 1833, he received brief notoriety in local presses when he initiated and led the Mashpee uprising.[3] But just five years later, Apess seems to have mysteriously disappeared; no record has been found of his subsequent activities, or even of his death.

As is evident from the above summary, the structure of Apess's story adheres precisely to the stringent pattern Brereton outlines of the prototypic conversion narrative. Not only does it include the standard success story progression from failure to fulfillment intrinsic to the norms of the Protestant conversion, but it also features sentimental circumlocutions, poetic diction, and scriptural references, typical of Christian rhetoric of the period. For example, Apess notes that while sitting in church as a young boy, he heard the word of God "spoken with divine authority, which not only drew tears of contrition from *me* but from many others" (122). As his personal conviction mounted, his descriptions became increasingly impassioned and ebullient, fraught with vivid contrasts of good and evil: "I groaned and wept; I had often sinned, and my accumulated transgressions had piled themselves as a rocky mountain upon my heart; and how could I endure it? The weight thereof seemed to crush me down; in the night seasons, I had fearful visions and would often start from my sleep and gaze around the room, as I was ever in dread of seeing the evil one ready to carry me off" (128). Throughout the passage, the salient imagery of weight and ponderousness is developed and intensified, mirroring the subject's inner agonizing burden. But once the regeneration occurs, the rocky geographical masses give way to a spontaneous poem:

> *O for such love, let rocks and hills*
> *Their lasting silence break;*
> *And all harmonious human tongues*
> *The Savior's praises speak.* (129)

In addition to poetic effusion, Apess frequently invokes the Bible to authorize and enrich his tale. He gains assurance, for instance, that his calling to the ministry is genuine when he receives a nighttime vision of an angel who "reads some extracts of John's Gospel" (132).

Although the structure of Apess's text follows the rigid requirements of the prototypic Protestant conversion narrative, the style of conversion he describes is not typical of those conveyed in early-nineteenth-century conversion narratives written by men. In a study of more than two hundred accounts of conversion between 1800 and 1830, Susan Juster discovered that men were usually forty years old when converted, tended to perceive God as an abstract system of rules and principles, and were frequently forced to abandon their self-sufficiency and rely on others during their conversion process. Women, by contrast, were usually twenty-five years of age when converted, generally experienced divine authority as a personal power, and often had to abandon family relationships and undertake the quest for salvation alone. Apess's process of conversion does not follow the pattern Juster predicts for men. Not only was he baptized at the age of twenty, but during the description of his conviction in the narrative, he continually stresses his desire for a personal relationship with God, which at one point he likens to "the dove [longing] for her absent mate" (128). Finally, throughout his narrative, Apess frequently emphasizes that his journey to salvation was done without the help or comfort of others: "I had none to take me by the hand and say, 'Go with us and we will do you good'" (128). In short, rather than adhering to the tendencies of the typical male convert, Apess seems to undergo precisely Juster's notion of the feminine process of conversion.

In another study of conversion narratives, Virginia Brereton found that unlike women narrators who tend to focus their stories principally on their angry and rebellious hearts before the conversion experience, men concentrate matter-of-factly on the effects of their regeneration—that is, the outward signs of change, such as the cessation of their drinking or gambling (*From Sin*, 38).[4] Although Apess does note that his drinking problem abated after his baptismal rededication to the Church, he—in a similar fashion to women converts—devotes more time appealing to his audience's emotions and underscoring his own by delineating the hardship, injustice, and wretchedness he and his tribal people have suffered. Because Apess's style of conversion does not follow the patterns Brereton and Juster describe, it calls into question whether their masculine categorizations should be more appropriately applicable or limited to white and middle-class writers. By presenting an unfamiliar type of conversion through a well-known narrative plot structure and fluidly moving between the expected and the unexpected feminine rhetorical postures, Apess engages in a double version of bifocality and thereby unseats accepted oppositional norms of gendered behavior and destabilizes conventional notions of Protestant identity.

Apess's ability to undercut status quo notions of identity may have been spurred in part by his Methodist leanings. A. Gregory Schneider affirms that

Methodist testimonials, to a much greater degree than those of other Protestant denominations, defied traditional modes of personal and social control: "Certainly acting out one's weakness as a mourner at the altar, braving the exposure of one's life and feelings in class meeting, . . . in the face of mocking worldlings at quarterly or camp meetings required believers to suffer and overcome [social] constraints" (*Way,* 118). The purging of one's heartfelt emotions—including acrimony and anger—as well as strong exhortations to others to transform their actions and beliefs, were endemic parts of the Methodist meeting in the early nineteenth century, and both men and women were expected to participate. In his narrative, Apess capitalizes on the unique permissions granted to Methodist converts to express emotion and rage and to encourage moral change in others. In so doing, he is able to defy standard norms of Protestant behavior and rhetoric, not simply for the sake of being rebellious nor solely for the purpose of recruiting others to the Methodist Church. Instead, through these experimental postures, he launches a political and religious directive against senseless racial discrimination: "It was thought no crime for old and young to hiss at the poor Indians, the noblest work of God, who had met with great misfortunes, and lost everything they had, by those very persons who despised them: yea, look which way they would, they could see no friends, nor even hear a pleasant sound from the lips of the white" (119). In a more telling example, Apess does not blame the devil, the will of God, or his grandmother for her severe beating of him but focuses pointedly on a particular worldly group: "My sufferings certainly were through the white man's measure; for they most certainly brought spiritous liquors first among my people" (121). In addition, rather than accentuate the waning of these feelings and unfortunate experiences following conversion, Apess emphasizes that even after becoming a preacher, he still "found men like adders, with poison under their tongues, hissing around me; and to this day, I find now and then one hissing at me" (132). Thus, while the well-known conversion narrative afforded Apess greater credibility and a larger audience, the less familiar emotion-filled Methodist and feminine-style testimonial enabled him to codify and give voice to his outrage at religious hypocrisy and racist discrimination, an outrage that is as justified after as before his conversion.

That Apess constructively utilized rather than rejected Protestantism and Protestant rhetoric was apparently not unusual for the many Native Americans who converted to Christianity from the seventeenth century to the present. Writing about the history of another New England tribe, James Clifford remarks: "Accounts of conversion as a process of 'giving up old ways' or 'choosing a new path' usually reflect a wishful evangelism rather than the more complex realities of cultural change, resistance and translation. Recent ethnohistorical scholarship has tended to show that Native Americans' response to Christianity was syncretic over the long run, almost never a radical either-or choice" ("Identity," 303). Thus, according to Clifford, Native Americans' conversion to Christianity may not have indicated a forfeiture or loss of their Indian identity. Yet, Clifford does not go into detail about how this syncretism actually happens or how it might impact the subject's sense of self. While William Apess certainly cannot be representative of all converted Native Americans, his narrative can shed some light on these questions.

The previous section of the chapter suggests that Methodism served a utilitarian purpose for Apess, providing him a structure, style, and ready audience for his political convictions without significantly altering or squelching his Pequot sense of self. While I believe that Methodism did fulfill a certain functional purpose for Apess, I contend that it served a much more integral purpose: it helped to form and mold his very identity. In his case, it was not an inherent sense of his own Pequotness nor even a rejection of that identity that — at least initially — shaped his sense of self. For him, it was the shame he received that first called him to mark his difference from others and that in turn caused him to identify with the fledgling early American Methodists who also experienced frequent shame from the established white circles. Later in this section, I will suggest that his connection with the Methodists sparked in him a critical, relativistic (bifocal) understanding of his own vexed and subjugated position in society; and it made possible a course of action for changing that position — that is, through public testimony and writing, to induce his white audience to gain a similar bifocal awareness of American society.

The fact that Apess constructed his identity through opposition should not be surprising. In writing about the social role of shame, early-twentieth-century psychologist Silvan Tomkins has argued that "whenever an individual, a class or a nation wishes to maintain a hierarchical relationship; or to maintain aloofness it will have to resort to contempt of the other. Contempt is the mark of the oppressor...In a democratic society, contempt will often be replaced by empathic shame, in which the critic hangs his head in shame at what the other has done, or by distress in which the critic expresses his suffering at what the other has done, or by anger in which the critic seeks redress for the wrongs committed by the other" (*Shame,* 139). Because it couches itself in empathy, shame masks the power relations upon which it is based more fully than does contempt and, as a result, is less easy to resist or reject. Unlike contempt or ridicule whose wounds are inflicted from outside, shame is experienced as an inner torment. This is because shame does not permanently renounce the object cathexis (that person or object of identification with whom the shamed individual aspires to please or identify). As Sedgwick and Frank note, "Without positive affect, there can be no shame: only a scene that offers you enjoyment or engages your interest can make you blush" ("Shame," 22). Thus, the effectiveness of shame lies in the fact that the oppressor (the one conferring shame) effaces itself and its own agency and causes the second person (who fears the loss of acceptance from and identification with the one projecting shame) to experience shame as self-inflicted, as "a sickness within the self" (Tomkins, *Shame,* 136). Hence, unlike guilt, which refers to what one *does,* "shame attaches to and sharpens the sense of what one *is*" and thus feels less easily modified (Sedgwick, "Shame and Performativity," 212). As a result of its ability to interrupt the shamed's identification with the shamer, shame constructs identity. Sedgwick writes, "shame and identity remain in very dynamic relation to one another, at once deconstituting and foundational, because shame is both peculiarly contagious and peculiarly individuating" (212).

According to Judith Butler, and as shown in the examples of Whitefield and Equiano, subjects are typically formed through an exclusionary matrix. Identifying with one subject position "requires the simultaneous production of a domain of abject beings, those who are not yet 'subjects,' but who form the constitutive outside domain of the subject" (3). As lower-class individuals, Apess, Equiano, and Whitefield experienced social repudiation. Yet, rather than accept that repudiated status and efface themselves completely, the men eventually took on a shamed position—that of the repentant, ridiculed Christian—thereby creating for themselves a recognizable social identity. Yet, unlike Whitefield who deployed this shaming to effect an exalted subject status, both Equiano and Apess continually vacillated between the shamed Christian subject position and repudiated Pequot nonsubject position, never assuming one at the total exclusion of the other.

Apess recounts in his autobiography that as a young child, he repeatedly witnessed whites' repudiation of indigenous people; and as a result, he initially not only failed to identify as a Native American, he was in fact terrified of having any association with his former tribal peoples. While collecting berries in the woods one day with his white foster family, he confronted some dark-skinned white women (who he wrongly believed were natives): "This circumstance filled my mind with terror, and I broke from the party with my utmost speed, and I could not muster courage enough to look behind until I had reached home" (10–11). His "great fear" can be explained by his realization (even as a young boy) that simply the word "Indian" could incur disdain and hardship and did not signify a recognizable subject position: "I thought it disgraceful to be called an Indian; it was considered a slur upon an oppressed and scattered nation, and I have often been led to inquire where the whites received this word, which they so often threw as an opprobrious epithet at the sons of the forest" (10). Apess's fear of repudiation and his realization of the despised status of the Native Americans (and therefore of himself) are accentuated repeatedly in his conversion narrative. Within the first two pages, he tells his white audience: "Little children, how thankful you ought to be that you are not in the same condition that we were, that you have not a nation to hiss at you, merely because your skins are white" (120). His statement not only discloses his disgust at the arbitrary derision he received, it also uncovers his awareness that the slurs were racially motivated, that he happened to possess the "wrong" skin color, and that whiteness was somehow aligned with subjecthood and even nationality. Viewed from the Euro-American perspective, he is excluded from the nation of America and effectively erased.

Although Apess may initially have accepted this contempted status and thus obliterated his own Pequot identity, this attitude did not remain constant. At various points in his life, he accepted and rejected the Euro-Americans' denigratory view of the Pequots, and he both embraced and denied his own Pequot heritage. In short, Apess did not fully jettison his Pequot past nor did he sever himself completely from the dominant Euro-American and Christian world. Instead he discovered and then joined a visible link between the two cultures: the Methodist Church. Oddly enough, he decided to join the Methodist Church (that is, to seek his salvation) not because it offered a total escape from social contempt but rather because it too involved a necessary experience with and acceptance of shame. Because the ridicule Methodists received was far less contemptuous than that foisted on the Native Americans and indeed impelled shaming (and thus the construction of an identity rather than the total repudiation of one), Apess connected the persecution he received as a Pequot with that he received as a Methodist and, as a result, constructed for himself an accepted social identity. Thus, not only does Apess underscore the ridicule the Methodists endured far more often than he details the freedom and comfort they offer from worldly concerns, but in virtually every description of persecution or personal torment that he presents, the repudiation he receives as a Pequot and the torment he suffers as a Methodist are either blurred or collapsed. One experience seems to flow seamlessly into the other.

The blurring of these two sources of ridicule is manifested in a passage where Apess expresses his frustration over the sectarian divisions in the Protestant Church and over the disdain most Protestants have heaped upon the Methodists: "This sectarian nonsense raged most bitterly, and I do suppose that they who could help it would not be willing for their dogs to go there to [Methodist] meeting, for fear of bringing disgrace upon themselves. I would to God that people were more consistent than what they are. Say, would you like to lose everything that was near and dear to you, merely because your skin is white? I had to do it, merely because I had a red one. Judge ye, if this is right; and if not, stop where you are, and cease to do evil and learn to do well" (126). In this passage, Apess connects the Pequots and Methodists by conflating two cases of ridicule, a "nonsensical" one dealing with sectarianism which quickly gives way to another more acrimonious one concerning Native Americans. The first indignation originates from the historically demeaning perception of the Methodists by the elite Protestant sector of white society. As noted earlier, Reformed Protestants resented the Methodists not only because they rejected the doctrine of predestination and a belief in an elected group of saved, but also because they subverted the traditional culture of honor and patriarchal sovereignty by promoting a more radical egalitarianism and a moral individualism. Meekness and righteousness monitored by an inner sense of guilt and emotional devotion to God were more significant in the Methodist community than exterior displays of land ownership, kinship ties, or material wealth. However, while the Methodist meetings might elicit jeers from the Protestant elite, they were well suited to the needs of the young Apess, who, already accustomed to disdain from white authority figures and unable to put forth any impressive displays of wealth or ancestry, must have felt akin to his Methodist brethren and sisters. Hence, although Apess may express a certain vexation over sectarian bigotry in the passage cited earlier, that resentment actually helped him to enter into and feel a sense of belonging in the Methodist (and by extension American) community. Moreover, it provided a convenient way to make sense of, to introduce and perhaps even to validate his longer-term terror over white prejudice and repudiation. He clearly uses the "safer" and more identifiable controversy (at least for his predominantly white audience) to carve out a much needed space for the more significant, volatile, and heretofore silenced one.

Just as the Methodists had a history of discrimination and persecution by the elite Reformed and Anglican denominations, the Pequots had continually faced repudiation and mistreatment by the Europeans since the colonists' arrival. Unlike most nineteenth-century white Protestant rhetors, who erase the existence of the Native Americans or invoke their supposed assimilation or annihilation to illustrate the pertinacious advance of the divine American republic, Apess excavates the presence and history of his fellow tribesmembers and of white racism to constitute a local, personal, and political act of resistance and empowerment. Prior to writing his conversion narrative and autobiography, Apess researched the historical roots of the derision he and his tribesmembers regularly received. In speeches and published writings, he broadcasted his findings, no doubt hoping to encourage his white and native audiences to connect the past treatment of the Indians to present policy and to elicit active attempts at change.[5] Perhaps more than any other New England tribe, the Pequots' encounters with whites had been particularly devastating. The 1637 Pequot War, the Pequots' "voluntary" participation on the colonists' side in the French and Indian War, their forced relocation and enslavement, and the systematic usurpation of their land by the U.S. government nearly decimated the tribe. Records indicate that what had been a thriving population of approximately thirteen thousand before the seventeenth-century European contact and what had been an indomitable tribe that ruled over virtually all of the southern Connecticut river valley had diminished to a paltry thirty or forty members by 1800 and to a mere ten by 1850 (Starna, "Pequots," 46). To intensify matters, even though the Pequots have never completely disappeared, their mention in government reports or in history books almost invariably affirms their extinction after the 1637 war. Apess's narrative brings forward the presence and history of a people who have been and still are effectively erased. He was able to do so not only by directly giving public speeches and appending historical accounts of the Indian-European relationship to his publications, but also more indirectly by drawing an admittedly uneven parallel between the historical plight of the Pequots and that of the Methodists within his conversion narrative.

Apess does more than simply create parallels over the issue of repudiation. In his description of his concern as a young regenerate over the state of his soul, he hints at a possible response to this form of persecution: "My heart now became much troubled, and I felt determined to seek the salvation of my soul..., though I had neither respectability nor character to lose but was like the partridge upon the mountain, a mark for them all to shoot at, and hiss at, and quack at—which often put me in mind of the geese and crows" (126). In this passage, Apess is referring to the calumny he received from his white foster family members, all of whom attended the Congregationalist Church. While this family fed him better than other white Reformed Protestant families with whom he had lived, they nevertheless resented both his Indianness and his proclivity for attending Methodist meetings. In fact, it is unclear in this passage whether his foster family made any distinctions at all between their two prejudices.

At least as significant as the interchangeability of these two sources of ridicule in this passage and Apess's unwillingness to separate them rhetorically as distinct aspects of himself is his bifocal reaction to the ridicule. On the one hand, Apess's claim that, after enduring racist derision and realizing his own sinfulness, he was put "in mind of the geese and crows" suggests that he did indeed imbibe the contemptuous view of Pequots and Methodists that his white Reformed Protestant family had foisted on him; certainly, geese and crows are not exalted creatures in Euro-American society. On the other hand, rather than signify his acceptance of an inferior or abject status, Apess's accentuation of the repudiation he sustained may ironically point to his own desire for empowerment. Ethnographer William S. Simmons notes that the Pequots considered all birds—and especially crows—to be *manitou* or sacred spirits who assisted in forming the universe ("Mystic," 143). Thus, if viewed from the Pequot lens, Apess may have selected the expression, to be put "in mind of the geese and crows," precisely for its doubleness, its hidden and enervating Pequot meaning. He may have been covertly reproaching the white Protestant Reformed elite for their truculence and suggesting that their actions may have worked against their assimilationist goals and served to magnify his tribal and Methodist devotion and his own sense of power.

Apess's ability to transform repudiation into an impetus for Pequot empowerment and for a Pequot connection with Methodism is borne out more obviously in another example. Immediately prior to the passage cited earlier, Apess reveals his complex commitment to both Pequotism and Methodism and his belief in the interrelatedness of those two seemingly diverse realms. Referring to the Methodists, he writes, "Persecution seemed to cement the hearts of the brethren and sisters together, and their songs were sweet. Their prayers and exhortations were like arrows sticking in the heart of their King's enemy, while the preachers poured the thunders of the law upon them, as if God himself had spoken to them" (126). Here, Apess overturns the dominant negative view of Methodists held by the Protestant elite, first by acknowledging their persecution and then by stressing that this derision served to strengthen rather than diminish them. Yet, interestingly, in this case, he buttresses his reversal by metaphorically aligning the Methodists' struggle with that of the Indians and by layering the transposed contrast between Methodists and other Reformed Protestants with a surprising comparison. An image historically denigrating to Native Americans — that is, "arrows sticking in the hearts" of elite white people — is suddenly toppled and associated positively with a Euro-American cause, Methodism.

Apess persists in promoting the comparison between the persecution of the Pequots and that of the Methodists because it proffers a possible means for his white audience to identify with the Pequots' difficulties. Or, to phrase it in terms of bifocality, the lens of Methodism helps his audience to place in focus and thus to make sense of the Euro-American oppression of the Pequots. Yet, seeing the Pequots clearly against a background of Methodists serves another purpose. As the Methodist-Pequot comparison gains sharper focus, it becomes significant precisely for its inadequacy; for certainly, the persecution of the two groups is not synonymous. By midcentury, the Methodists rose to national prominence and prestige. Circuit riders traveled throughout the South and the West to establish a national network of annual conferences, quarterly meetings, love feasts, and weekly classes. Numerous well-ordered and tree-lined camp meetings were erected all over the American rural landscape. In describing the Weslayan Grove camp meeting in Massachusetts, for instance, one historian writes: "The pure, exhilarating air under the shade of the tall oaks, the hearty greetings of old friends and acquaintances, the customary exercise of walking, and above all, the animating devotions of the occasion, enlivened spirits and sharpened appetites" (Weiss, *City*, 27).

Unlike the Methodists who enjoyed resort-like camp meetings and gained in prosperity and power during the first half of the century, the Pequots, throughout the antebellum era, faced economic hardship, material want, and extreme emotional anguish. Notes Apess, "We suffered thus from the cold; the calls of nature, as with almost nakedness; and calumny heaped upon us by whites to an intense degree" (120). Perhaps what is worse is that because they were pushed out of the sight of whites, few whites recognized or cared about their suffering. If Apess's narrative is any indication, many Indian children were taken from their birth families and hired out to labor for "adopted" white families in return for their upbringing. Adults lived in tents and other substandard housing outside of town or subsisted as the most despised of servants in gentry houses (O'Connell, "Introduction," lxii). Moreover, owing to the lack of economic opportunity on their local reservations or communities, the Pequots were frequently compelled to seek menial jobs in the fishing, whaling, or shipping industries or to become indentured servants or fieldworkers on faraway white-owned farms (Campisi, "Emergence," 125–28).

While the Pequots had virtually no recourse to capitalize on their marginalization, the Methodists in many ways were fortified by a ready presence of enemies. In his 1896 novel, *The Damnation of Theron Ware,* Harold Frederic emphasizes that Methodism needed religious opponents, hecklers, scoffers, and other worldly people because they "brought upon the scene a kind of visible personal devil, with whom the chosen could do battle face to face" (234). Furthermore, Gregory Schneider points out that the out-of-town location of Methodist camp meetings was deliberate and advantageous: "By setting their moments of spiritual family enjoyment apart from the world, the Methodists aimed to make manifest a sacred, inner space that was morally at odds with those on the outside. Such a separation implied an appeal to the outsiders to change their moral identifications" (*Way*, 98). Certainly, for Apess, the contrast between the power available to the Pequots to deal with their persecution and marginalization and that bestowed upon the Methodists must have been striking and must have sparked a desire for retribution. Yet, rather than abandon the Pequot struggle, surrender his Pequot identity, or refuse contact with whites, Apess — in a somewhat similar way to the Methodists — chose to employ shame as an opportunity for change, moral suasion, and empowerment. Apess achieved this empowerment by making a variety of cross-cultural or bifocal links, in an effort to capture his white audience's empathy, to prick their sense of Christian guilt and duty, and perhaps to spur them to political action.

As the narrative progresses, Apess goes beyond pointing out instances of bigotry and making integral but superficial connections between the Methodists and Pequots, and moves toward asserting a larger vision of America, one propelled by his dual Methodist-Pequot loyalty. Yet, in order to envision this new nation, Apess (as in the case of Olaudah Equiano) had not only to undercut dominant notions of race but also to overturn the dominant, racist, and nationalist rhetoric of the era: manifest destiny. Writes Apess near the end of his narrative, "But, reader, I acknowledge that this is a confused world, and I am not seeking for office, but merely placing before you the black inconsistency that you place before me—which is ten times blacker than any skin that you will find in the universe... If black or red skins or any other skin of color is disgraceful to God, it appears that he has disgraced himself a great deal—for he has made fifteen colored people to one white and placed them here upon this earth" (157). Through this searing display of irony, Apess reverses the standard racist representation of African Americans as different from and inferior to Native Americans, forges a new community of people of color, and redefines them as God's chosen people. Thus, the pejorative use of the term "black" is at once rejected in its association with skin color and reassigned to "a confused world" of bigotry and racism. Color is transformed from serving as an *outer* marker of one's race and power to a signifier of one's *inner* attitude toward race and difference. Apess's stress on one's interior over one's exterior mirrors, in some sense, the Methodists' concern with the individual believer's inner convictions over his or her outer displays of wealth, kinship, or prestige. Moreover, significantly, such an emphasis confounds and trumps the emerging nationalist-expansionist rhetoric of manifest destiny that propagates white Protestant Americans as God's chosen people.

Although the term "manifest destiny" was not officially coined until the mid-1840s, the concept had been utilized since the eighteenth century and brought pointedly into U.S. political circles at least a decade earlier by Jacksonian Democrats to justify their territorial acquisitions and their removal of Native Americans who resided east of the Mississippi. According to Thomas R. Hietala, two separate but related expansionist or manifest destiny myths circulated during the antebellum era: "The expansionists... perpetuated the convenient myth of a vacant continent, invoking an image of North America as an uninhabited, howling wilderness that the new, chosen people had transformed from savagery to civilization during their predestined march to the Pacific. Others recognized that the continent was not empty and that Indians and Mexicans had occupied much of it prior to American ascendancy but stressed that the United States, in seeking to expand, sought only what was best for these dispossessed races" (*Manifest,* 132). While the latter myth emphasizes a humane interest in nonwhite peoples as a primary motive for the appropriation of the North American continent and the former myth celebrates a contrived vision of a vacant land mass, both views are preoccupied with attaining a white racial homogeneity in the continent and with asserting Anglo-Saxon superiority. Sacvan Bercovitch contends that because this typology of American mission wed Protestantism with the advancement of civilization, technology, individualism, and the middle class, it formed "a web ... which allowed virtually no avenue of escape" (*American*, 168). Apess's narrative, however, calls Bercovitch's claim — or at least its sweeping application — into question, for Apess not only refused to use the rhetoric, but his published narrative, his physical presence in New England, and his accentuation of the cruel behavior of white Protestants in his narrative gave the lie to the validity of both expansionist myths.

Interestingly, Apess's refutation of this Protestant rhetoric of manifest destiny did not represent a split from Methodism; in fact, it may have been spurred in part by his involvement with this particular sect. Russell E. Richey asserts that unlike the more powerful Reformed Protestants, the Methodists were wary of nationalism and manifest destiny: "Notions of America as God's chosen people, of a covenant between God and nation, of eternal purposes being worked out through the American experiment, of America as the light to the world, of religion as requisite to national prosperity, of American history as itself sacred, of the millennium as an American affair — notions certainly available to Methodists had they wanted to adopt them — are absent" (*Early*, 39–40). Perhaps because their ministers were circuit riders, roaming on horseback a hundred-mile radius of often rugged terrain on horseback, American Methodists "oriented themselves to America as continent rather than as nation: to its physical environment, its lands rather than its polity; to geography rather than *civitas*" (12). Given the Methodists' emphasis on the availability of grace to all believers regardless of race, sex, or class and their stress on the continent's physical rather than political geography, their perspective on North America was necessarily not as exclusionary or oppressive as the dominant nationalist-expansionist view held by elite Reformed and evangelical Protestants. No doubt the Methodists' view of the country as divided or bounded only by geography rather than by race was appealing to Apess and enabled him to construct a new vision or identity for the continent of North America. His new social vision merged spirituality with political activism to empower rather than to erase native peoples: "I believe there are many who would not hesitate to advocate our cause; and those too who are men of fame and respectability — as well as ladies of honor and virtue ... Do not get tired, ye noble-hearted —

only think how many poor Indians want their wounds done up daily; the Lord will reward you, and pray you stop not till this tree of distinction shall be leveled to the earth, and the mantle of prejudice torn from every American heart — then shall peace pervade the Union" (160–61).

In addition to overturning the racial coding of the rhetoric of manifest destiny and U.S. nationalism, Apess's new social vision combats what Maggie Sale has also shown was a gender-specific typology ("Antebellum," 700). Indeed, for Francis Parkman, one of New England's Romantic historians and a contemporary of Apess, the rhetoric of American mission was not solely a matter of race; it was also determined by gender. Rejecting the idea of the American Indian as noble savage, Parkman wrote, "The Germanic Race, and especially the Anglo-Saxon branch of it, is peculiarly masculine, and, therefore, peculiarly fitted for self-government" (qtd. in Horsman, *Race*, 184). In contrast to Parkman's statement, Apess's call for "ladies of honor and virtue" to participate in taking antiracist action and to forge a new divine republic certainly speaks to his awareness of women's palpable presence within both the Methodist Church and the union as a whole.

It is possible that Apess's acknowledgment of "ladies" in his narrative may not be directed solely at white women. Contemporary ethnohistorian Jack Campisi reports that the Pequot women in the early nineteenth century both outnumbered the men (by a ratio of eight to one in 1800) and held the most commanding leadership positions within the tribe ("Emergence," 127–28). In addition to serving as signers of various petitions to the state, Pequot women controlled the lease of land and crop sales, helped to maintain a council house, and took an active part in community affairs. As Campisi points out, "women acted as chiefs, [even though] the values of the surrounding white communities did not allow them to be accorded the title of chief or the status of leadership" (128). Apess's ease with powerful women is evident in the inclusion in his book, *The Experiences of Five Christian Indians,* of the conversion stories of four Pequot women (along with his own) and in his frequent commendation of his aunt Sally George for her spiritual leadership and strength (150). Moreover, Protestantism — particularly Methodism — was amenable to strong feminine leaders. Perhaps more than any other Protestant denomination, Methodism offered women opportunities for leadership roles as deaconesses, lay preachers, missionaries, prayer leaders, and Sunday School teachers (Dayton, *Discovering; Holiness*). Apess's social vision unites an antipathy for all varieties of prejudice and scorn with the realization of a landscape replete with white, native, and other nonwhite women and men; and it is a vision propelled rather than repulsed by a profound Methodist spirituality.

Apess's social vision is impressively inclusive, dynamic, and expansive, galvanized rather than thwarted by his relationship to Methodism. The journey he narrates in his conversion story is at least two-directional in its path, revealing a process of inter-reference between two traditions. By exploring the surprising commonalities and stark disjunctures between the Pequots and Methodists, Apess creates a complex, multilayered system of bifocality that ultimately exposes some of the less than laudatory manifestations of dominant values held by the Protestant elite (and no doubt by many Methodists as well) and forces his white audience to recognize the presence and worth of Native Americans on this continent. By setting each group against the background of the other, Apess maintains in some measure a dialectic between two cultures, a dialectic that serves to interrogate, alter, and improve dominant perceptions of both groups. Thus, rather than signifying a surrender to the dominant system of thought or a mere instrumental use of it, Apess's interaction with Methodism provides a glimpse into the way intercultural knowledge can offer reservoirs for renewing antiracist values and for promulgating effective and humane social change.

Chapter Three

Ladders and Quilts

Catharine Beecher's and Harriet Beecher Stowe's Visions of the Christian Subject and Nation

Although writing from a more privileged class and educational background than that of William Apess and Olaudah Equiano, Harriet Beecher Stowe and her older sister Catharine Beecher — like these male predecessors — nevertheless wrestled with the rigid dualisms inherent in Protestantism. As Kathryn Kish Sklar has eloquently argued, Catharine Beecher not only accepted the good-evil dualism embedded in Protestant theology, she "also exaggerated and heightened gender differences" that were soon to become endemic to an overwhelmingly Protestant U.S. society (*Beecher,* 153). Similarly, critical scholars writing about Harriet Beecher Stowe's 1859 novel, *The Minister's Wooing,* have contended that Stowe invests her narrative with a fundamental feminine-masculine opposition or conflict. Dorothy Berkson, for example, asserts that in this novel, "a repressive, dogmatic, paternalistic Old Testament creed . . . give[s] way to the liberating influence of a compassionate, matriarchal New Testament Christianity" ("Millennial," 246). Similarly, Lawrence Buell notes that *The Minister's Wooing* is founded upon a long series of thematic polarities that are personified in various characters: Burr's skepticism versus Hopkins's faith; Virginie's Catholicism versus Mary's Protestantism; and finally Hopkins's masculine, speculative theology versus Mary's feminine, intuitive piety. And more recently, Joan Hedrick argues that "by virtue of her immersion in a women's culture defined largely by rituals of nurturance and motherhood, Stowe developed an egalitarian vision implicitly at odds with the pastoral model of her father and explicitly challenging the male clerical establishment" ("'Peaceable,'" 308).

Thus, both of the Beecher sisters underscore the way in which Protestantism — as well as American society and its members — is organized in terms of a series of hierarchical dualisms such as good/evil, man/woman, activity/passivity, head/heart, reason/passion, and soul/body. The first term of these binaries is not only privileged over the second one, but it is typically designated as the norm of cultural meaning. Yet, did the two sisters ultimately reinforce, undercut, or overturn dominant binaries that were repressive to women and other minority groups? And were the two women's responses to Protestant binary thinking similar or different?

Relying on the argument already advanced by Sklar, the first half of this chapter argues that Catharine did not just tacitly accept these religiously infused cultural dualisms; she promoted them as imperative for the general well-being and advancement of society. Moreover, she went so far as to assert that they must be maintained through the self-sacrifice of American women, lower-class servants, and nonwhites. While she romanticized the power and esteem of women and others' subservient roles and glorified them as the key to U.S. freedom and security, she herself nevertheless refused to assume such a subservient position. The second half of the chapter explores Stowe's novel, *The Minister's Wooing*, and asserts that while she — like her sister — constitutes a binary-laden world, she does so in order to undercut these binaries. As did William Apess in his conversion narrative, Stowe forms a more conciliatory, fluid, expansive, and pluralistic, socioreligious vision than critics have previously allowed. In addition, she implicitly critiques Catharine's affirmation of the masculine-feminine opposition as well as her belief in the necessity of complete self-abnegation for the good of society by invoking a social and interpersonal model of mutuality and acceptance. Thus, Stowe undermines what she sees as Protestantism's and Catharine's principles of exclusion, elitism, and Common Sense reason while simultaneously absorbing their strengths under her new, more tolerant, mobile, heterogeneous, and inclusive individual subjectivity and nationalist vision. Yet, although Stowe's vision is less self-contradictory, adversarial and dualistic than is Catharine's, it too at times advances exclusionary and oppositional thinking, thereby calling into question the ability of anyone during this era to transcend Protestantism's hierarchical dualisms.

During Stowe's formative years, her older sister, Catharine, exerted at least as powerful an influence on her as did her father. Shortly after Catharine founded the Hartford Female Seminary in 1823, Harriet joined her there, first as a student and then, from 1827 to 1832, as a teacher and administrator. During these years, Harriet experienced her initial conversion and began writing. Along with other family members, the two sisters moved to Cincinnati in 1832, where they wrote both alone and together. Thus, Catharine's philosophy—much of which was formed during the Hartford and Cincinnati years—was certainly intimately familiar to Harriet.

As Kathryn Kish Sklar noted in her biography of Catharine Beecher, although Catharine quibbled with various aspects of her father's Reformed faith, she actually remained loyal to much of the Calvinist belief system. For example, despite her rejection of the innate depravity of children, Catharine nevertheless endorsed "a vision of a world divided sharply between good and evil" (*Beecher,* 262). Although she may have "believed that she was taking great risks in asserting human goodness," she ended up concocting a world in which (like that of the Calvinists) the majority was not allowed to enjoy their goodness (263). The reason for this view was that despite her belief in greater human choice in the salvation process, she nevertheless aligned herself with the Calvinist belief in absolute submission to God and a higher moral structure. And finally, even though she virulently balked at her father's and the Calvinists' insistence on the amount of guilt she should feel for her sins, she still proceeded to shame those who she felt were not following proper Christian roles.

Interestingly, however, Catharine begins her 1836 *Letters on the Difficulties of Religion* by recognizing the presence and validity of a wide array of believers and nonbelievers:

> The writer has had opportunities of mingling, on social and familiar terms, with persons of a great variety of moral and religious sentiments. Among all denominations of Christians, who agree on the fundamental truths of Christianity, she has found persons of intelligence, learning, and piety, whose friendship has been highly prized. — Among Unitarians, Universalists, Swedenborgians, and Catholics, she has found amiable, conscientious, and intelligent friends. Even among Infidels,

Atheists and entire skeptics, there have been found those, whose domestic character, fine natural endowments, and real friendship, have been appreciated and valued as they deserved. (v)

While Catharine professes a friendly sentiment toward all peoples, a clear hierarchy emerges in her statement. The first group to which she refers (those
Christians who hold fundamental truths) is obviously superior to the other
groups as evidenced by her praising of their education, intelligence, and devotion and by the categorization of her friendship with them as "highly prized."
The second group of believers (Unitarians, Universalists, Swedenborgians, and
Catholics) may be "amiable, conscientious and intelligent," but her affection
toward them is clearly curtailed as a result of their rejection of certain "fundamental" truths and their concomitant stubbornness and ignorance. In fact,
because of their unwillingness to turn properly to God, they are not far removed from the final group of nonbelievers whose character traits are more
qualified than those of the first group and whose friendship is bounded and
appreciated only "as they deserved." Thus, despite her initial division of American society into three groups, in reality, she demarcates them into two. As she
notes later in the book, there are essentially two classes of believers: those
who give "to God the first place in . . . [their] affections" and therefore are saved
and those who "do not believe that men are in any danger of being *lost forever*
and therefore do not suppose that they need to do anything to be saved" (330–
31). Thus, what initially may appear as tolerance for a diverse range of views
actually results in a rigid hierarchical dualism of the good and the bad, the
saved and the damned.

   Beyond bifurcating the world of religious believers, Beecher also subdi-
vides humanity into two distinct and opposing genders, and she surprisingly
consigns men to a superior position: "man the head, protector, and provider —
woman the chief educator of immortal minds — man to labor and suffer to
train and elevate woman for her high calling, woman to set an example of
meekness, gentleness, obedience, and self-denying love, as she guides her children and servants heavenward" (*Woman's*, 184). In this sense, many of Catharine's writings (especially those with an overt agenda about religious and domestic obligation) apparently endorse binarily structured gender relations that
later scholars, Barbara Welter in particular, have systematized as the Cult of
True Womanhood, a cultural ideal promulgated beginning in the 1830s (*Dimity*). Women, according to this ideal, should be characterized by the virtues of
piety, purity, submissiveness, and domesticity and should remain in the pri-

vate realm of the home. Men, by contrast, were to operate in the public sphere of commerce, law, education, and politics and could embody the principles of action, independence, aggression, and intelligence.

Recent feminist historians have underscored that this gender ideal was more prescriptive than descriptive or innate (Kerber, "Separate"); and interestingly, Beecher, writing in 1836, also realizes that men and women require continual socialization, self-discipline, and self-sacrifice to inculcate and maintain the "proper" behavior for their gender. Consequently, she spent much of her life penning advice books, treatises, and other writings designed to instruct readers of their appropriate conduct; and she developed a range of strategies for persuading them of the necessity and value of this dualistic gendered paradigm. One of her most frequent strategies is to hyperbolize the social, political, economic, and religious importance of this gendered hierarchy: "Society could never go forward, harmoniously, nor could any craft or profession be successfully pursued, unless these superior and subordinate relations be instituted and sustained" (*Treatise*, 2). Indeed, despite its egalitarian emphasis, the future of the U.S. political system itself, she believes, depends upon a hierarchical and dualistic social order:

> Now the principles of democracy require . . . that distinctions of superiority and subordination shall depend, not on accidents of birth, fortune, or occupation, but solely on those relations, which the good of all classes equally require . . . It is, indeed, assumed, that the value of the happiness of each individual is the same as that of every other; but as there must always be occasions, where there are advantages which all cannot enjoy, there must be general rules for regulating a selection. Otherwise, there would be constant scrambling among those of equal claims, and brute force must be the final resort . . . The democratic rule, then, is that superiors in age, station, or office have precedence of subordinates. (*Treatise*, 124)

Surprisingly, in this passage, Beecher not only presupposes the value of hierarchical relations in a democratic society but also proclaims the "brute" destructiveness of egalitarianism. For Beecher, unequal social relations help to mollify a potentially chaotic, anxiety-ridden, and rapidly changing American society. The antebellum rise in urbanization, industrialization, racial tension, and immigration served to uproot what she saw as the previous, more stable and homogeneous agrarian society. While the above passage highlights the deference of children to elders, employees to employers, church members to ministers, or citizens to legislators, the most significant and prevailing social distinction for Beecher, as Sklar points out, was that between the two genders:

"[Beecher] led her readers to conclude that by removing half the population from the arena of competition and making it subservient to the other half, the amount of antagonism the society had to bear would be reduced to a tolerable limit" (156). Moreover, by raising the gender binary to a transcendent level, Beecher was able to erase in a single stroke all of the other political, racial, class, regional, and sectarian divisions that were threatening to rip the nation apart. Beecher made it seem that by adhering to this simple dichotomous prescription, Americans could stabilize a fractious society and function as a beacon of hope to the remaining world: "already the light is streaming into the dark prison-house of despotic lands, while startled kings and sages, philosophers and statesmen, are watching us" (*Treatise*, 12).

Because woman was cast in the inferior role in this dualism, Beecher expended much energy highlighting the benefits and significance of her place and function. According to her, although woman is relegated to the private sphere, the influence she wields on family and other loved ones has far-reaching worldly and eschatological impact:

> Now the family state is instituted to educate our race to the Christian character, — to train the young to be followers of Christ. Woman is its chief minister, and the work to be done is the most difficult of all, requiring not only intellectual power, but a moral training nowhere else so attainable as in the humble, laborious, daily duties of the family state.
>
> Woman's great mission is to train immature, weak, and ignorant creatures, to obey the laws of God; the physical, the intellectual, the social, and the moral — first in the family, then in the school, then in the neighborhood, then in the nation, then in the world. (*Woman's*, 175)

For Beecher, woman need not enter the pulpit, cast ballots, or hold public office to alter the course of history and improve society. By concentrating woman's sphere of influence on the home (that is, to "matters pertaining to the education of their children, in the selection and support of a clergyman, in all benevolent enterprises, and in all questions relating to morals or manners" [*Treatise*, 9]), her power — Beecher believed — would ironically be more pervasive. In a (perhaps feeble) attempt to solidify her argument further, Beecher even went so far as to downplay men's greater economic and political power and to claim that their role was less influential than that of women: "There is a moral power given to the woman in the family state much more controlling and abiding than the inferior, physical power conferred on man" (*Woman's*, 181).

Even more ironic than the supposed global impact of woman's narrow focus on the home is Beecher's contention that woman's power stems from her complete selflessness. "The principle of subordination," she stresses continuously, "is the great bond of union and harmony through the universe" (*Woman's*, 188). Such harmony is achieved because, for Beecher, woman's "chief concern is, not mainly to save self, but rather to save [herself] by laboring to save others from ignorance of God's laws" (*Woman's*, 176). Self-sacrifice, then, entails not only relinquishing any hopes for a professional nondomestic career or public position of leadership but also impeding any selfish desires or "lower propensities": "We are not to aim at destroying our appetites, or at needlessly denying them, but rather so to regulate them, that they shall best secure the objects for which they were implanted. We are not to annihilate the love of praise and admiration; but so to control it, that the favor of God shall be regarded more than the estimation of men" (*Treatise*, 159). In addition to instructing her women readers to regulate and control their bodily appetites and desire for praise, Beecher calls for the complete suppression of anger: "A woman can resolve, that, whatever happens, she will not speak, till she can do it in a calm and gentle manner. *Perfect silence* is a sage resort" (138). Squelching one's anger is particularly laudable in Beecher's eyes because it involves the resistance of temptation that, for her, is the only true indicator of self-sacrifice. To be virtuous when one is not tempted to act otherwise does not constitute self-sacrifice; one's worldly or selfish desire must be consciously abandoned for the higher "Christian" or moral goal. While perfect submission or obedience to God's will is impossible, it is the "*determination* to obey" divine volition in the face of temptation that sets the true, virtuous Christian apart from all others (*Letters*, 138).

Beecher's emphasis on self-discipline and self-sacrifice parallels and in some ways eclipses the same emphasis made by Calvinists such as Whitefield and Equiano, who believed complete self-renunciation to be a prerequisite of conversion. Whereas the Calvinists deemed self-sacrifice as one of the manifestations of regeneration (providential favor and the ability to convert others being other evidences of sanctification), Catharine viewed it as "the only means of individual salvation and cultural regeneration" (Sklar, *Beecher*, 249). In this sense, Beecher's demands (particularly for women who by virtue of their subordinate social station were required to do more sacrificing than men) were even more exacting than those made by Whitefield and her father's religious contemporaries. But, as in the case of her transcendent use of the gender binary, her focus on self-sacrifice helped to simplify for antebellum U.S. women what may have seemed like an increasingly complicated system of social conventions and codes of conduct. And similarly, their compliance to this ideal promised great rewards, for Beecher contends that as a result of their self-sacrifice, "every occasion for clashing, and collision, would cease, and the whole universe would be united in feeling and action" (*Letters,* 130).

Self-sacrifice, as Beecher well knew, does not come easily. Thus, she called for women, through their example and direct instruction, to inculcate this quality in their daughters. Yet, even in the absence of proper maternal role models, women and girls could imbibe their divinely prescribed role and the concomitant virtue of self-sacrifice through commonsensical readings of the Bible. First promulgated in the late eighteenth century by the Scottish philosophers Thomas Reid and Dugald Stewart, and then coopted by nineteenth-century conservative and liberal Protestants alike, Common Sense philosophy prescribed a moral system in which one's conscience determined all mental and moral judgments and served to guide the individual through life's turmoils. Put simply, this philosophy (or antiphilosophy) originated as a response to David Hume's skepticism and argued that perception is a dynamic activity in which sense seizes immediately on the external object and establishes a continuous contact between mind and nature. In addition, common sense advocated a psychology of intuitive realism. According to Bozeman, " 'Judgment' was not to be understood as a datum transmitted to the mind by the senses, but as an a priori enrichment and validation of sensory information, evincing itself by 'a strong and irresistible conviction and belief' " (*Protestants,* 10). Whereas late-eighteenth and early-nineteenth-century strict Calvinists accepted that the human mind had been utterly blinded by the Fall, Common Sense Protestants believed that humans came equipped with an intuitive ability to make moral judgments.

While Common Sense philosophers' emphasis on the individual conscience was less hierarchical than was the traditional Calvinists' belief in the minister as ultimate spiritual authority, they nevertheless reinforced other elements of the Calvinist tradition by affirming the importance of the social community and the reciprocal correlation between internal piety and external morality. Moreover, in some ways, the control over individual agency in Common Sense thought was more insidious than that in Calvinism in that one's conscience, unlike a minister, could never be fully resisted or escaped.

Although Common Sense philosophy theoretically stressed individuality (indeed one's conscience reigned supreme), in no way did Beecher (or the other Common Sense thinkers for that matter) intend for individuals' consciences to give rise to divergent views and methodologies. For her, the common sense method of the Bible assumes "to be true that which has much positive evidence in its favor, and which secures all the good without any of the risk of a contrary course" (*Letters,* 68). While Beecher never defines what she means by "evidence," it is clear that she means for her readers to interpret the Bible as conservatively and literally as she does. If, during a Bible-reading, inconsistencies or contradictions present themselves, one should (Beecher cautions) not question the book's veracity but instead assume "it is one's own want of knowledge that creates the difficulty, rather than the unworthiness of the record" (*Letters,* 70). And she goes even further to emphasize that "no one has a right to assume that anything in it is inconsistent, false, or absurd, till he has proved that there is no other assumption possible" (71). But in order to do that, the person must "understand the original languages of scripture... [and] know the customs, habits, country, manner, controversies, and philosophy of the age in which the different books of scripture were written" (71). In short, contesting scriptural truths would require finances, education, and leisure time only a select few American women possessed. Thus, Beecher was effectively calling for women to read the Bible literally and uncritically, that is, to receive it as was presented by the most traditional Protestants of her era.

Beyond appealing to common-sense readings of the Bible, Beecher also resorts to the use of shame to mold women into their proper roles. As Eve Sedgwick has argued, shame does not serve merely as a constraining or destructive force; it also functions to individuate and constitute the self. Unlike shame, contempt involves the total rejection or repudiation of the other's humanness and cuts off communication between the oppressor and oppressed. Shame, on the other hand, entails a connection between the two parties and, as a result, is less easy to combat or reject. Thus, through the use of shame, Catharine Beecher was able to wield considerable power and influence over women's processes of identification. By promoting the transcendence of the feminine self-sacrificing identity she promulgates, and by associating it with the well-being of a democratic, Christian, and moral society, she simultaneously encourages her readers to seek identification with an object cathexis (in this case, a moral nation) and effaces her own agency in the process of identity-construction. Further to obfuscate her own power position, Beecher continually asserts her own adherence to this gendered identity, her own adoption of the proper submissive feminine role. For example, after proclaiming woman's need to "follow Christ in self-denying labors," she notes, "I have sacrificed all my time, all my income, my health, and every plan of worldly ease and pleasure" (*Woman's,* 86). Thus, Beecher performs a multilayered self-effacement: simultaneously denying her agency in the construction of woman's identity, an identity defined by its self-effacement, a self-effacement she then claims to follow.

Moreover, in keeping with the mechanism of shame, Beecher interrupts the identification process when she locates an individual transgressing the rigid boundaries of femininity, and not surprisingly, she underplays her personal dislike of these unfeminine women and highlights their offense to others, in particular to men and God:

> Every man of sense and refinement, admires a woman as a woman; and when she steps out of this character, a thousand things that in their appropriate sphere would be admired, become disgusting and offensive.
>
> The appropriate character of a woman demands delicacy of appearance and manners, refinement of sentiment, gentleness of speech, modesty in feeling and action, a shrinking from notoriety and public gaze, a love of dependence, and protection, aversion to all that is coarse and rude, and an instinctive abhorrence of all that tends to indelicacy and impurity, either in principles or sorrow. (*Letters,* 22)

As was shown in the examples of Equiano and Apess, identity, for Beecher, gets formed through a logic of repudiation: woman is defined by what she is not. Indeed, according to her, the good Christian woman represents the exact antithesis of the unfeminine woman, and the exemplar of this mannish female is the free-love advocate and anarchist Fanny Wright. Beecher detests Wright's public role and radical views on religion, family, and the state as well as "her great masculine person, her loud voice, her untasteful attire, . . . [her] bare-faced impudence, . . . [and her] brazen front and brawny arms" (*Letters,* 231). Indeed, none of Wright's personal features or traits seems salvageable in Beecher's eyes; the core of her very being is unacceptable. Yet, as Judith Butler notes, "The 'I' who would oppose its construction is always in some sense drawing from that construction to articulate its opposition; further the 'I' draws what is called its 'agency' in part through being implicated in the very relations of power that it seeks to oppose" (*Bodies,* 123). According to Butler, when an individual defines itself in opposition to another being or group, that individual necessarily is informed by or constituted through its opposer.

Thus, although Beecher frequently proclaimed her own selfless femininity, in many ways, her own daily life screamed the opposite and was in fact more closely akin to the life of Fanny Wright than to the ideal of True Womanhood. As Sklar points out, "She was a writer on the moral education of children, but had no children herself; she was a competent religious writer, but had not experienced conversion; and she urged young women to become teachers, but was herself not willing to teach. The only consistent element in Catharine's life was her role as a publicist of self-sacrifice since she believed that her personal life was one of self-denial and self-sacrifice" (*Beecher,* 186). Not only did Beecher's unmarried status and lack of a permanent domestic residence allow her greater mobility and a life outside the private sphere not enjoyed by most American women nor enjoined by the feminine ideal she promoted to others, it also enabled her to compete with her father and brothers on their own ground: "She who had been asked to submit [and demanded others to submit] now assumed a male role and asked others to submit to her as their spiritual mentor" (64). Thus, Beecher was able to achieve public power by maintaining a strict fissure between her rhetoric and practice, that is, by promoting an ideal that she herself refused to follow.

Beecher's ideology of self-sacrifice afforded her the opportunity for public acclaim and leadership and for transgressing dominant codes of conduct, but it did not offer the same opportunities to the bulk of her readers. While American women under this ideology might ostensibly serve as the purveyors of middle-class, domestic morality and the virtuous saviors of a troubled nation, they nevertheless were closed out of a host of career and leadership opportunities as well as political, legal, and economic rights. Moreover, their own voices, feelings, and desires became their enemies, as women were precluded from expressing themselves freely. Given her refusal to follow these prescriptions, Beecher herself demonstrated the losses incurred by the feminine ideal she so vehemently advocated.

Unlike Catharine, who promoted a rigid gender binary which she herself did not follow, Harriet Beecher Stowe, drawing from her own lived experience, simultaneously affirmed and undercut the binaries that her sister, for the most part, publicly supported. Prior to writing *The Minister's Wooing,* Stowe had undergone a series of disappointments, challenges, and traumas that propelled her to rethink the Calvinist Reformed faith of her father and its codification of women. The sudden death of her mother, the severe interrogation she received by a local minister upon her conversion, her slow-developing but dramatic empathy for the plight of the American enslaved (and especially the mothers suddenly severed from their children), the unexpected deaths of her brother George and her sons Charley and Henry, as well as her own inability to fulfill her domestic responsibilities adequately and be a noted American author at the same time all served to unseat her childhood devotion to Calvinism.

Yet, rather than reject the Reformed tradition entirely, Stowe pays homage to it by including mention in her novel of three of the most prominent Calvinist-based theologians in New England history: Jonathan Edwards, Joseph Bellamy, and Samuel Hopkins.[1] Bellamy and Hopkins differed from Edwards in their emphases, tone, and mode of presentation,[2] but they all converged in their loyalty to the Calvinist tenet that all humans are so intrinsically corrupt that, unless redeemed by the unmerited operation of divine grace, they are deserving of damnation. By incorporating into her narrative this historical chain of religious thinkers, each of whom espoused and altered some of his predecessor's views, Stowe affirms the longevity of Calvinist thought, yet also confirms that theology has been and must continually be reconfigured to suit the social and political happenings of the time. Hopkins's Calvinism, she infers, is an outgrowth of an old (and now dated) order: "The system of Dr. Hopkins was one that could have had its origin in a soul at once reverential and logical—a soul, moreover, trained from its earliest years in the habits of thought engendered by monarchical institutions. For although he, like other ministers, took an active part as a patriot in the Revolution, still he was brought up under the shadow of a throne, and a man cannot ravel out the stitches in which early days have knit him" (23). In this passage, Stowe negotiates between two seemingly opposing claims: one that theology is socially and politically constructed and the other that it conforms to humans' natural spiritual inclinations. Hopkins's hierarchical views are in keeping with "the noblest capabilities of [human] nature" as well as a consequence of his upbringing "under the shadow of a throne." By simultaneously reserving the natural applicability and origins of religion and insisting upon its historical contingency, Stowe retains the essence of Christianity while granting herself (and others) license to reshape it.

Consequently, despite Stowe's belief in the outmoded quality of Calvinism, she refuses to forsake it altogether. As witnessed in the above passage, Stowe goes to some pains to accentuate the valuable aspects of Calvinism—its "reverential and logical" character and its engendering of a "loyal" and "noble" capability.[3] As is evident in the rest of the novel, Stowe clearly reveres the close-knit solidarity of the Puritan-Calvinist community where "theology was the all-absorbing interest" (87). During the course of the narrative, virtually every character, from the noble heroine Mary to the enslaved Digo and Candace, earnestly engages in a hearty discussion over Hopkinsian theology. Another indication of Stowe's refusal to jettison Calvinism entirely is her complex and ambivalent depiction of Dr. Hopkins. Undoubtedly, Hopkins's rebuking of Simeon Brown's slave trade, which he does at the risk of losing the most prominent members of his church, is commendable in her eyes. In addition, the fact that Mary Scudder (the protagonist) venerates his sermons and that he ultimately withdraws his marriage agreement with her to permit her to marry James (the man whom she passionately loves) at least somewhat endears him and his Calvinist principles to the readers. After all, by liberating Mary from her connubial obligation, he is fulfilling the dictates of his doctrine of Disinterested Benevolence; in other words, however reluctantly, he does obviate his most precious earthly desire for the benefit of Jim, Mary, and the entire Newport community.

Although Stowe may see Hopkins's willingness to comply with the strictures of his own stringent theological system as meritorious, she is also quick to pinpoint in this novel the many problems with Disinterested Benevolence in particular and Calvinism in general. Stowe's biggest complaint with Calvinism comes through in the famous "rungless ladder" passage[4] in chapter 6:

> There is a ladder to heaven, whose base God has placed in human affections, tender instincts, symbolic feelings, sacraments of love, through which the soul rises higher and higher, refining as she goes, till she outgrows the human, and changes, as she rises, into the image of the divine. At the very top of this ladder, at the threshold of paradise, blazes dazzling and crystalline that celestial grade where the soul knows no self no more ... This highest step, this saintly elevation, which but few selectest spirits ever on earth attain, ... for which this world is one long discipline, for which the soul's human education is constantly varied, ... to which all its multiplied powers tend with upward hands of dumb and ignorant aspiration, ... had been seized upon by our sage [Hopkins] as the all of religion. He knocked out every round of the ladder but the highest, and then, pointing to its hopeless splendor, said to the world, "Go up thither and be saved!" (87–88)

By eliminating all but the bottom and top rungs of the ladder, Hopkins creates a fixed binary and thus occludes the possibility of differing degrees of faith or regeneration. While such lofty and rigid requirements for conversion might have worked more comfortably in a small, isolated, closely contained, deeply religious, and technologically simpler Puritan community, they are not readily applicable to the more populated, diverse, and pressure-ridden New England of Stowe's own times. Even Newport in the late eighteenth century feels the strains of a world market system, higher scholarly theological criticism, and political disputes over labor divisions and slavery. As a result of these formidable environmental changes and challenges to religious authority, New England theology — in Stowe's mind — needs to be renovated but not dismissed.

Other than being more openly conciliatory and dialectic, Stowe's position on Calvinism was not very different from that of her sister. Because Catharine never experienced the conversion demanded by Reformed thinkers, she too disagreed with the stringent demands of the Calvinist conversion process and in particular with the amount of self-scrutiny and guilt required of the unregenerate. In fact, in an 1828 letter to her brother Edward, she wrote, "I wish I could catch my inward woman and give her such an inspection and exposition, but she is such a restless being that I cannot hold still long enough to see her true form or outline" (qtd. in Sklar, *Beecher*, 79). Unwilling to submit herself to the vulnerability and humility entailed in self-analysis, Catharine downplayed the inward focus of Calvinism and focused more pointedly on outward manifestations of morality. By emphasizing proper character formation and behavior rather than inner piety, Catharine was able to appeal to those unable to follow Calvinist conversion standards and "to design a more appropriate national system of morality and ethics" (79).

Stowe too sought to widen the appeal of Reformed Protestantism and its hopeless ladder theology.[5] But she did so not by shearing her faith of its inward focus but instead by calling for a richer, more variegated view of salvation. Rather than focus exclusively on the endpoint (the moment of regeneration), ministers — Stowe infers — should consider the fluctuating, lifelong process toward human sanctification. Because of their emphasis of product over process and part over totality, the ministers are not only bolstering a rigid elitism (comprised of the "few selectest spirits"), they also are denying their very responsibilities as servants of God (Caskey, *Chariot*, 185). In other words, according to Stowe, these ministers are tragically oblivious to their obligation to assist church members in mounting the everyday ladder rungs that she believes would inevitably lead them toward salvation. Instead, preachers such as Hopkins worry over abstract theological questions and over the ultimate state of regeneracy of their members' souls. A vivid example occurs when the word arrives in Newport that James Marvyn has drowned at sea (Hedrick, *Stowe*, 144).[6] Upon hearing the news that this beloved member of the community has unexpectedly perished, Hopkins expresses no concern over the emotional or spiritual well-being of James's family and loved ones and instead "musingly" inquires, " 'What was his spiritual state?' " (317).

The salvation question resonates powerfully with Stowe personally, as it did with many nineteenth-century women. Large epidemics, expanded travel opportunities by sea, high infant mortality rates, along with greater religious disillusionment, made the probability immense that a loved one would die in an unregenerate state. Stowe's own life and faith were affected deeply by such tragedies. Her sister's fiancé, her brother George, her two sons Charles and Henry, all died suddenly with their souls in questionable conditions. Stowe herself continually grappled with the certainty of her own salvation because she never met the clear-cut conversion requirements demanded by Calvinism[7] and because she had difficulty believing that God, as the author of sin, would condemn an individual to hell for sinning. As a result of her disenchantment with Calvinism's exclusionary foundational principles, Stowe's position more closely resembles Arminianism,[8] which recognizes the individual as active rather than passive in her or his salvation. For Stowe, grace is not arbitrarily or capriciously dispensed like the royal prerogative of a sovereign ruler, but tendered freely to all people as the gift of a loving parent to his or her children. According to Geoffrey Nuttall, Stowe's shift from Calvinism to Arminianism can be attributed to her own evangelical fervor, her own desire to augment the numbers of God's chosen people. He writes, "The theology of Calvinism arises, naturally and properly, as a theology of the people of God within the household of God. An Arminian theology arises equally naturally and properly, as a theology of mission to the unbeliever" (77).[9] Whereas Hopkins, Edwards, and George Whitefield held that the awakened sinner is more odious than the completely unregenerate one, Arminianism holds that sinners can reasonably expect to be saved if they work as God would want them to do and obey His will.

Stowe's subscription to Arminianism is borne out in her detailed explanation of the conversion process of two of the most sympathetically portrayed characters in the novel—Jim Marvyn and Candace. Unlike the typical Calvinist convert, Candace neither experiences a miraculous conversion nor assents to Calvinist theological doctrine as divine truth. In particular, she ardently denounces the biblical creation story and the concept of original sin. She exclaims,

"I didn't do dat ar', for one, I knows. I's got good mem'ry, — allers knows what I does, — nebber did eat dat ar' apple, . . . Don't tell me!"

It was of no use, of course, to tell Candace of all the explanations of this redoubtable passage, — of potential presence, and representative presence, and representative identity, and federal headship. (139)

Interestingly, in this passage, Candace rejects one form of individualism only to supplant it with another. According to Calvinism, the individual is utterly alone in his or her road to salvation — traveling with "no interceding relation" on this worldly plane (341). Yet, even more challenging is the fact that the individual is not only severed completely from others but is a representative individual, a symbolic version of the depraved Adam or Eve. Candace, on the other hand, views herself as unrepresentative of anyone but herself; thus, her view of individuality more closely resembles that implicit in Republicanism where human beings are seen as unique, inherently worthy, and deserving of all individual rights and liberty. In fact, she accepts Christianity only after she hears about Christian people, like Hopkins, treating other slaves as unique individuals by working toward their emancipation and redemption. For her, conversion is an individual's act of free and deliberate choice: " 'I's set out to b'liebe de Catechize, an' I'm gwine to b'liebe it, — so!' " (140). Moreover, Candace's assertive personality and physical strength, while playing directly into racialized stereotypes of the "mammy" figure, nevertheless directly contradict the Calvinists' notion of federal headship of Adam over Eve because Adam (and by extension, all men) had the priority in creation. As the narrator notes, "A whole woman's rights convention could not have expressed more in a day than Candace could give in a single look or word" (178). Despite this character's unorthodox means of conversion and Stowe's racialized depiction of her, Stowe clearly does not want the reader to question Candace's faith — for the narrator comments that her "very thorough profession of faith was followed . . . by years of the most strenuous orthodoxy" (140). Moreover, as Joan Hedrick points out, many of Candace's spiritual views — especially those relating to Christ's love and grief — echo sentiments Stowe herself expressed in correspondence to bereaved loved ones (" 'Peaceable,' " 315).

Like Candace, Jim undergoes an unorthodox salvation process brought about, in part, by his extensive traveling, which invested him with "those new modes of speech, those other eyes for received opinions and established things, which so often shock established prejudices" (26). Referring to Hopkins's speculative theories, James notes, "it is too narrow to take in . . . this world of ours.

Nobody that has a soul, and goes round the world as I do, can help feeling it at times, and thinking, as he sees all the races of men and their ways" (72). Because his thinking is informed by cultures and peoples far removed from New England, James is not able to identify with Hopkinsian Calvinism and is deemed an infidel by the Newport religious elite. Mary, however, refuses to label him as such and offers him spiritual advice and her Bible before he sets sail on a three-year voyage. Responding favorably to her nonjudgmental ministrations, Jim promises Mary that he will exert effort toward his own salvation through Bible-reading (34, 38).

James's effort pays off when he comes across a Bible story that responds to many of his religious solicitudes. Toward the end of the novel, he recounts his interpretation of the story to Mary: " '[Jacob] saw a ladder in his sleep between him and heaven, and angels going up and down. That was a sight which came to the very point of his necessities. He saw that there was a way between him and God, and that there were those above who did care for him, and who could come to him to help him' " (517). Jacob's ladder provides a direct contrast to Hopkins' rungless one, because it promises a wide array of helpers who will nurture and guide James toward salvation. Through this metaphor, Stowe underlines two significant points of her own theology. First, she accentuates Horace Bushnell's concept of "Christian Nurture," which holds that conversion is a lifelong development and is propelled by the influence of others. Toward that end, she also offers a countermetaphor to Jonathan Edwards's famous harrowing image of the unbelieving sinner who dangles perilously as a spider over the pit of hell: "O sinner! Consider the fearful danger you are in: it is a great furnace of wrath, a wide and bottomless pit, full of the fire or wrath, that you are held over in the hand of that God, whose wrath is provoked and incensed as much against you, as against many of the damned in hell. You hang by a slender thread, with the flames of divine wrath flashing about it, and ready every moment to singe it" (Edwards, *Selections,* 165). Edwards's threatening vision is reinforced by Catharine in her writing. Repeatedly, she warns women that unless they follow their prescribed responsibility to save themselves and others, "terrific hazards, and more awful and universal ruin" will follow (*Letters,* 91). While Edwards and Beecher expend most of their descriptive energy detailing the horrors of the underworld, Stowe, by contrast, spends her time fortifying and peopling the spider's web so that it will foster a more stable and tight-knit community of "spiders" who, working together, build networks of webs stretching toward the higher spiritual realms of salvation.

In an attempt to reempower the individual, Stowe calls upon him or her to sidestep theologians and to read the Bible actively for his or her unique purposes. James's pragmatic remarks about the Bible are typical of Stowe's thinking: "'There is a great deal in it that I cannot understand, a great deal that seems to me inexplicable; but all I can say is, that I have tried its directions, and find that in my case they do work, — that it is a book that I can live by; and that is enough for me'" (520).

While Jim's and Candace's conversions are similar in that they are both self-induced and self-actualized, they differ in at least one notable respect. Jim, as the free, white, middle-class man, is highly literate and can therefore secure his salvation through the act of critical reading. As an uneducated slave woman, Candace, on the other hand, must gain her regeneracy through direct observation and experience. Although this difference in the characters' conversions indicates Stowe's awareness of the disparity in privileges available to the two new believers, it also (on a darker note) may suggest Stowe's (perhaps unconscious) assumption that nonwhite characters are less sophisticated than white people in their spiritual and social outlooks.

Despite their racialized differences, the examples of Candace and Jim affirm that for Stowe, salvation can happen through a variety of methods, efforts, and mediations. Both figures are assisted by others in their processes of sanctification. In her writings, Catharine Beecher also underlines how important it is for the saved to help others to "secure endless happiness in the life to come" (*Woman's*, 43), but her method contrasts sharply with the more tolerant one implemented by Mary Scudder in Stowe's novel. Whereas Mary sees value in and even falls in love with the unregenerate Jim, Catharine, in her letters to nonbelievers and skeptics, frequently resorts to fairly combative attacks, reminiscent of George Whitefield. Writing to an agnostic, she poses the question: "Do you not allow that if you found a man really believing new and curious contrivances to be the effect of chance, and acting and talking on this assumption, you would think him a lunatic?" (*Letters*, 39). At another point, she refers to skeptics as "ignorant and incompetent" (70). Later, she reasons, "When men embrace and endeavor to propagate opinions injurious to the interests of society, it is the duty of all good citizens to throw the whole weight of their influence against them; to make their opinions appear absurd and discreditable, and if possible to use legal means to prevent their usurping the places of property, devoted to the extension of opposing sentiments" (*Letters*, 320).

The difference between Stowe's and Beecher's methods of ministration illustrates the contrast that contemporary psychologist Judith Jordan has commonly observed in patterns of interpersonal relations. Beecher's strategies resemble in many ways what Jordan terms as "masculine" or dominant methods of dealing with conflict. According to Jordan, dominant individuals or groups are able to maintain power by suppressing conflict; and they achieve this repression through several strategies: (1) by shaming the person expressing the alternative view; (2) by propounding a myth of harmony and unity (so that any disagreement by the subordinate is construed as a sign of personal failure or inadequacy); and (3) by articulating rules for conflict that effectively silence or denigrate claims made by nondominant voices ("Courage," 5). Stowe's methods, by contrast, support mutual intersubjectivity, which involves (on the part of both or all participants) the "motivation to understand another's meaning system from his or her frame of reference and ongoing and sustained interest in the inner world of the other" (Jordan, "Meaning," 83). Neither party is present merely to serve as a vessel for the other's projections or as the caretaker of the other's needs. In other words, mutuality requires full parity and equality. Whereas Beecher professes tolerance but then attempts to eradicate existing differences in her community, Stowe in her novel uses difference to create new opportunities, new knowledge.

In order for mutuality to be achieved, Stowe had to dismantle the rigid dualistic hierarchies that Beecher vehemently endorsed — especially that between the public and private spheres. In *Domestic Individualism,* Gillian Brown argues that the principal reason Stowe opposes slavery so vehemently in *Uncle Tom's Cabin* is that slavery "disregards th[e] opposition between the family at home and the exterior workplace. The distinction between work and family is eradicated in the slave, for whom there is no separation between economic and private status" (15). In other words, according to Brown, Stowe's abolitionism is motivated in part by her desire to strengthen and maintain the illusory boundary between the pure (white), feminine sanctity of the home and the shiftless, chaotic, and ungodly otherness of the public marketplace. Yet, because Stowe realizes that the public-private dualism is no longer stable or fortifiable, she takes a more radical step in this novel and supplants the market economy with a matriarchal domestic economy "built on an excess of supply rather than the excess of demand" (24).

While *Uncle Tom's Cabin* marks the beginning of Stowe's prioritization of a domestic economy, *The Minister's Wooing* includes a much more ambitious one. From the onset of the book, she glories in the inclusion of foreign and public market elements in the home. George Scudder and Jim Marvyn are both world-traveling merchants who bring back to their Newport homes not only such material goods as African gold rings (9),[10] Cantonese tea cups (18), foreign corals and shells (29), Indian perfumes (187), and all sorts of other " 'cur'us kind o' tings' " (143), but who also carry with them enriched world outlooks owing to their distant travels.[11] In addition to sending Newport characters out into the world market system to enlarge their visions and to bring back foreign items to be welcomed, included, and assimilated into the domestic community and economy, Stowe also widens the scope of her narrative plot so that it allows for foreign people and public figures to enter easily into the small Newport environment. Prissy Diamond, the town dressmaker, brings gossip via her seamstress sister to Newport women, from the highest state officials, including the celebrated Adams family.[12] African slaves arrive regularly by ship to the Newport harbor, and townsfolk such as Hopkins and Mary visit them frequently. The French aristocrat Virginie de Frontignac, Senator Aaron Burr, and the renowned theologian Samuel Hopkins all either visit or live in the Scudders' Newport home.

Stowe invites and integrates the public, secular world market system into the private, intimate, more sacred community of Newport. For her, the public is neither a unified, seamless sphere nor in rigid opposition to the private. Indeed, the public world/private community polarity is continually blurred as a result of her own broader theological and evangelical designs. The conventional dichotomy of public, masculine, secular versus private, feminine, sacred is especially clouded in the Newport community where women, such as Mary Scudder and Candace, seem more suited to minister openly to the Newport community than even Hopkins or Stiles, the town's celebrated male theologians. Thus, to maintain the equations of public equals masculine and secular, and private equals feminine and sacred, advanced by Catharine Beecher, is to obscure Stowe's vision of the public role of Protestant religion in society as well as to efface the public role of women in the remaking of nineteenth-century religion. In addition, Stowe troubles the traditional public/secular and private/sacred split within the individual self. Unlike Beecher, who advises women to squelch their emotions and voice, in Stowe's novel, an individual's private religious sentiment is of little merit if it is not expressed and tested in a public arena. The wealthy slaveowner and slave-trader Simeon Brown fancies himself "submissive to the Divine will, to the uttermost extent demanded by the extreme theology of that day" (58); yet when the Doctor asks him to relinquish his slaves for "the glory of God" (158), he renounces his faith in Hopkins's system of theology and is exposed as a religious hypocrite. Private feelings cannot and should not be isolated from the public arena.

In fact, in this world, the stronger the individual's "private" religious convictions, the more influential and respected is his or (more often) her public voice. As Virginie's love of God and Christ grows, so too does her prominence in the Newport community. When Mary asks her mother if the French woman can stay in their home for an unspecified duration, Katy (a woman known for her munificent hospitality) becomes "flurried and discomposed at the proposition" (399). Shortly after Virginie's stay commences in the Scudder home, Prissy criticizes her for her fashionable tastes and notes the gossip of the townspeople: " 'They say, when she speaks French, she swears every few minutes' " (439). Prissy's criticism of Virginie's fashionable tastes is not only culturally specific but also religiously targeted. Nativist-oriented Protestants typically deplored what they saw as Catholics' devotion to artistry and artifice. However, by the novel's end, Prissy points out that Virginie's " 'a master-hand for touching things up. There seems to be work provided for all kinds of people, and French people seem to have a gift in all sorts of dressy things, and 'tisn't a bad gift either' " (559). Even Katy seems to accept Virginie unreservedly. Virginie's friendship with Mary and other members of the Newport community benefits her in that she gains self-esteem and a deeper piety, but it also assists Mary and others. After all, it is Virginie who first shows the wisdom to warn Mary of the dangers of marrying Hopkins, and by doing so, she implicitly points out the shortcomings of Mary's unquestioning devotion to Calvinism. Stowe wants to envision a community that is demarcated by its inclusion of a variety of mutually supportive peoples under a shared faith in Christ.

In addition to her promotion of intersubjective mutuality, Stowe's vision differs from that of Beecher in another crucial way. Whereas Beecher counsels women to accept the Bible unquestioningly and literally, Stowe suggests that — if anything — women have a more critical and insightful ability to comprehend the Bible than do men. Throughout the nineteenth century, the Bible proved to be a powerful ally to many women combating the androcentric world of theology. Because of their increasing literacy levels and educational opportunities, vast numbers of women were now able to read critically and interpret the Bible for themselves. Thus, they could now more easily bypass the authority of ministers. During this period, women and the Scriptures were so closely associated with one another that at times they became almost interchangeable (Tompkins, *Sensational*, 164–65). In *The Minister's Wooing*, Mary is intimately aligned with the Bible and with God's will. James, Hopkins, Ellen, Virginie, and Cerinthy Ann all consult her on their deepest spiritual misgivings, and she routinely offers them either scripturally grounded advice, verse recitations, or a copy of the Bible itself. Indeed, one wonders if the title of Stowe's book rightly refers to Mary and her wooing of the community to her brand of Christianity rather than to Hopkins and his love for Mary.

Stowe goes further than simply casting women as the Bible-bearers and - givers, she also revises the traditional masculinist interpretation of the Scriptures by having characters point out its many examples of strong women, such as Deborah, Huldah, and Anna (364). To push this point further, Stowe creates fictional, present-day women who are formidable spiritual agents. Both Mary and Candace exhibit not only profound spiritual wisdom but also an ability to foresee the future. Early in the novel, Mary envisions an accurate future image of James as a regenerate "grand and noble man" — "not the man that he is but the angel [he] may be" (130). Even after James had supposedly been dead for some months, Candace rightly prophesies, " 'I dunno 'bout de rest o' de world, but I ha'n't neber felt it in my bones dat Mass'r James is r'ally dead, for sartin' " (447). In short, Stowe has women reclaim the Bible for themselves by featuring their own prophetical heritage within it, by asserting their present spiritual affinity to it, and by encouraging them to appropriate it through their own translations and interpretations of it.

In addition to valorizing the spiritual agency of women and to offering a new, more woman-oriented biblical hermeneutic, Stowe uncovers the overt and subtle ways Calvinism represses women. Far from the passive, self-renouncing, and subordinate True Woman that Beecher promulgates, the virtuous women in this novel are assertive, self-sufficient, and possessing ample quantities of "faculty." On page three, we learn that Katy Scudder can harness a chaise, row a boat, saddle and ride any horse as well as cook and sew to perfection. To top if off, she manages an extremely well-organized and efficient home, complete with boarders, hired men to feed, and frequent visitors. In *Reconstructing Womanhood*, contemporary critic Hazel Carby reveals how the nineteenth-century, middle-class, Anglo-Saxon True Christian Woman fundamentally depended, for the preservation of her pure, unsullied image, on the dirty work done by nonwhite slaves or lower-class servants. Stowe's ideal woman, by contrast, does her own servile labor without any assistance from slaves or servants: "she shall not have a servant in her house. . . . and yet you commonly see her every afternoon sitting at her shady parlor-window behind the lilacs, cool and easy" (2–3). On the one hand, her notion of faculty is rather disconcerting, especially given that Stowe herself had difficulty completing her domestic chores without servant assistance. Yet, on the other hand, it also resembles what Jean Baker Miller calls "agency-in-community," which means "being active, using all of one's resources without the connotations of aggression" (17). Such an ability is especially significant for women in a Protestant society who are typically told not to use their powers fully and freely and are made to see their own self-determined actions as wrong, evil, or selfish.

Although Stowe clearly wants her readers to admire the remarkable faculty of such women as Prissy, Katy, and Mary, who are capable of achieving enormous amounts of labor without the least hint of consternation or acrimony, she also unmasks the way in which the pure, abstract Calvinist theology depends upon the unappreciated industry of women. While Hopkins sits at a desk "covered with pamphlets and heavily-bound volumes of theology" contemplating the greater metaphysical questions, Katy and Mary are scrubbing floors, washing clothes, baking, pickling, and preserving (59). Stowe hammers home this conspicuous contrast in her physical description of Hopkins, who "apparelled in the most faultless style, with white wrist-ruffles, plaited shirt-bosom, immaculate wig, and well-brushed coat, sat by Mary's side, serenely unconscious how many feminine cares had gone to his getting-up" (167). As the narrator highlights later, he is completely oblivious as to how hypocritical and self-serving it is for him to extol the virtues of passivity, piety, and submissiveness to his feminine congregants: "The Doctor little thought, while he, in common with good ministers generally gently traduced the Scriptural Martha and insisted on the duty of heavenly abstractedness, how much of his own leisure for spiritual contemplation was due to the Martha-like talents of his hostess" (168).

In many ways, *The Minister's Wooing* represents Stowe's reclamation of Martha as the more realistic yet misunderstood ideal Christian woman. Yet, typical of Stowe's conciliatory and inclusive approach, she does not completely banish the Mary ideal either. In fact, Mary Scudder, at different points in the book, embodies both the Mary and Martha types. Early in the novel, the fictional Mary is described in strikingly similar terms to her scriptural namesake. Just as the biblical Mary sits at the feet of Jesus listening intently to his message, the fictional Mary also listens "in rapt attention, while her spiritual guide, the venerated Dr. Hopkins, unfold[s] to her the theories of the great Edwards on the nature of true virtue" (22).

Contrary to traditional biblical interpretation, Stowe's depiction of the Mary ideal is less than sublime. The problem, according to Stowe, with this feminine ideal (an ideal made popular by her older sister) is that it can entail a destructive self-effacement. The more that Mary submits to the Hopkinsian notion of Disinterested Benevolence, sacrificing her own worldly desires for the glory of God, the more stolid she becomes: "the thousand fibres that bind youth and womanhood to earthly love and life were all in her as still as the grave" (375). While transitory forms of self-renunciation may work productively for artists and philosophers during moments of creativity, it does not serve Mary well who suffers from "an internal paralysis" — "a state not purely healthy, nor realizing the divine ideal of a perfect human being made to exist in the relations of human life" (375, 376). Stowe's perspective on self-sacrifice contradicts directly that of her sister, who counseled women to view the "chief end and aim of this life" as influencing others and, if need be, sacrificing "every earthly plan and enjoyment" (*Woman's,* 83). Beecher's model is decidedly nonmutual, whereby "power over" or the ability to exercise dominion or to dominate is idealized, while Stowe's more mutual model conceptualizes power as "the capacity for flexibility, responsiveness, adaptation, receptivity, creativity, activity and change through connection" (Surrey, "Empathy," 3).

For Stowe, Christianity should result not in passivity and self-abnegation but instead in active, romantic love and embodied sexuality. Love, according to Stowe, represents "the noblest capability of [one's] eternal inheritance" and provides the lover with a "glimpse of heaven" (122). Stowe, then, validates feminine desire, suggesting, through the example of Mary, that women can and should be both desiring and spiritual agents (the two forces of desire and religion having the same divine source). Mary tells Aaron Burr that for her Christianity is "a living form" (224), but it is not until James returns alive from his long voyage that she begins experiencing it as this living form. Immediately after she encounters Jim, she places her "throbbing" palm in his "strong, living, manly hand" and her body in his arms (506). In order to become a complete living and loving being, she must not only recognize her body but also learn to reject the notions of "self-denial and self-sacrifice [that] had been the daily bread of her life," and to tune out "every prayer, hymn and sermon, from her childhood, [which] had warned her to distrust her inclinations, and regard her feelings as traitors" (511). In other words, Mary had to become like the biblical Martha, to take action and to give voice to her own feelings and opinions. Indeed, although her Christian name suggests her likeness to the biblical Mary, her surname, "Scudder" ("scud," meaning to run or move quickly), points to a more active, Martha-like disposition. Mary is a dynamic combination of two seemingly disparate personae.

In addition to dealing with the Mary-Martha polarity, Stowe also has Mary reconcile an even more fundamental opposition. Beyond striving to deny Mary's voice and actions, Calvinism threatens to fragment her very subjectivity. Mary's dutiful compunction to marry Hopkins seems directly at odds with her love for James. As the narrator puts it, "her sensitive nature [is] divided between two opposing consciences and two opposing affections" (538). The basic tenets of her faith seem to put her at a no-compromise, either/or position. But interestingly, although Mary eventually marries James rather than Hopkins, she is not obliged to choose one side at the total expense of the other. At the novel's end, Mary remains the lover and spouse of Jim as well as the "revered and dear" friend of Hopkins, and as both Jim's wife and Hopkins's friend, she still retains the core of her religious devotion. In short, Stowe bypasses the traditional inner/outer, either/or binary—public religious duty versus private individual desire—by showing that one's subjectivity can contain a variety of feelings, compulsions, and beliefs. Mary can be a devotee of Hopkinsian theology while simultaneously following the dictates of her own heart.

Thus, unlike Catharine, who underscored the importance of consistency, Stowe embraces the simultaneous existence of opposites. Albert Rothenberg has argued that the capacity for an individual to hold equally operative notions is one of the hallmarks of creativity. In her novel, Stowe validates this ability in a prominent metaphor that encompasses discrete particulars and clashing contradictions under a unifying form. After Mary announces her betrothal to Hopkins, the women of Newport partake in the traditional engagement ritual of quilting, an activity involving the delicate arrangement of "fluttering bits of green, yellow, red, and blue" into an expansive whole. As the narrator comments, a woman's "busy flying needle stitched together those pretty bits, which, little in themselves, were destined, by gradual unions and accretions, to bring about at last substantial beauty, warmth, and comfort" (436). In contradistinction to Hopkins's ladder or Catharine's notion of complete self-renunciation, a quilt signifies a nonhierarchical, nonlinear, and inclusive image. At any given moment, the quilt maker or onlooker can focus on one patch without completely losing or suppressing the others. Thus, Mary (like the poet Walt Whitman) can "contain multitudes" of varying impulses, beliefs, and feelings. The narrator writes: "In all the system which had been explained to her, her mind selected points on which it seized with intensest sympathy, which it dwelt upon and expanded till all else fell away. The sublimity of disinterested benevolence, — the harmony and order of a system tending in its final results to infinite happiness, — the goodness of God, — the love of a self-sacrificing Redeemer, — were all so many glorious pictures, which she revolved in her mind with small care for their logical relations" (342). Mary's subjectivity is marked by copiousness, tolerance, flexibility, expansion, and permeability; it neither completely rejects any ideas nor advocates any which it cannot sincerely praise at that moment, and it is open to new shifts in thoughts and historical happenings.

Stowe herself followed a similar pattern in her own thinking. When her son Charles accused her and her brothers (his uncles) of being inconsistent and contradictory in their thinking, Stowe answered him in a letter:

> Uncle Henry and Uncle Tom . . . differ[ed] in many points with the received orthodoxy of their day — but they made no noise about it — they preached what they sincerely did believe and left what they were in doubt about to the further teachings of Gods [sic] Holy Spirit. Clinging to Christ making definite efforts to bring souls into union with him they found work enough for man or angel to do without chasing after or fighting over disputed theological subtleties and noble christian churches have grown up under their labors. What I, and your uncle Henry believe and teach is not either slovenly, or inconsistent, and we are neither of us dishonest.[13] (qtd. in Caskey, *Chariot*, 198–99)

William G. McLoughlin affirms that Henry Ward Beecher, Stowe's famous brother, was known for his "massive inconsistency": "When Beecher was told that what he had preached one Sunday was contradictory to what he had preached the previous Sunday, he replied, 'Oh, yes! Well, that was last week!' Or, as he put it another time, 'Life is a kind of zig-zag'" (*Meaning*, 30–31). Yet McLoughlin is also quick to add that Stowe and her brother "did make sense" to their audiences, and few were dismayed (as was Stowe's son) by their contradictions (32). For Stowe, contradictions and expansion in one's thinking are perfectly understandable and necessary given the constant flux of personal experience and history.

For Stowe, an emphasis on process and pragmatics is preferable to the linear forms of logic and hierarchical and inexorable thinking engendered most fully by the systematic Reformed theology. The narrator notes that the preaching of New England Calvinist ministers "was animated by an unflinching consistency which never shrank from carrying an idea to its remotest logical verge" (336). Interestingly, this capacity to push logic to its furthest extremes and to advocate the sacrifice of one set of views for another was not limited to Puritans like Hopkins or to real-life Protestants like Catharine. Stowe has Aaron Burr, the most skeptical, heretical thinker in the novel, fall prey to this deleterious mode of thought.[14] In fact, the narrator notes that "self-denial is not peculiar to Christians. He who goes down often puts forth as much force to kill a noble nature as another does to annihilate a sinful one" (418). Later, Burr and Hopkins are further likened to one another; they both possessed "a perfect logic of life, and guided themselves with an inflexible rigidity by it" (482). Like Hopkins and Catharine Beecher, Burr buys into the either/or binary: either he can pursue his own inner desires (and attain worldly success), or he can lead a pious and selfless life. And his downfall is that unlike Mary, he fails to take full advantage of the quilt form and to trust that God will assist him in weaving all of his richly varied and seemingly contradictory impulses into a purposeful and successful life. In other words, Burr's tragic defeat stems in part from his ignorance that Protestant Christianity and personal satisfaction are not mutually exclusive.

As an outgrowth of this expansive conception of subjectivity and religion, Stowe envisions a more inclusive earthly society. Once again, the quilt as a metaphor works appropriately for Stowe's concept of a community. Galvanized and unified by a common faith in God, Stowe's community hosts a variety of different types of people. Candace (African-American freed slave), Virginie (aristocratic French Catholic), Prissy (working-class seamstress), Zebedee Marvyn (farmer), Hopkins (revered theologian), Jim (world-traveling merchant), Cerinthy Ann (a rationalizing, reluctant believer), and even at one point a Jewish rabbi (222) are all stitched into the fold of this expanding society. Stowe's inclusive, expansive social vision is somewhat remarkable, given the novel's pre-Civil War date (1859) and her family background. Her father and sister were both vitriolic in their anti-Catholicism and frequently vented their xenophobic fear of the rise in immigration. In fact, Catharine was up front about her purpose in teaching American (read white, middle-class, native) women to be better housewives: "to eliminate the influx of ignorant and uncleanly foreigners into our kitchens" (*Woman's*, 51). Furthermore, Stowe's inclusive community is progressive in its demand for the active participation of and appreciation for strong, Martha-like women, who also do not deny their more passive, pious sides.

The benefits of Stowe's brand of (inter)nationalized Christianity are that it allows for a greater diversity of people and ideas and a greater voluntarism than before. Candace's spiritualism is at least as valued as Hopkins's Calvinism. "Natural" Christians such as Mary are as welcomed as "self-made" ones such as Jim and Candace. Moreover, while there are acceptable exclusionary limits to the community (Aaron Burr and Simeon Brown are deservedly castigated), no boundaries are ever permanently fixed. Patches can always be appended to Stowe's grand quilt. The narrator, as well as Virginie's son, shows Burr mercy at the end of the book, and Burr is described in later life as sleeping with the New Testament under his pillow, thereby leaving open the hope for his redemption and reentry into the Christian community.

Despite the many benefits of Stowe's community vision, it also includes some shortcomings. Stowe's evangelism, like any form of evangelism, could easily transform into a coercive and stultifying power. Unbelievers either convert or exit the community in this novel, and there seems to exist no space for serious resistance or disgruntlement. Cultural, racial, attitudinal, labor, and class differences are relatively benign. Unlike the scriptural Martha, no one complains openly about anything. As Judith Butler argues, a certain amount of disunity and disavowals within a subject—and by extension, within a given community—is necessary and even beneficial in that it recognizes rather than covers over the subject position as a site of converging and agonistic relations of power:

> It is doubtless true that certain disavowals are fundamentally enabling, and that no subject can proceed, can act, without disavowing certain possibilities and avowing others... The ideal of transforming all excluded identifications into inclusive features—of appropriating all difference into unity—would mark the return to a Hegelian synthesis which has no exterior, and that, in appropriating all difference as exemplary features of itself, becomes a figure for imperialism, a figure that installs itself by way of a romantic, insidious, and all-consuming humanism. (*Bodies*, 116)

Such insidious romanticism is at its worst in Stowe's novel when even the slaves are portrayed as fervently devoted to their masters, to Protestant religion, and to the United States. In chapter 17, Candace and Digo engage in a theological discussion that directly mimics and, in a sense, pays homage to their masters. When Zebedee grants Candace her freedom, she responds by announcing her desire to remain the Marvyns' even more obedient servant: " 'I'll allers put three eggs in de crullers, now; an' I won't turn de wash-basin down in de sink, but hang it jam-up on de nail; . . . — I'll do eberyting jes' as ye tells me. Now you try me an' see ef I won't!' " (177).

The dignity of labor, which Candace's statement exemplifies, has been a longstanding article of Protestant faith. James Marvyn, Samuel Hopkins, and Mary Scudder obviously are gifted in their relative occupations, and each is rewarded in terms of money, prestige, and reputation for their abilities and efforts. Although these characters' economic advancement is shown to be a direct result of their Protestant faith, it also equally seems to be a result of their white race and middle-class status. Despite their hard work and religious zeal, nonwhite and lower-class characters do not so readily transcend their economic statuses. Candace remains a servant for the Marvyns throughout her life, and Miss Prissy seems destined to stay a poor, lifelong dressmaker. Thus, a hierarchical class structure remains. In addition, nonwhite and non-middle-class characters are not portrayed with the same moral seriousness as white characters. The agonizing and complicated spiritual dilemmas of Hopkins, Ellen, Mary, and James are drawn out in much greater sympathetic detail than those of Candace, Digo, or Miss Prissy. In fact, when Digo and Candace debate theological issues, they are described with animal imagery. Candace emits guttural howls and bristles her feathers like a hen, and Digo's stomach is likened to that of an ostrich (276–77). Undoubtedly, Stowe intends for Candace to be a laudable character and significant religious spokesperson.[15] Nevertheless, the marked representational (not to mention speech) differences between her and the white, middle-class protagonists exposes Stowe's nascent racist and classist tendencies and uncovers the limitations of her all-inclusive, egalitarian communal vision.

By aligning herself with U.S. Protestant nationalism, Stowe at times falls victim to the troubling ideology of the dominant culture and its binary, hierarchical thinking. Unfortunately, her more conciliatory, diverse, and expansive vision seems to have been intended mainly for white, middle-class subjects. Despite these grievous shortcomings, Stowe stitches out more sites of mutuality for women and nontraditional Christians than did her sister Catharine. While Catharine promoted a masculine public-feminine private hierarchy and the total self-abnegation of women and other minority groups, Stowe deliberately worked to blur the male-female, public-private binaries in part by espousing an active and public role for women. Rather than reinforce her call for a universal, self-sacrificing feminine identity through shaming tactics and an appeal to Common Sense reasoning as did Beecher, Stowe advocated a more diverse feminine subject in part by valorizing greater religious tolerance and respect for individual differences. Yet, despite these strengths, Stowe ultimately was unable to overcome completely her own racial, class, and pro-Christian biases. Engrossed in a shifting, nonuniform but pervasive Protestant culture and existing in a dynamic historical moment, it was difficult not to be complicit with parts of dominant and dualistic thinking, while simultaneously proffering possibilities for subverting or modifying it. Like the quilt maker, Stowe artfully threads a variety of colorful patches — the praiseworthy as well as the dubious — into a copious, expansive, and inclusive whole; and as a result, she provides us with one glimpse of the manifoldly diverse and sometimes tangled threads of nineteenth-century American women and Protestantism.

Building on the more egalitarian emphasis of evangelical Protestantism, both Harriet Beecher Stowe and William Apess were able to dismantle the oppositional binaries inherent in Calvinism that Olaudah Equiano attempted to transcend. Through a focus on cultural interaction rather than domination, Stowe and Apess were able to thwart the dominant rhetorics of domesticity and manifest destiny by envisioning an expansive nation comprised of active and diverse members. The individuals examined in the following chapter incorporated even more variegated and extreme forms of liberal and evangelical Protestantism to advance their antiracist and antisexist agendas.

Chapter Four

Uncovering the "Mother-Heart of God"

The Cultural Performance of the
Christian Feminists

According to her *Narrative,* Sojourner Truth (then called Isabella Van Wagener) once encountered a woman who, after witnessing her master kick her young child around "like a foot-ball," sought revenge on him during his final illness:

> She was very strong, and was therefore selected to support her master, as he sat up in bed, by putting her arms around, while she stood behind him. . . . She would clutch his feeble frame in her iron grasp, as in a vice; and, when her mistress did not see, would give him a squeeze, a shake, and lifting him up, set him down again, as hard as possible. If his breathing betrayed too tight a grasp, and her mistress said, "Be careful, don't hurt him, Soan!" her ever-ready answer was, "Oh no, Missus, no," in her most pleasant tone — and then, as soon as Missus' eyes and ears were engaged away, another grasp — another shake — another bounce. . . . Isabella asked her, if she were not afraid his spirit would haunt her. "Oh, no," says Soan; "he was so wicked, the devil will never let him out of hell long enough for that." (84)

Such a story would have been compelling — if not terrifying — to nineteenth-century white and black audiences for curiously similar reasons. As Annalucia Accardo and Alessandro Portelli have pointed out, domestic slaves such as Soan were particularly disturbing because they represented a curious combination of "visible subordination and secret subversion": Paradoxically, the house slave was "both a member of the slave population and a part of the master's household, yet . . . an outsider to both" ("Spy," 78). Those slaves not living in the "Big House" mistrusted the house slaves because of their close proximity and relation to the master; yet, this very intimacy also instilled fear and suspicion in the master. Thus, the house slaves were potentially terrifying precisely because they knew and understood the master's vulnerabilities and resided in the same intimate domestic setting; yet they were, like the field slaves, ever-aware of their bonded state. Hence, because they operated within—instead of outside of—the master's private space, these figures risked being coopted into the system and labeled accommodationists or sellouts by those outside; yet they also harbored the possibility for insurgency, or what Ruether and McLaughlin call "radical obedience."

It is precisely this double bind or potential—to operate in docility or in secret rebellion—that makes these figures so intriguing yet so often misunderstood. Moreover, this liminal, shifting quality is also what makes them appropriate symbols for a prominent group of nineteenth-century thinkers, whom I call the Christian feminists. Unlike more secular feminists such as Elizabeth Cady Stanton and Susan B. Anthony who functioned at least partially outside the dominant system of the Protestant Church, Christian feminists operated within mainstream Protestantism and sought "to make religion less sexist [and thus more empowering for women], not to make women any less religious" (Brooks Higginbotham, *Righteous*, 139). Yet, what was the Christian feminists' relationship to the mainstream Church? Did the Church serve to empower or to contain them? What strategies did this group use to gain a voice within or to transgress this highly conservative institution?

This chapter will respond to these questions by exploring the formation of feminine identity by three different groups: conservative Protestants; white Christian feminists, and African-American Christian feminists. In an effort to project and mobilize the nation as a superior, homogeneous, Protestant worldly force, mainline conservative Protestant leaders constructed the Church as a unified arena. They achieved this combination of uniformity and harmony by promoting the separate spheres and true womanhood ideals, ideals founded on the suppression of feminine autonomy and agency. In response to these ideals, the predominantly white, Christian feminists incorporated a stance of radical obedience. By straddling two seemingly opposing systems of thought—woman's rights and evangelical Protestantism—these thinkers were able to select tropes and knowledge from as well as to gain a critical and comparative perspective on both systems in order to create a familiar yet dissident rhetoric of their own, one that was both acceptable to large audiences of women and effective in securing limited social and religious reform. Finally, the African-American Christian feminists, because of their prevailing negative social image, had not only to achieve at least as convincing a Christian demeanor or "politics of respectability" (Brooks Higginbotham) as their white counterparts did but also to invent unique strategies for combating the racism as well as the sexism of the Protestant Church.

While the term "conservative" has numerous political and religious meanings, in this study, it will refer to those Christian ministers, leaders, and writers who subscribed to the following set of beliefs: a general distrust of evangelicalism; an acceptance of the literal and infallible truth of the Scriptures; a belief in the authority of an educated clergy; and most important, an adherence to the ideals of separate spheres and true womanhood (the beliefs that woman should remain in the private realm of the home and be pious, pure, submissive, and domestic). Although most of the conservative thinkers I consider were members of the Calvinist-based Reformed denominations such as Presbyterianism and Congregationalism, others were followers of other nonevangelical denominations. And even though Protestant conservatives were often virulently anti-Catholic and would rarely concede to any points of agreement with Catholics, on the crucial features listed above, the two groups converge.

Another distinguishing feature of conservative Protestants and Catholics alike is the belief in the rightness of Christianity for the expanding nation. Rather than accentuate the multifariousness of Christian theology, practice, and subjects (as Stowe did), conservatives tended to underscore the uniformity of Christian thought and the homogeneity of its followers. Thus, they minimized the sectarian or creedal conflicts and controversies within their own ranks (Weber, "Two-Edged," 116). Exhorted one, "Not only is controversy, for the most part, unedifying, and very inappropriate to the gentler sex; but it often diverts them from profitable contemplation and important duties. Besides, it is apt to make them opinionative and dogmatical; and to lead them . . . into the scale of party than into that of true religion" (Winslow and Sanford, *Benison*, 82). Another writer, warning against sectarian divisions among Christians, declared that the true Church "is indestructible, and holds a sacred commission to conquer the world by the power of holiness and love. God is in its principles and its sacraments, in its members and its government, and the *different denominations* demonstrate their claim to membership in this spiritual household" (Peck, *True,* 278–79; italics mine). Contemporary historian Janette Hassey notes that conservatives "somehow agreed to disagree on a variety of issues in order to join forces on what they perceived to be the essentials" (5–6). One of the most significant essentials was the issue of woman and its corollary metaphor of separate spheres.

The most popular venue used by conservatives to express their views concerning woman was the advice book. Advice books proved particularly appropriate for their needs for a number of reasons. First, as Nicole Tonkovich has asserted, nineteenth-century U.S. advice literature was typically designed to "present morally grounded codes of behavior characterized as natural 'law,' and [to] promise that adherence to these 'laws' will smooth otherwise difficult social interactions" ("Advice," 65). Advice literature's reliance on natural law and its goal of prescribing a code of moral behavior corresponded perfectly to the conservative agenda of constructing a homogeneous, harmonious, and moral nation. Second, not only was the didactic literature popular in the late nineteenth century, but Christian advice books as a subgenre also burgeoned—particularly those produced by prominent conservative clergy. George Burnap, for example, served as pastor of a large Baltimore church and authored more than thirty publications; according to the *Dictionary of American Biography,* his *The Spheres and Duties of Woman* (1848) enjoyed "a large circulation" (Johnson, 3:292). Harvey Newcomb's *How to Be A Lady* (1846) (an earlier edition of *Christian Character: A Book for Young Ladies*) sold 34,000 copies. Congregationalist Hubbard Winslow, who succeeded Lyman Beecher at Bowdoin Street Church in Boston, commanded considerable acclaim in New England, and his advice books were "extraordinarily popular, many thousands of copies being printed" (Johnson, *Dictionary,* 20:396). Contemporary historian Frances Cogan maintains that during the mid-century years, the *Bibliotheca Americana* listed more titles for advice books than for any other genre; and she further contends that since the middle class comprised about 75 percent of the population, these books, with their intended middle-class readership, may have served to set the cultural tone and code of conduct for the bulk of U.S. society (*All-American,* 14–16).

In keeping with Cogan's hypothesis, advice writers themselves foresaw their work as possessing the utmost significance and a potential long-term influence. In the introductory chapter of his advice book, Jesse T. Peck declares:

[We] are responsible to coming generations, as we verily believe, to the end of time; for should the duration of the work be long or short, we feel that its effects must extend beyond our present power of estimation. No man writes merely for the passing hour. His book may pass from the notice and the memory of the world, but if he has gained a single reader, as he surely will, the thoughts, and feelings, and impulses he has produced or revived, have entered into the life-current of the future, and become a part of the characters and destinies of unborn generations. (*True,* 35)

Enthusiastic predictions by the writers and large sales, however, may not necessarily confirm that these books were read carefully, approvingly, or even at all. If the handwritten inscriptions in most of these books are any indication, many were probably distributed to young women as gifts by doting parents, protective older siblings, or concerned local ministers; and because the women did not purchase or select these books for themselves, whether they read them completely or how they received them is open for speculation. Annotations, when they existed at all, were minimal. Yet, despite the question over the readership of these books, we can (with fair certainty) surmise that the (intended) readers were well-versed in the books' general content — and especially in the spheres trope. In fact, advice writers frequently point out that much of their books' content had previously been delivered in sermons or public lectures. Furthermore, given the marked uniformity of these books' rhetoric, it seems relatively certain that their ideas and language were familiar to churchgoing women.

Advice writers addressed young (unmarried or newly married), middle-class, and probably white women, who considered themselves regenerate or soon-to-be-saved Protestants. Early in the advice book, writers typically issue a brief but dramatic plea for conversion, warning women that if they do not make haste in securing their salvation, "there will be the force of the long-established habit of sinning to contend with, meshes of evil to unravel, and all that mingled texture of light and darkness, which originates in a polluted heart ... to separate thread from thread" (Ellis, "Daughters," 217). Yet the remaining bulk of the book proceeds under the assumption that its readers are self-identified or preparing Christians; therefore, the book's purpose is not so much to proselytize to skeptics as to guide already or hopeful Christian women in the optimum moral conduct of life.

Although most of the authors covered an array of practical topics, such as fashion, education, courtship, marriage, household economics, friendships, and leisure activities, they undergirded these topics with their notion of the ideal woman and its accompanying separate spheres metaphor. Without fail, every conservative writer featured this metaphor, most often within the first few pages of the book. As did Beecher in her books, these writers affirmed that man and woman have been divinely ordained to equally important, complementary, but starkly opposing, realms. Women are relegated to any form of activity that occurs inside the newly privatized household of the emergent middle class; men, by contrast, are assigned to the competitive and chaotic public world of politics and capitalist enterprise. Morgan Dix, rector of Trinity Church in New York City, articulated it this way:

> Man's is the outer life, woman's the inner.... He is eminently the doer, the creator, the discoverer, the defender. His intellect is for speculation and invention; his energy for adventure, for war and for conquest.... The man's work for his home is, to secure its maintenance, progress, and defense. The man's duty for the Commonwealth, is to assist in the maintenance, in the advance, in the defence [sic] of the State. The woman's duty, as a member of the Commonwealth, is to assist in the ordering, in the comforting, and in the beautiful adornment of the State. (*Lectures*, 19–20)

A strict oppositionality forms the driving force behind Dix's and other conservatives' constructions of masculine and feminine identity. Man is the public agent, woman his private assistant; and more important, such a binary serves not to divide the nation but to unite and galvanize it. "Christian women, believe me," writes Stephen Dana, "you can best give us what we need, by being most unlike ourselves" (*Woman's*, 110).

As Dix's passage cited earlier attests, the public-private gender polarity was more than a religious issue, serving to keep a burgeoning feminine congregation out of leadership positions; it also helped to forward the existing American political and economic systems. Contemporary theorist Rebecca Chopp notes that the liberal-capitalist ideology of the nineteenth century demanded that "the public arena ... represent not only individual rights and freedoms, but market exchange. This public, in order for the autonomous individual to exist, depends upon the private sphere in the form of woman's place, not only to take care of procreation, but increasingly to absorb the private values that the bourgeoisie has to deny, things like friendship, tradition, religion and kinship" (Chopp, *Power*, 113–14). In order for the (male) citizen to operate independently in the battleground of commerce and politics, private domestic management, child-rearing, and low-level manual domestic labor must be kept distinct from and unrelated to the public realm.

Historian Betty DeBerg has argued that the emergence of this gender dualism marked a shift from the early industrial era of the previous century when men defined themselves through several key roles: patriarch; landowner or skilled laborer; and warrior (14). The movement away from the farms and into the city (and a wage economy) disrupted this traditional understanding and function of manhood. Fewer men could own large tracts of land, pass down their wealth or skills to their sons, or demonstrate physical prowess. Thus a new notion of manhood, which maintained men's superior position over women yet was more congruent with the changing economy, emerged. No longer able to be the heroes on the battlefield defending their family honor, men instead became the economic warriors, in a business world increasingly depicted "as an unsavory and strenuous world in which ruthlessness and aggression were prized" (DeBerg, *Ungodly*, 18). A fixed income, a middle-class home, and a virtuous wife and family replaced bravery, physical strength, and property as the markers of successful manhood. Moreover, assigning women to the private sphere worked to assuage the moral and ethical conflicts in capitalism. "Uneasy about the profit motive, about exploiting those less fortunate, about using deceptive means to sell their goods, about ruthless and often unfair competition against other businessmen" (19), the home was constructed as the refuge from the vicious world of business. By remaining in the private sphere, women did not threaten masculine power or identity.

To compensate women for being excised from the world of work and politics, the home and women's influential role within it were glorified in hyperbolic terms. Writes Reverend Daniel C. Eddy, "Home is woman's throne, where she maintains her royal court, and sways her queenly authority. It is there that man learns to appreciate her worth, and to realize the sweet and tender influences which she casts around her...; and there she fills the sphere to which divine providence has called her" (*Young*, 23). Not only did woman ostensibly have the power to influence her family members, but ironically by remaining within the home, she had the power to influence the public realm beneficially. As William Thayer writes, "Indeed such is woman's influence, we may add, that she decides social morality. If her standard of excellence is high, the society in which she moves will be elevated. If otherwise, the morals of the community will be loose. Let her treat religion lightly, and the men will rail about it as infidels of the lowest school" (*Good*, 55).

Historians have noted that the notion of woman as the moral exemplar and of man as the undisciplined wayward sinner (unable to affect virtue without woman's guidance) was newly fashioned in the nineteenth century (De-Berg, *Ungodly,* 20). Traditional Christianity had typically portrayed woman as the Eve figure, the deceiver and sexual temptress, while men were considered morally sound creatures of the spirit and intellect. Thus, despite the conservatives' pronouncement that separate spheres and the ideal of womanhood were divinely ordained, they were in fact constructions that in part served to bolster a growing capitalist economy and a fragile, unstable masculine identity. Yet, beyond exaggerating the power and appeal of woman's role, conservatives had to develop a number of other strategies to persuade women to assume and remain in their prescribed role.

The most obvious way of achieving this end was to underline the spheres' divine ordination or naturalness. "Men are born to be the providers in the home; they are formed *by nature*... for every species of toil. Theirs is the battle of life on sea and land. The home with its quiet, its obscurity, its sanctities, is for woman: she is *made* to grow up in the shade" (O'Reilly, *Mirror,* 359; italics mine). Or, as others put it, God stamps upon the sexes "original marks of difference" (More, "Excerpt," 291) and "supplies principles which are rooted in the soul, and sway the conscience" (James, "From Friend," 463). Naturalizing this gender ideology was effective for its seeming benignity. As opposed to a system (like Calvinism) where authority figures demand certain behaviors from their subjects, this system claims that individuals are naturally suited to these roles and thus should be able to follow them effortlessly and without exterior controls. Believing they were following nature or divine decree, individuals would monitor themselves. Antonio Gramsci has argued that coercion alone is not enough to sustain a hegemonic relationship. Consent is always necessary for the rulers as well as for the ruled. The woman's consent was needed both as a prevention and as a cure for the conservatives' guilt; her acceptance of the ideal as "natural" formed the foundation of the conservatives' "consent" to themselves. Both groups, then, on some level had to identify with the ideal; constructing it as "natural" or "god-given" better ensured that identification.

Once consent has been gained, shame becomes the mechanism by which the ruler and ruled monitor each other and themselves. Thus, because the true womanhood ideal was posited as "natural" and thereby something all women should follow, conservatives could make shaming claims such as if they rejected it, they were "guilty of a deeper sin against our Heavenly Father, and the human family whose happiness he has in some measure committed to [their] trust" (Ellis, "Daughters," 256). Thus, did woman stand to lose well-being and fortune not only in this material world but also in the more lofty and significant one hereafter. As one adviser cautioned: "But permit us to remind you that your wrong is against the infinite God! It is His will that you have disregarded! His law that you have violated!... What fact is at this moment so terrible as that He who is infinite in holiness, in justice, and in goodness, now looks down upon you with disapprobation! You are a rejecter of Christ, and God (to those out of Christ) is a consuming fire!" (Peck, *True*, 274). As in the above passage, Sarah Gould forewarns wayward women, "think—if for a moment you can bear the thought,—what will be the desolation, shame, and anguish of those wretched souls, who shall hear those dreadful words [on judgment day]: 'Depart from me, ye cursed, into everlasting fire, prepare for the devil and his angels'" (*Golden*, 45). Hence, these advice-givers performed a peculiar sleight-of-hand. Initially, they offered to their readers a benevolent, loving god who benignly issues edicts through the individual's conscience and natural inclinations; but as soon as the woman rebelled against these inclinations, God reemerged in his fiery Calvinist guise, with a furor even the unsparing Jonathan Edwards would admire.

If the threat of God's wrath were not enough to keep woman in her place, conservatives also shamed her into thinking that transgressing her role could cause more than her own damnation. It would impel the ruin of her loved ones. Warned Daniel Wise, "If you unfit [your husband] for his work by the peevishness of your temper,—you cripple his energies,—discourage his heart,... God will curse you in soul and in body, and in all probability both you and he will fail of heaven" ("Bridal," 141). Even more startling is the fact that woman's downfall could lead to the demise of the democratic nation: "Countries so unfortunate as to sanction by custom the want of female virtue, become a prey to tyrants, and remain in hopeless political slavery" (Winslow and Sanford, *Benison*, iv).

While failing to lead a fully virtuous life or to instill morality in others was worthy of castigation, deliberately adopting an alternative role—particularly that of the feminist—was worse. Conservatives assigned these women every invective from "Amazonian disputants" (Wise, "Young," 85) to "scum and froth of the pot which rise to the surface" (Tyler, "Papers," 57) to "leprous dregs of corruption" (Burnap, *Sphere*, 204). The following passage represents a typical denunciatory depiction of the feminist:

Oh how fallen... is she when, impatient of her proper sphere, she steps forth to assume the duties of the man, and, impelled by false zeal, with conscience misguided, does as even man ought not to do—when forsaking the domestic hearth, her delicate voice is heard from house to house to house, or in social assemblies, rising in harsh unnatural tones of denunciation against civil laws and rulers... What a sad wreck of female loveliness is she then! She can hardly conceive how ridiculous she appears in the eyes of all sober, discreet, judicious Christian men, or how great the reproach she brings upon her sex. (Winslow and Sanford, *Benison*, 24–25)

Beyond profaning the divine order and defiling middle-class propriety, feminists were particularly disturbing for conservatives whenever they refused to be self-sacrificial. As demonstrated in the moral writings of Catharine Beecher, self-sacrifice was a defining feature of the true womanhood and separate spheres ideology. While both the conservatives and Beecher endorsed woman's self-sacrifice, the conservatives' construction of this "virtue" was—if anything— more restraining and severe than that advocated by Beecher. Women were not asked simply to quell unkind words, they were told to "endure any amount of suffering, of toil, and even of injury... [and not to] listen to those unthinking women who tell you [that] you will be trampled upon unless you assert your rights, and speak for yourself" (Wise, "Bridal," 122). Beyond being asked to "avoid egotism... [and] to suppress their own claims" (Winslow and Sanford, *Benison*, 11), women were instructed to construe their heartfelt, nonrational feelings—even those induced by religion—as "spurious... a delusion of Satan" (Newcomb, *Christian*, 15) and their spiritual enthusiasm as "a mere animal fever, ... a wandering of mind, bordering on delirium, which exaggerates realities, and embodies shadows" (Winslow and Sanford, *Benison*, 131).

According to conservatives, true Christianity should impel women to act more rationally, soberly, and, above all, more obediently toward men. Rather than focus on her own religious affections, a good Christian woman should enter fully "into the spirit of her husband's vocation" and focus solely on his salvation: "Then your husband, viewing his crown, radiant with stars, shall gaze upon its brightness, and think, perchance, how much, under Christ, it owes its adornments to you" (Wise, "Bridal," 141). Indeed, one writer seriously advocated that woman play the role of ventriloquist, thereby effacing her very being entirely. Make the husband "appear the sole director; like the statue of the Delphic god, which was thought to give forth its own oracles, whilst the humble priest, who lent his voice, was by the shrine concealed, nor sought a higher glory than a supposed obedience to the power he would be thought to serve" (Gould, *Golden,* 241).

Because women were to identify utterly and selflessly with their husbands, friendships with other people were expressly forbidden. According to conservatives, a woman's friendship should be "confined to one;...the conjugal, which in its perfection, is so entire and absolute an union of interest, will and affection, as no other connexion [sic] can stand in competition with" (81). The danger of nonspousal intimacies is that "they induce [the woman] to be over-confidential and to tell the affairs of her home to one who is not of her own household. Then, too, by mining up one's love as if it were a piece of citron, and giving a little of it here and a little of it there, there is left a portion not altogether desirable which is to be given to Prince Charming" (Ashmore, *Side,* 122–23). In keeping with this ban on all nonconjugal friendships, women were never to question or distrust their husbands. Even in cases where the evidence of misdoing or wrong sentiment was irrefutable, the woman should keep this information "from every living soul" (O'Reilly, *Mirror,* 113).

Conservative writers buttressed their insistence on feminine self-sacrifice with references to meek biblical women who are "remarkable [for] their strictly feminine deportment. From the *wife* of Abraham to the *wife* of Aquilla, there was none who forgot her subordinate station" (Winslow and Sanford, *Benison,* 175–176; italics mine). Although Sarah and Priscilla definitely made accomplishments on their own, it is their role as the subservient spouses of men that is underscored. In similar fashion, when confronted with the stories of other biblical women who enjoyed even more clear positions of leadership than did Sarah or Priscilla, conservatives downplayed or denigrated their power: "Deborah, though she was a very wise woman and judged Israel, did not go at the head of the army. Huldah was endowed with the prophetic gift; but she does not stand forth prominent in the civil and religious history of the Jews. Anna, though she devoted herself to the service of God in the temple, did not at all go beyond the bounds of female modesty and propriety. Miriam led the songs of her countrymen after the triumph at the Red Sea. The daughters of Philip by no means stand forth in any public capacity" (Duren, "Place," 26–27). Determined to sustain a simplistic and oppositional notion of gender, conservative writers attempted to reinterpret strong biblical women—sometimes wrenching them into an unrecognizable form—to make them conform to the true womanhood model.

Although they managed to locate and manufacture biblical support for their claim, the conservatives' edict of feminine self-sacrifice is actually curious when pondered more fully. According to them, woman's primary allegiance is not to God but to her husband. Moreover, even though she is to remain supposedly within her divinely ordained, "natural" sphere, she should squelch her equally "natural" emotions, friendships, intellectual curiosity, and independence. Thus, for the conservatives, submission and piety hold very specific this-worldly and male-oriented connotations. Woman is caught in a double bind. Set up as the moral guardian of the wayward male in a Christian environment where ostensibly "all distinctions disappear" (Peck, *True,* 326), woman must abdicate her own spiritual development and even her entitlement to salvation to ensure those of her undeserving spouse. More ironically, such a prescription was pronounced during the supposed golden age of democracy, self-reliance, and individualism. While most conservatives simply ignored the idea of woman's civil rights (preferring to concentrate solely on sacred matters), a few like George Burnap boldly rejected it:

> The position of woman is a question of expediency, not of abstract, original right. The first dictate of natural justice would seem to be, that the natural rights of man and woman should be equal. But this assertion must be received with considerable modification...., for no one becomes a citizen in the fullest sense, no one has the right of suffrage until he has reached the age of twenty-one... So, after all, under the freest constitution, political rights are determined by expediency. Woman has a right to precisely that position which is most conducive to the welfare of that community to which she belongs. (*Sphere,* 191)

Thus, while man has the right to full citizenship (including property and suffrage rights), woman must be content to serve the "common" good, which, despite its inclusive name, does not include her.

According to conservatives, when women should receive an education, it should not be for the cultivation of the intellect or an independent profession but for the perfection of their subordinate roles as housekeeper, wife, and mother (Thayer, *Good,* 34). Furthermore, for those few conservatives who concede that women should be trained in a vocation, they specify that it should be sewing, weaving, housekeeping, laundering, or tutoring, which they should exercise only in the event of an economic emergency or spousal death (Wise, "Young," 182) and which offer no threat to male power. Thus, despite their casting woman as "the lowly vine, which needs support for itself" (O'Reilly,

Mirror, 360) or the poor "bird...with cropped wings" (Graves, *Twenty-Five,* 31) who rests in "the home with its quiet, its obscurity, its sanctities" (O'Reilly, *Mirror,* 359), conservatives simultaneously commanded her to assume enormously strenuous domestic tasks. Counseled Ashmore, "I know it is hard when there are beautiful, high, and noble thoughts that we would like to enjoy alone than to have to sweep a floor, or mend a gown, or bathe a baby, but the doing of any of these gently and cheerfully is better than thinking high thoughts — it is living them" (Ashmore, *Side,* 77). Similarly, Graves asserts: "The greatest evil is that the idea of washtubs, house-cleaning, scrubbing floors, blacking stoves, washing dishes, baking bread, broiling meat, and doing the hardest kind of home work, does not enter into the idea of [woman's] education. But lily fingers loaded with gold rings, pale faces, slender forms tightly laced... [wrongly] makes up the education" (Graves, *Twenty-Five,* 37). Jesse Peck put it most succinctly, "labor here, rest in heaven; [that] is the motto of the true woman in the Church" (*True,* 307).

Thus, upon closer examination, the main components heralded as essential to the true womanhood ideal — domesticity, piety, passivity, and submissiveness — were not what they were initially touted to be. Enduring "any amount of suffering" (Wise, "Bridal," 122) and ignoring the husband's misdeeds does not seem congruent with the image of the quiet, obscure, tranquil home. Following the dictates of her husband and squelching her own religious emotions does not seem to lead toward greater piety. A life replete with washing, scrubbing, broiling, blacking, and baking seems antithetical to the pure, passive woman image. Finally, submission is not so much to God as to a woman's husband. In short, the true womanhood traits served the greater autonomy and power of men than the advancement of women's spiritual state or the glory of an ethereal god.

Given the stringency and sexism of the Protestant ideal of womanhood, the question arises as to why intelligent women not only joined the Church but assumed active roles within it. By the second half of the nineteenth century, close to 75 percent of churchgoers were women; by century's end, women comprised the overwhelming majority of the U.S. missionary force. They helped to found numerous benevolence organizations and served as the principal educators in Sunday schools. As early as 1870, 165 women listed themselves as ministers (Hassey, *No Time,* 9), and many more served as prayer leaders, deaconesses, and evangelists. Unlike Beecher, who gained prominence and power by inculcating a conservative Protestant rhetoric to which she did not follow in practice, many of the Christian feminists never achieved public fame and were sincere practicing believers. Did their conversions serve to thwart or empower them? Was there a way in which nineteenth-century Christianity and women's rights were congruent, at least for certain groups of women? If the two systems of thought were so incompatible, then why was such an inordinate number of active middle-class women so attracted to Protestantism?

In the past three decades, a number of noted historians have given various responses to these questions. Perhaps the first historian to identify the crucial role of gender in the transformation that took place in U.S. Protestantism between 1800 and 1860 was Barbara Welter in her 1965 article, "The Feminization of American Religion." She writes,

> In the period following the American Revolution, political and economic activities were critically important and therefore more "masculine," that is, more competitive, more aggressive, more responsible to shows of force and strength. Religion, along with the family and popular taste, was not very important, and so became the property of the ladies. Thus it entered a process of change whereby it became more domesticated, more emotional, more soft and accommodating— in a word, more "feminized."... Feminization, then, can be defined and studied through its results—a more genteel, less rigid institution—and through its members—the increased prominence of women in religious organizations and the way in which new or revised religions catered to this membership. (*Dimity,* 84)

For Welter, women, domesticity, religion, family, and anti-intellectualism are fully entwined with one another and wholly distinct from the world of men, politics, business, and aggressive competition. Indeed, according to Welter, little if any interchange was evident between these two opposing realms. Consequently, because they lacked access to primary modes of power or positions of authority, women were compelled to remain unwilling but passive victims of this social-gender bifurcation and were relegated the less significant aspects of society: religion and family.

To support her claims, Welter does not consider the writings of Protestant women; instead she cites numerous sermons and advice books composed by conservative clergymen. As a result, she neglects the women's sides of the story and (perhaps unconsciously) gives credence to the clerical view. While Welter correctly interprets the ministers' injunctions as degradatory and onerous to women, she nevertheless consents to their conception of society as dualistic and of woman as accepting religion out of weakness rather than choice. More-over, according to her, women did not realize, when they thronged to their community revivals, that they were unwittingly contributing to their own loss of power and dignity: "Whether in the divine or human order, woman was constantly urged to be swept away by a torrent of energy, not to rely on her own strength which was useless, to sink into the arms of Jesus, to become absorbed and assimilated by the Divine Will—in other words, to relax and enjoy it. The fantasies of rape were nourished by this language and by the kind of physical sensations which a woman expected to receive and did receive in the course of conversion" (*Dimity*, 92–93). Although Welter's agenda is undoubt-edly feminist (in that she openly critiques a masculine-controlled Christian institution), she nevertheless reinforces an antifeminine notion of woman-hood by portraying nineteenth-century women as agencyless beings, mere putty in the hands of wily clerics, unable to take any constructive part in fash-ioning their own destiny. Although she was the first to express it, Welter's view that women were the acquiescent prey to the socioreligious shift in the nine-teenth century has been appropriated and developed by other scholars.[1]

Another thesis that became widespread among women's historians emerged in Nancy Cott's 1977 book, *The Bonds of Womanhood: "Woman's Sphere" in New England, 1780–1835*. Whereas Welter views the rupture between private and public spheres as real and fixed, Cott finds the two realms intersecting in cru-cial ways: "The canon of domesticity... constitut[ed] the home as a redemp-tive counterpart to the world. Yet the ultimate function of the home was in the world. It was to fit men to pursue their worldly aims in a regulated way. The accent on individual character and self-control in the canon of domestic-ity simulated and underpinned individual economic struggle, just as women's vocations simulated men's" (98). Although the domestic or separate spheres ideology defined women and men as well as the home and marketplace op-positionally, these antipodes were actually less distinct. Furthermore, unlike Welter, Cott does not depict women as dupes of conniving clerics. For her, "Christian belief had a self-perpetuating force that was not likely to be dis-rupted by experience that would provide alternative and equally satisfying explanations" (136).[2] Thus, not only was women's affinity to Protestantism understandable but it also afforded them a means of self-affirmation and em-powerment. Cott contends that religious activities (in particular, Christian women's societies and reform organizations) emboldened women to define self and to forge a viable, feminine-centered, and socially acceptable community. She claims:

> Religion stretched before the convert a lifetime of purposeful struggle, holding out heartening rewards. It provided a way to order one's life and priorities. . . . Religious identity also allowed women to assert themselves, both in private and in public ways. It enabled them to rely on an authority beyond the world of men and provided a crucial support to those who stepped beyond accepted bounds — reformers, for example. . . . Religious faith also allowed women a sort of holy selfishness, or self-absorption, the result of the self-examination intrinsic to the Calvinist tradition. In contrast to the self-abnegation required of women in their domestic vocation, religious commitment required attention to one's own thoughts, actions and prospects. (139–40)

For Cott, the more diligently Christian ministers sought to promote and safeguard "feminine" values, the more legitimate and likely it became for religious women to scrutinize those values. By doing so, women also came to question their assigned gender roles and sought to expand them.

Thus, through their participation in the Church, women who had "previously held no particular avenue of power of their own — no unique defense of their integrity and dignity" — found a means of gaining a new sense of self and even a political consciousness (200). Yet, paradoxically, Cott also declares that, in the long run, Protestantism with its ideology of separate spheres "restrained women's initiative because of its central distinction between womanly self-abnegation and manly self-assertion" (195). Because separate spheres thinking "deprived the sexes of their common ground, [it] opened the door to antifeminist and misogynist philosophies" (195–96). Thus, it is in Cott's work that the basic vexed relationship of Protestantism and feminism comes to the fore. While Welter implies that the force of religion was too overpowering for women to surmount and thus to formulate a feminist consciousness, Cott proposes that feminism and Protestantism did at times converge and collide. However, she refuses to leave this tension unresolved; for in her view, Protestantism formed an advantageous but temporary stage for incipient feminists.

The Protestant ideology of domesticity helped to galvanize in some women a group consciousness that in turn caused them to recognize a common identity and finally to assert their own political rights. Yet, in order for women to achieve what Cott sees as the final and preferable goal of becoming secular feminists, they ultimately had to disengage themselves from "the convincing power of evangelical Protestantism" (204): "What precipitated some women and not others to cross the boundaries from 'woman's sphere' to 'woman's rights' is not certain; but it seems that variation or escape from the containment of conventional evangelical Protestantism—whether through Quakerism, Unitarianism, or 'de-conversion'—often led the way" (204).

Cott sets up a feminist teleology with secular feminism as the treasured culmination. Those who managed to reach that goal are decidedly superior to those who remain within the confines of Christianity. By setting up a hierarchical dualism between feminism and secularism, Cott (and Welter for that matter) ends up promoting the idea that the two systems of thought are fundamentally at odds. Moreover, she runs the risk of ignoring not only the overlapping ideas of—but also the complexities and contradictions within—both systems and of occluding the work of those suffragists who never extricated themselves from Christianity.

In this chapter, I will demonstrate that the interplay between and within these supposedly antipathetic groups was more fluid and mobile than many scholars have understood. In an analysis of advice writing and religious commentaries written by Protestant feminists (most of whom were women and lifelong Christians), I argue that through the selective miming of a variety of Christian and critical discursive practices—evangelicalism, historical criticism, and liberal individualism—these writers forwarded a unique women's rights message of their own. While their message may not have been revolutionary in the sense that it overturned major systems of thought, it was radically obedient. As a result, the adherents of this strategy were able to reach a large audience of Christian women that the secular feminists could not.

What I have in mind by miming is not a simple reiteration of, or subordination to, dominant Protestant thought but instead "an insubordination that appears to take place within the very terms of the original and which calls into question the power of origination" (Butler, *Bodies,* 45). Thus, miming repeats the origin only to displace that origin as origin. The Christian feminists reiterated the conservative ideals of true womanhood and separate spheres and, by doing so, reinterpreted those norms and simultaneously exposed them as privileged, constructed interpretations rather than innate, divinely decreed, natural laws. In short, they functioned as "domestic slaves," or secret rebels; and by unseating the conservatives' grounds of decidability within the rubric of the Church itself, Christian feminists deferred conservative authority and thereby reconstructed the Church not as the uniform arena that conservatives posited but as a site of multifarious, competing, and unifying discourses or a critical arena of debate and exchange.

Like the conservatives, the Christian feminists glorified woman's influential social role. Proclaimed Lillie Devereux Blake, "The national housekeeping is all out of order for want of that virtue, love of order, and, above all, conscientiousness which woman especially represents" (*Woman's*, 147). The key to woman's ability to "clean up" the home and (by extension) society is her devotion to Christ and her evangelical ability. "Dear girls," advised Frances Willard, "CHRIST is the magnet of humanity, and she has found the best vocation, and the highest, who brings most souls diseased within the healing power of His immortal Gospel" ("How," 41). Later in the same advice book, she made another statement that could easily have been issued from the pens of conservatives: "The home is but the efflorescence of woman's nature under the nurture of Christ's Gospel" (55). Similarly, in another work, she underlined the power of woman's maternal instinct: "Mother-love works magic for humanity... Mother-hearted women are called to be the saviors of the race" (qtd. in Hardesty, "Minister," 97).[3] Implicit in Willard's statement is the conviction that women are aligned with virtue and Christianity and are destined to improve those around them. Noted Elizabeth Oakes Smith, "In [woman's] shape there is flexibility, a variety, more graceful, ethereal, and beautiful, appealing more intimately to that something within the soul of man, that goes onward to the future and eternal — a softening down of the material to the illusions of the unseen" ("Woman," 22–23). Finally, as did the conservatives, the Christian feminists tended to view men and women as different yet complementary. As one writer put it: "The man has more of the material nature, woman more of the moral; he excels in animal life, she excels in the spiritual; he is more coercive, she more persuasive; he is exterior, she interior; he is self-loving, she loving; he is more theological and speculative, she more religious and practical; he is doctrinal, she devotional; he distrusts, she trusts; he walks by sight, she by faith; he has more head, she more heart" (Miller, *Woman*, 15).

In addition to endorsing the conservatives' view of woman as pivotal to the moral progress society, as aligned with Christianity, and as fundamentally different from man, Christian feminists also typically dressed in ways conservatives would approve. Hannah Whitall Smith, for example, earned the honorific, "angel of the churches," because of her blond hair, tall stature, and "charming" Quaker attire (James, *Notable,* 3:314). Correspondingly, Elizabeth Oakes Smith was commonly depicted as "very feminine in appearance, with brown hair and eyes and a small mouth with full lips; she was a popular performer" (James, *Notable,* 3:310). Also tall, Amanda Berry Smith was known to be a "smooth-skinned woman with a well-proportioned body that she chose to clothe in a simple, Quaker-like dress and scooped bonnet" (Dodson, "Introduction," xxxiii), and Sojourner Truth reportedly clothed herself often in Quaker garb (Stetson and David, *Glorying,* 131). Finally, Frances Willard's dresses were "ladylike and fashionable, usually 'black or brown velvet or silk' with 'a blue ribbon or a touch of white or ivory lace at the throat,' and a tasteful bonnet that she removed when she spoke'" (Campbell, *Man,* 130). Willard's and the other Christian feminists' conservative exterior appearance was crucial in dispelling the conservatives' claim that suffragists were "Amazonian... [and were] mutilating fair womanhood in order to assume the unnatural armor of men" (*Young Lady's Guide,* 101). As Ruth Bordin notes, Willard (and indeed all of the Christian feminists) "preached and exemplified a womanliness and domesticity that [at least initially] did not challenge existing cultural values" (11).

This traditionally feminine demeanor no doubt enabled Willard and other Christian feminists to gain more readily public forums and favorable receptions. Frances Willard, president from 1879 to 1898 of the Woman's Christian Temperance Union (W.C.T.U), the largest organization of women in the nation's history, was so celebrated that one historian called her, "Woman of the Century" (Hardesty, *Women,* 25). As lay preachers and lecturers, Elizabeth Oakes Smith, Amanda Berry Smith, Hannah Whitall Smith, and Sojourner Truth often spoke to enthusiastic crowds numbering in the thousands. These women indeed represented some of the most skilled and successful public speakers of the nineteenth century. Although their use of conservative rhetoric and physical appearance may have served to increase their public following, the question remains as to whether their conservative trappings ultimately undermined their concern for women's rights.

Contemporary historian Karlyn Kohrs Campbell argues that such a performance by Willard and others constituted "rhetorical alchemy," or "relabeling... proposals in ways that transformed them from demands for social change into reaffirmations of traditional arrangements and values" (*Man,* 126). Nancy Hardesty advances a similar interpretation, claiming that Willard's argument "raises serious theological and sociocultural problems. It is based on and perpetuates cultural stereotypes of women's role as derived from biological differences ... That concept obviously tends, for the majority of women, to circumscribe their sphere to marriage and maternity within the confines of the home and the nuclear family" ("Minister," 100–101). Finally, Lori D. Ginzberg contends that while conservative Christian ideology may have granted some women a personal and "cultural authority" in the postmillennial fervor of the 1830s and 40s, it had "lost most of its radical potential" after the Civil War; as a result, women, like Willard and her organization, W.C.T.U., that in the late nineteenth century still relied on a rhetoric of female values, ended up reinforcing conservatism and lobbying for "repressive" legislation (for example, the 1873 Comstock law, Sunday blue laws, censorship regulations, prohibition, and increased punishment of prostitutes) (*Women,* 206).

While the Christian feminists did fall prey to repressive conservative values, Ginzberg's and Campbell's interpretations may nevertheless be reconsidered. The W.C.T.U. included many chapters spanning the country and globe, each with different legislative and social goals. Ruth Bordin notes that rather than social purity legislation, Willard's most ardent interests included labor rights for women, a free kindergarten movement, better municipal sanitation, federal aid for education (as a way of providing schooling for blacks), separate correctional institutions for women, Protestant ecumenicism, and, of course, female suffrage. Claims Bordin, "Willard's journals show her consistent preoccupation with the woman question from her earliest years, but the temperance question is mentioned only rarely" (*Willard,* 69). Betty DeBerg argues that because "Willard's rhetoric and strategy used an appeal to 'home protection,' which was an extension and adaptation of the ideology of separate spheres," she provided the opportunity for many of the W.C.T.U. members to venture into the world of politics and social reform. Indeed, "many respectable middle-class women were radicalized by their participation in the W.C.T.U." (*Ungodly,* 29). Similarly, Bordin suggests, "through the vehicle of a militant temperance organization designed as a vital protection for the home and children [Willard] permitted women to do whatever they wished in the public sphere and compelled men to praise them for it" (11). Thus, the conservative rhetoric and demeanor may have served as women's "tickets" into the public sphere of politics.

While Willard, Oakes Smith, Whitall Smith, Berry Smith, and Truth undoubtedly represented some of the most skilled and successful public figures to deploy such a performative strategy, this means of persuasion was probably not uncommon among lesser known feminist women. In *Searching the*

Heart, Karen Lystra offers as an example the personal situation of Elizabeth Boynton Harbert, who was a wife, mother, and suffragist, to suggest how common women were able to transgress sex-role expectations by reframing them rhetorically to allow for their own greater maneuverability: "Elizabeth regularly left her home and family for woman's suffrage conventions, and W.C.T.U. conferences, but by offering to return home at any moment she translated her 'violation' of feminine sex-role obligations into a long-distance 'fulfillment' of them. By confirming to both herself and her family that they were the priority, she offered self-abnegation in theory but self-assertion in practice" (144). Thus, to judge all Protestant feminists solely by the legislation advanced by the conservative wing of one of its largest movements (two million members in 1897) is to overlook the variegated quality of as well as the radical goals pursued by its more liberal members and leader.[4]

Critics' sweeping dismissal of Christian feminists' political efficacy also ignores the diverse array of creative and sometimes self-contradictory tactics that they employed in the service of social and religious reform. But the Christian feminists' self-contradiction differs from that performed by Catharine Beecher. Beecher's self-contradiction took the form of the old parental, patronizing adage, "do as I say, not as I do." Not only did she command women to remain within their sphere and shame those who veered away from it, but she also neglected to point out her own violation of the spheres ideology. Furthermore, although she spearheaded a campaign to employ and mobilize single white women to teach in the West, she instructed them to spread the conservative spheres ideology to Western residents and Native American women. The Christian feminists, by contrast, openly combined a range of contradictory secular and religious rhetoric strategies to expand, rather than constrain, the rights and opportunities for women and to create greater mutuality among Protestant believers and between feminists and Christians. In the next sections, I demonstrate that by relying upon principles drawn from the Weslayan holiness movement, the Christian feminists mimed perfectionistic evangelical leaders, and by incorporating liberal historical criticism, they entered into and subtly undermined the conservative circles of biblical scholarship.

According to Mark A. Noll, the term "evangelical" has always been a plastic one, signifying slightly different things for various sects; yet a wide array of faiths — Catholic and Protestant, independent and denominational, dispensational and antidispensational, mainline and fundamentalist — did adhere to its underlying principles (*Between,* 1–2), which included an acceptance of the Bible's divine authority and a belief (based on faith) in "the miraculous birth, death and resurrection of Jesus to save men [sic] from damnation" (McLoughlin, *American,* 6). In general, evangelicals underscored Christ's atonement and the individual's free will to accept or deny faith in God. Whereas orthodox Calvinists (such as George Whitefield) conceived of God as a merciless ruler who admits to Heaven only a predestined few, evangelicals held that all individuals share a moral sensibility and a common consciousness of their freedom to choose; thus evangelical preachers launched their pleas for conversion expecting people to be capable of responding to them. In other words, anyone, in the evangelical view, can will to be, and thus can be, saved. Hence, the goal of nineteenth-century evangelicalism was to save souls; and (as was evident in Harriet Beecher Stowe's novel) its emphasis was on pragmatics rather than on speculative doctrine.

Virtually all of the Christian feminists were involved in evangelical churches. Frances Willard, for example, was a lifelong member of an evangelical Methodist Church. A descendant of a long line of Quakers, Hannah Whitall Smith converted to a perfectionist strain of Weslayan Methodism when in the 1860s she met her husband, Robert Pearsall Smith. Both she and her spouse became conspicuous and influential evangelists in the Keswick Movement in Britain. Although raised in a strict Calvinist family, Mary Ashton Rice Livermore married an evangelical Universalist minister and converted to his faith as a young woman. Lillie Devereux Blake, the great-great-granddaughter of the eminent Jonathan Edwards, was heavily involved in an evangelical Methodist Episcopal Church. Julia A. J. Foote, Virginia Broughton, and Mary Cook joined evangelical black Baptist denominations as well. A member of the African Methodist Episcopal Church, Amanda Berry Smith practically became synonymous with evangelical sanctification during her celebrated missionary and preaching career.

One reason for women's special attraction to evangelicalism was its deemphasis on an educated male clergy. Because this form of religion was in its nascency and thus lacked enough educated clergy to meet its immediate aim of converting the nation, midcentury evangelical denominations sanctioned the use of lay preachers and prayer leaders and championed the right of individuals (including women) who were genuinely called by the Holy Spirit to minister and evangelize to do so. Hence, as opposed to the conservatives who placed a premium on high educational standards for clergy and on a literal reading of the Scriptures, evangelicals emphasized personal experience and spiritual calling over formal theological knowledge (Dayton, *Discovering*, 87). This accent on experience and calling directly facilitated the entry of women into leadership roles within the Church. Although in the late nineteenth century such higher educational institutions as Oberlin College, Boston University, and Garrett Biblical Institute were increasingly admitting women into their theological seminaries, women enrolled in higher theological institutions was still a rare occurrence. Consequently, while women may not always have been able to compete with men in terms of formal education, they could rival them in the realm of experience.

Christian feminist advice writers often featured women's singular propensity for excelling in the religious world of experience. Hannah Whitall Smith, for instance, opened her book by retreating from pedantic theological speculation and aligning herself with daily praxis: "I do not want to change the theological views of a single individual. The truths I have to tell are not theological, but practical. They are, I believe, the fundamental truths of life and experience, the truths that underlie all theologies, and that are in fact their real and vital meaning" (*Christian's*, 1). Frances Willard sounds a similar theme when she writes: "Men preach a creed; women declare a life. Men deal in formulas, women in facts. Men have always tithed mint and rue and cummin [sic] in their exegesis and their ecclesiasticism, while the world's heart has cried out for compassion, forgiveness and sympathy. Men's preaching has left hearts hard as nether millstones. . . . Men reason in the abstract, women in the concrete. A syllogism symbolizes one, a rule of life the other" (*Woman*, 47).[5] Despite their protestations to the contrary, these women were projecting a theology of their own — one that specially valorized women's lives. By cloaking themselves with the banner of feminine experience rather than with that of masculine theology, they were able not only to theologize without disrupting their "feminine" status but also to travel authoritatively in the most exalted and socially acceptable evangelical circles. In addition, by appealing to personal experience as the "true" foundation of all theological systems, Willard and Smith were in a sense usurping the lofty authority of male theologians and tendering a new woman-centered and experience-based theology of their own.

Evangelicalism's stress on commonplace experience as opposed to abstruse systems of theology also spurred a potent emotional fervor and an experimental zeal in its religious gatherings. Dayton asserts that because revivalists were willing to transgress conventional modes of worship,[6] they were more open to experimenting with new feminine roles in the Church (*Discovering*, 87). Furthermore, revivals frequently served as hotbeds of passionate emotions; individuals—male or female—could swell with intense religious sentiment at any moment and speak, sing, or act out in previously unsanctioned ways. Eliza B. Rutherford, for example, was suddenly struck by the spirit at a camp meeting in Ennis, Texas. She recalled, "On Jan. 10th, 1892, God called me to preach the gospel. He plainly revealed to me that I was to do the work of an Evangelist. When I recognized His voice calling me to this work, I answered: 'Here am I Lord! I am wholly consecrated to Thee. I belong to Thee to go where and when you want to send me and by your power will do your whole will'" (qtd. in Dayton, *Holiness*, 65). At the time of her momentous revelation, Rutherford was married to a lower-income farmer and had rarely ventured beyond her small Texas hometown. The Holy Spirit precipitately impelled in Rutherford both a sudden willingness for mobility as well as an emphatic justification for renegotiating her entire life.

Just as the traditional Anglican clergy of the eighteenth century had complained about George Whitefield's revivals, nineteenth-century conservative Christians shunned the profound intimacy and feeling engendered by nineteenth-century camp meetings because they "feared the power of the passions to break down the boundaries of groups or 'classes' within a community... They were concerned at the mixing, 'shaking together,' and 'pressing out of their place' of the various sorts of groups which were supposed to be separate and distinctive in their behavior—men and women, old and young, higher and lower" (Sizer, *Gospel*, 63–64). Thus, within the revivalistic arena, religious ardor functioned as a common denominator in leveling sex and class differences (Hassey, *No Time*, 52). Moreover, Sizer adds, "what was private, namely the emotion connected with the intense experience of conversion, was being ushered into the public sphere" (69). Women, as the appointed proponents of conversion and religious fervidity, were thus boldly traversing into a newly transforming public arena.

Not only did evangelicalism help to shift public-private boundaries, it also embodied the potential to spur attacks on traditional authority. Scholars such as George M. Thomas and Paul E. Johnson have attested that revivalism defined and legitimized a new cultural and economic order. Writes Thomas, "Petty capitalists, yeoman farmers and laborers all flocked to revival... because it articulated new freedoms from local paternalistic institutions" (87). For evangelicals, the world could now be sliced in a different way: real versus non-

Christians, according to the level of their spiritual enthusiasm; and this new (albeit simplistic) manner of separation often cut across old gender, class, and race lines and inspired various forms of civil and social disobedience. A recent scholar explicates the reason for this cultural and attitudinal transformation:

> A moral theory based upon the dictates of conscience offers little room for ethical compromise; and a commitment to a moral law that is above man's law would countenance the overthrow of iniquity at all costs. . . . Radicalism is more a product of the heart than of the head; and this was an age when the radical heart was encouraged . . . The evangelical emphasis on the committed heart, combined with the insistence on the faithful performance of moral duty, with the popular literary fascination with sentiment, led many to the conclusion that disinterested moral vehemence and sacrificial devotion to a good cause were essential to good character. (Meyer, *Instructed*, 30)

Hence, while women may not have been given a legitimate public role in society, they could authoritatively devote themselves to revivals and other evangelical endeavors and thus gain a measure of public agency and power.

Mary P. Ryan confirms that women frequently attended revivals alone and converted to Christianity before the men in their family. Consequently, at least for a time, women "exercised a degree of religious autonomy during seasons of revival . . . ; [and] in addition to constituting the majority of revival converts, were also instrumental in a host of other conversions among their kin of both sexes" ("Women's," 91). Although Ryan's study predates this study's period of consideration, narrative accounts of late-nineteenth-century women preachers confirm her findings. For example, in 1905, Eliza Rutherford, an ordained minister of the Methodist Protestant Church, wrote that at the time of her conversion, her husband not only smoked, drank, and refused to attend church, but he was thoroughly "disgraced" by his wife's active role in the camp meetings. Only after a year of steady patience and ministering on Eliza's part did he finally convert (Dayton, *Holiness*, 66). Moreover, since women were first in the process of conversion and, as Willard phrased it, were "climbing more rapidly than men . . . [to] the heights of spiritual power, with souls more open to the 'skyey influences' of the oncoming age" ("How," 50), they helped to form a new transcendent, woman-dominated, and woman-oriented community. John Smith, a historian of the Holiness evangelical movement, affirms that "forty years before the time of woman's suffrage on a national level, a great company of women were preaching, singing, writing and helping to determine the policies in this religious reform movement" (qtd. in Dayton, *Dis-*

covering, 97). Contemporary historian Donald Dayton writes that the *Guide to Holiness* (a newspaper edited by evangelist Phoebe Palmer) customarily included within it support for active feminine participation in the Church; one typical issue read, "When the Pentecostal light shines most brightly, women do the bulk of the common-school teaching. They are also principals, professors, college presidents and are admitted to all the learned professions.... When the light shines clearly, they have equal rights with men, by whose side they labor for God's glory" (qtd. in *Discovering,* 97).

After 1865, women partook more formally in the revivalistic evangelical movement as lay, itinerant, and ordained ministers, hymn and prayer leaders, missionaries, deaconesses, Sabbath-school teachers, conference delegates, and committee members of local, state, and national religious associations. The Methodists—the largest U.S. evangelical denomination in the latter half of the nineteenth century (Schmidt, "Reexamining," 76)—established three training schools (the Chicago Training School for City, Home, and Foreign Missions; the New England Deaconess Home and Training School; and Scarritt Bible and Training School) designed primarily to teach women to assume important roles in the evangelical movement.[7] Thus, given the number of women in evangelical leadership positions, many of these Christian feminists met with, heard about, or were converted at the hands of other Protestant women. Frances Willard, for example, became sanctified at a revival given by Phoebe Palmer. Mrs. E. J. Sheeks felt the Spirit move her to the ministry after hearing Mrs. M. L. Woolsey preach at a camp meeting at a Cumberland Presbyterian Church in Tennessee (Dayton, *Holiness,* 90). Amanda Berry Smith found inspiration in the sermons of Hannah Whitall Smith, Laura Bowden, and Sarah Smiley and in Phoebe Palmer's *Guide to Holiness* (*Autobiography,* 213). Evangelicalism, then, represented one locale where women held (sometimes for several generations) equal or superior positions of authority and influence. As a result, it proved a particularly enticing realm—both in terms of rhetoric and action— for women seeking greater power and mobility.

Whitall Smith, Berry Smith, as well as many other Christian feminists were particularly attracted to one of the more extreme and controversial doctrinal principles of evangelical-revivalistic Protestantism: perfectionism or holiness. Perfectionism holds that consecrated believers would grow in grace until they reach a virtually sinless state. One of the appeals of this doctrine, particularly for women, was that it offered its followers a form of self-abnegation that differed significantly from the concept of self-sacrifice advanced by conservative clergy. While feminine submission for conservatives meant following the dictates of one's husband or father; for perfectionism, it meant absolute trust in God's will. Because achieving holiness (also known as perfection or sanctification) was a lifelong process involving numerous challenges and rewards, its followers were licensed to grow and move in new directions. Rather than perceive conversion as the desired final goal, perfectionists insisted that believers must continue, throughout their lives, to improve in their devotion; as a result, its followers not only were given permission to develop and change in response to God's calling but also were licensed to obey God's will over and above the will of all other earthly beings. As Barbara Epstein notes, "religious zeal was legitimate[,] protesting male authority was not. Only in the name of something as deeply held and long established as orthodox religious belief could women bring themselves to challenge the supremacy of their husbands and fathers" (*Politics,* 61–62).

Christian feminists often availed themselves of this propitious chance to shun domineering male figures or masculine traditions. For example, after receiving sanctification, African-American Christian feminist, Julia A. J. Foote, declared, "Man's opinion weighed nothing with me, for my commission was from heaven, and my reward was with the Most High" ("Brand," 208). Similarly, in her advice book, Willard counseled her young reader to think of herself as "a daughter of God, whose duties are first of all, to her own nature and to Him by whom that nature was endowed" ("How," 59). Interestingly, Willard listed a woman's fealty to self even before her obligation to God, and she implied that the dual responsibility to self and God is mutually reinforcing. Hannah Whitall Smith was even more specific than Willard about what this loyalty to God and self entails. She instructed her women readers to "learn, from Luke 14:26–33, and similar passages, that in order to be a disciple and follower of your Lord, you may perhaps be called upon to forsake inwardly all that you have, even father or mother, or brother or sister, or husband or wife... It often happens that the child of God who enters upon this life of obedience, is sooner or later led into paths which meet the disapproval of those [s]he best loves" (*Christian's,* 56).

Paradoxically, obedience to God offered the possibility for disobedience to man, and because of this divinely ordained opportunity to defy men, Christian feminists viewed their own position as advantageous when compared to that of non-Christian women. Wrote Virginia Broughton, "women according to the flesh are made for the glory of man, but when recreated in Christ or born of the Spirit, they are recreated for such spiritual service as God may appoint through the examples given in his Word" ("Twenty," 39). Indeed, Broughton herself initially had to face considerable opposition from her husband when she decided to become a missionary. When he asked her to give up missionizing, Broughton retorted, " 'I belong to God first, and you next; so you two must settle it' " (qtd. in Brooks Higginbotham, *Righteous*, 132). Thus, for these women, total submission to God may not have been perceived as oppressive or confining because it allowed them to oppose the more pertinacious problems generated by men in this world in a seemingly licit manner.

The Christian feminists' allegiance to God was significant because for them the deity was conceived as being especially profeminine. Whitall Smith, for instance, repeatedly drew the analogy of God as the loving mother or parent and the consecrated believer as "a child in the Father's house" (*Christian's*, 21). In her advice book, Abba Goold Woolson speculated, "I sometimes think God must be a woman — He is expected to forgive so much" (*Woman*, 302). Indeed, in many cases, Jesus came to supplant the husband as the woman's dearest friend, companion, and soul mate. Sojourner Truth remarked about Jesus, " 'I saw him as a friend, standing between me and God, through whom, love flowed as from a fountain' " (*Narrative*, 69). Similarly, during the Civil War, Amanda Berry Smith was known to sing a hymn with the lyrics: "I am married to Jesus / For more than one year / I am married to Jesus / For during the war" (*Autobiography*, 81). Evangelicalism's image of Jesus as a loving partner was enticing for the Christian feminists because it offered them an alternative not only to the stern, merciless Calvinist god but also to their demanding and dominating spouses. Thus, these women could bypass oppressive forms of male authority without shirking their Christian true woman image.

Another feature of perfectionism that was particularly appealing to women was its postmillennial focus, or the view that Christ's return will happen only when complete social harmony is achieved on earth. For them, sanctified, ever-perfecting individuals would aid in effecting the millennium, a prelapsarian state of ultimate harmony on earth. History, then, was seen as the progressive unfolding of victory. As a result, the millennial order was linked to secular progress — the advance of Christianity and the goals of civilization being synonymous. Thus, as George M. Thomas affirms, "revivalism radicalized . . . mainstream Protestantism. A moral citizenry must actively construct the Kingdom of God. Viewing themselves blessed by God with foundational documents of democracy, Christians were to push forward and directly transform the nation" (*Revivalism*, 78). Christian feminists not only imbibed this postmillennial-reformist thrust, they particularized it to women's benefit. Their perspective on this goal differed from that of the conservatives who deemed women's millennial role as one fully sacrificial to men. As historian Janette Hassey notes, these women "tried to change unjust conditions in society and stressed service to others, thereby enlarging the female sphere of action in socially acceptable directions" (*No Time*, 8; italics mine). Indeed, under the encompassing and familiar aegis of Christian authority, female missionary reformers and deaconesses ventured into orphanages, prisons, hospitals, and neighborhoods of all classes as well as into foreign lands. In addition to expanding their sphere of action, these women also included in this progressive historiography the special advancement of woman. As one of the Christian feminist advice writers, Mary A. Livermore, put it, "There is not one country like America. The youngest of the family of nations . . . whose far-reaching future no prophet's eye can see, women stand on higher vantage-ground than ever before" (*What*, 53–54). While Livermore's depiction of woman as the locus and gauge of human and religious progress smacks of manifest destiny rhetoric (a point that will be taken up later in the chapter), it is ambitious for the scope of its vision and significant in its assignation of woman as the focal point.

Although white women's involvement in the evangelical movement had its definite shortcomings, it was pivotal in securing for them an acceptable public role. Frances Willard commented in 1889 that at least two-thirds of the world's Christian disciples were women, and many historians have also alluded to the unusually high percentage of women working in missionary and reform organizations. In 1896, for example, women comprised 1,000 of the evangelical Salvation Army's 1,854 American officers. By 1882, at least 16 women's missionary societies had dispatched 694 single female missionaries and raised almost six million dollars (Brereton and Klein, "American," 175), and Barbara Welter declares that by 1880 women constituted more than 57 percent of the active missionary force ("She Hath," 118). For the Christian feminists, women's entry into domestic and foreign missionary movements was significant not only because it helped to spread the gospel but also because it demonstrated the benefit and power of women's movement into the public sphere. As Willard affirmed, "[Woman] will come into government and purify it, into politics and cleanse its Stygian pool, for woman will make homelike every place she enters, and she will enter every place on this round earth" ("How," 55).

Thus, rather than jettison prominent terms of the conservative true womanhood ideal — piety, purity, submissiveness, and domesticity — the Christian feminists retranslated them in more expansive ways. Instead of signifying total obedience to man in the service of God, piety for the Christian feminists meant total obedience to a profeminine God, a god vehemently opposed to sexism. As Mary Dodge asserts, "A gospel that preaches masculine self-gratification as manly religion, the lowest womanly subserviency to man as the sole womanly way of doing God service, is not . . . to be lightly let slip. Its improbabilities, its inconsistencies, its monstrosities [have] seemed to go down sweetly like the grapes of Beulah" (5). For them, total submission did not entail the complete obfuscation of woman's uniqueness and agency. Argued Elizabeth Oakes Smith, "The individuality of each is a great law of God, and a woman is better when she acts out of her own spontaneity, tenfold, than when she attempts to conform to any theory" (111). As evident from Blake's concept of "national housekeeping" and Willard's idea of woman purifying the "Stygian pool" of the U.S. government, the Christian feminists invested the notions of domesticity and purity with new national implications.

This retranslation or miming of conservative norms of womanhood was not the only strategy the Christian feminists deployed. In addition to contesting conservatives on the evangelical-pious front, they also combated them in the realm of biblical scholarship by calling into question their use of the Bible to justify their true womanhood ideal. Unlike secular feminists such as Elizabeth Cady Stanton who believed the Bible was thoroughly denigrating to women, Christian feminists contended that the Bible could be read toward feminist ends. Mary Cook, an African-American Baptist, contended, "As the Bible is an iconoclastic weapon — it is bound to break down images of error that have been raised. As no one studies it so closely as the Baptists, their women shall take the lead" (qtd. in Brooks, "Feminist," 52).

In order to tap into the Bible's radical potential, Christian feminists needed to undercut the conservatives' method of biblical interpretation. Eschewing hypothetical, metaphorical, or symbolic readings of the Bible, conservatives believed that scriptural passages were equivalent to facts in nature — patent, unambiguous, and rationally evincible. According to them, "biblical writers perfectly portrayed what they saw and experienced. Once the modern interpreter understood the established usage of the words in the biblical account, the interpreter was brought into direct contact with the event itself. To read the biblical words was to encounter the biblical thought or deed just as if the interpreter had had direct experience of it" (Rogers and McKim, *Authority*, 291). Yet the conservatives' dedication to literalism was not upheld consistently. As demonstrated earlier in the chapter, they typically touted those passages, such as Ephesians 5:22 and 1 Timothy 2:11, that call for women's self-abnegation, silence, and obedience to males as literally and universally true but ignored or downplayed the significance of any passages contrary to that position.

Thus, the Christian feminists set out to refute what the conservatives believed was a disinterested, literal method of biblical interpretation or translation and to highlight their inconsistent use of that method. Toward that end, they obviated the conservatives' practice of what Donna Haraway (in an unrelated context) has labeled "the god-trick of seeing everything from nowhere" and promoted an openly situated method of scriptural scholarship ("Situated"). For example, Lillie Devereux Blake claimed, "when women interpret the Scriptures they find a very different meaning from that which men . . . give to it" (*Woman's*, 17). Or, as Willard eloquently expressed, "The mother-heart of God will never be known to the world until translated into terms of speech by mother-hearted women" (*Woman*, 46–47). For her, biblical exegesis was not a universal science but a method that changes over time: "[It is] one of the most time-serving and man-made of all sciences. . . . It is in no sense an inspired work, but grows in breadth and accuracy with the general growth of humanity" (23–24). Yet, neither Blake nor Willard advocated a radical relativism, or biblical interpretations based solely upon uninformed personal predilection. For them, women translators provided a much needed check and a more incisive perspective on masculine scholarship: "We need women commentators to bring out the women's side of the book; we need the stereoscopic view of truth in general, which can only be had when woman's eye and man's together shall discern the perspective of the Bible's full-orbed revelation" (Willard, *Woman*, 21). In other words, additional viewpoints serve to illuminate rather than to fragment complex textual meaning—to contribute to a fuller, more diverse, and egalitarian vision of God and, by extension, of society.

Beyond debunking the conservatives' objective, literal, and disinterested method of biblical interpretation, the Christian feminists also developed a new, more feminist method of interpretation, one that refused to overuniversalize select passages and to suppress others. Toward this end, they drew from a relatively new form of academic biblical scholarship: historical criticism. They were particularly attracted to this form of criticism because, in keeping with their own conciliatory stance, it sought to reconfigure traditional ways of understanding the Bible without completely rejecting its basic truths. As noted in the previous chapter, historical criticism or historismus emerged in German universities in the eighteenth century as a Romantic reaction against the Enlightenment's emphasis on natural law (Brown, *Rise*).[8] Mark S. Massa explains,

> While the doctrine of natural law had achieved almost canonical status in the Western intellectual tradition by the eighteenth century, the heralds of the romantic revolt against "formalistic" patterns of thought saw in it an affront to the dignity and unique historical efficacy of human activity within history. Permanent, transcendent categories outside or "above" the arena of historical activity appeared purely arbitrary to the new lovers of history and its vagaries, and seemed to be doubtful bases for judging the ethical meaning of contingent temporal activity. (*Briggs*, 4)

For these academic religious critics, history alone—not some abstract philosophy or theology—formed the most reliable guide to the ultimate questions of human concern. God, then, was viewed as radically immanent within the historical process itself; and because of their immanentist current, historical-critical thinkers stressed God's presence within human cultural development and called for the conscious adaptation of religious ideas to modern life (two trends strikingly akin to some of the postmillennial emphases of U.S. revivalism).

Historical criticism revolutionized not only the accepted notion of the Bible as espousing ahistorical, universal, and immutable truth and the traditional literalist form of biblical scholarship but also the orthodox approaches to historical thinking and notions of self in relation to God and society. In 1905, Oscar Wilde epitomized historical criticism as "part of that complex working towards freedom which may be described as the revolt against authority" (*Rise*, 5). Similarly, contemporary historians such as Grant Wacker have dubbed it as "the dynamite that ultimately exploded the entire edifice" of late-nineteenth-century thought ("Demise," 127).[9] Part of its revolutionary impetus was to reorient the focus away from a sovereign (masculine) deity toward the individual as the prime mover in this present historical realm. In other words, historical critics perceived history as an ever-changing progression of time and society that the contemporary individual could rationally understand and manipulate toward subjectively desired ends. In short, rather than succumb to the dictates of an eternal, fixed god as expressed in the completely factual, transhistorical Scriptures, individuals (male or female) could now adjust their behavior to the exigencies of the sociohistorical context according to the intensity of their inner feelings.

As was evident in Stowe's endorsement of it in *The Minister's Wooing* (see chapter 3), religious feminists found this novel hermeneutical method amenable to their agenda for a variety of reasons. First, it impelled the individual to take action in this newly desacralized world rather than wait for supernatural intervention or clerical guidance. Thus, using their own initiative, Christian feminists began actively to engage in biblical scholarship. Their first tactic was to resuscitate those biblical passages conservatives typically repressed. For example, they regularly emphasized the New Testament verse Galatians 3:28, arguing that it "fixes no limits, prescribes no bounds, names no places, occasions, subjects or duties, but affirms in general and unqualified terms, that there is neither male nor female, but that all are one in Christ Jesus" (Lee, "Woman's," 6–7). And in the Old Testament, they focused on Joel's prediction (Joel 2:28) that "women's active preaching and prophesying would be a leading feature of the gospel dispensation"[10] (qtd. in Dayton, *Holiness*, 5), to justify stronger leadership roles for women. These advice writers regularly apotheosized such figures as Miriam, Huldah, Hilkiah, Noahdiah, Anna, Priscilla, and Phebe as exemplary women. Cook's description of the warrior and prophetess Deborah serves as a representative example: "Her work was distinct from her husband's who, it seems, took no part whatever in the work of God while Deborah was inspired by the Eternal expressly to do His will and to testify to the countrymen that He recognizes in His followers neither male nor female, heeding neither the 'weakness' of one, nor the strength of the other, but strictly calling those who are perfect at heart and willing to do his bidding" (qtd. in Brooks, "Feminist," 39).

The Christian feminists' valorization of consequential biblical women is intriguing, for not only does it redress the conservatives' tendency to minimize or ignore these figures' importance but it also marks their miming of the conservatives' favorite practice of "prooftexting." In other words, at the same time that these women criticize the ministers' uplifting of certain (albeit submissive and self-effacing) biblical women and passages as universally true, they offer some counterverses and figures of their own. On the one hand, such a reversal seems patently hypocritical; for indeed, they are engaging in the practice of those conservatives with whom they disagree. On the other hand, the Christian feminists do not offer their prooftexts as the sole and absolute truth (as did the conservatives) but as possible alternatives to those traditionally offered. Thus, they unseat conservative norms and, by doing so, reveal another in a heterogeneous array of tactics that can be used to foster a more expanded biblical hermeneutic and (by extension) vision of womanhood. Through miming, they carve a distinct and acceptable place for women in the realms of biblical scholarship, church leadership, and traditional Christian theology.

A second way Christian feminists used historical criticism to overturn conservative biblical norms was to question the authority of traditional scriptural translation. Prior to the rise of historico-critical scholarship in the United States, Protestants wholly opposed tampering with the Common Version of the Bible. Yet, as early as the 1850s, scholars such as Richard Chenevix Trench insisted that the "interest in the historical Bible had uncovered hordes of new information that could not be ignored. The limits of the King James Bible, despite its profound beauty, had to be addressed" (Cmiel, *Democratic*, 122). By the 1890s, radically new translations and interpretations of the Bible — including the well-publicized Revised Version, Julia Smith's translation, as well as Stanton et al.'s *The Woman's Bible* — emerged. Just as liberal scholars interrogated the authorship and translations of the Scriptures, Christian feminists also considered the possibility of forged or mistranslated biblical passages; and because conservative ministers commonly adverted to the restrictive New Testament epistles, these women focused most particularly on them. Ellen Battelle Dietrick, for example, questioned the validity of the antifeminine portions of Paul's books because they did not correspond to other parts of his writing where he lauds active, commanding women: "In view of the whole of what is given us as Paul's life and letters, we must pronounce the woman-despising passages palpable forgeries and very bungling forgeries at that" (*Women*, 106–7).

Other writers quibbled with male scholars' proclivity to translate and interpret passages according to their own sexist whims and prejudices. B. T. Roberts noted, "To make a word mean one thing in one passage, and then something else in essentially the same connection, for the purpose of making the writer support our views, violates the principles of right interpretation" (*Ordaining*, 23).[11] And Christian feminist writers offered a bevy of illustrations, such as the following by Frances Willard: "it is objected that Paul specifies (in

2 Tim. 2:2) men only as his successors: 'And the things that thou hast heard of me, the same commit thou to faithful men, who shall be able to teach others also.' But the word translated 'men' is the same as that in the text, 'God now commandeth men everywhere to repent' and even the literalists will admit that women are, of all people, 'commanded to repent'!" (*Woman*, 34). Fannie McDowell Hunter argued a comparable and frequently made claim: "The word translated 'servant' occurs twenty times in Paul's writings. Sixteen times it is translated 'ministers.' Three times it is translated 'deacon.' Only once it is translated 'servant' and it is rather singular that the single exception is where the word is used in reference to Phebe. The same Greek word is used where it is said of Paul that he was made a minister" (qtd. in Dayton, *Holiness*, 27).

Willard also compared multiple translations to one another in order to uncover both the androcentric bias of male translators as well as the inaccuracy of the translation process. For example, she pointed out that while the King James Version of 1 Timothy 2:11 reads, " 'Let the woman learn in silence with all subjection,' the more recent Revised Version phrases it, " 'Let a woman learn in quietness with all subjection' " (*Woman*, 38) — the latter admonition being significantly less severe than the earlier one.[12] Thus, unlike Stanton who believed that the Scriptures could never be resuscitated to benefit women, the Christian feminists trusted in the latest translation methods to transmute the Holy Book into a decidedly less antifeminine text.

A third and final way Christian feminists used historical-critical principles to unseat conservative thinking was to consider more fully the historical context of scriptural verses. Not only did historical criticism assert the meaning of the original witness over later masculinist dogmatic usurpations, but it also made the assimilation of the text to present church and clerical interests more cumbersome. Furthermore, the Bible suddenly became subject to historical scrutiny and consideration and was viewed as a product of historical evolution, offering insight into the divine while also bearing the thought patterns and presuppositions of the time of its composition. Historical-critical biblical critics thus took on the task of segregating the " 'dross' of the human package from the divine treasure" (Massa, *Briggs*, 9) and began to question the authorship and historical nature of some of the most sacred books of the Bible. For these thinkers, the Bible's words do not transparently reflect God's message, but, as Andrews Norton (a nineteenth-century, liberal U.S. theologian) declared, they "are only human instruments for the expression of human ideas" (qtd. in Gura, *Wisdom*, 13). As such, personal biases, historical vicissitudes, and the peculiarities of the language itself color and transfigure the original intent of the godhead. As a result, in their view, the Bible's words do not always necessarily reflect God's intended revelation, and they chastised the conservatives for their propensity of refusing to historicize the Scriptures. For example, Frances P. Cobbe insisted that clergy who accept the Pauline injunction for wifely submission as universal truth should therefore be

> bound to attach the same authority to a parallel passage in another Epistle, wherein the same apostle commands slaves to obey their masters, and actually sends back to his chain a runaway who in our day would have been helped to freedom by every true Christian man or woman in America. . . . In our day, men habitually set aside this apostolic teaching, so far as it concerns masters and slaves, despots and subjects, as adapted only to a past epoch. I am at a loss to see by what right, having done so, can claim for its authority, when it happens to refer to husbands and wives. (*Duties*, 124–25)[13]

Similarly, Willard bemoaned ministers who demand woman's silence in the church as commanded by Paul but overlook the apostle's specific exhortations against braided hair, gold, pearls, and expensive attire (*Woman*, 20).[14]

Using the new tenets of historical criticism, Christian feminists sought to interpret the offending New Testament verses (such as 1 Timothy 2:11) the conservatives hailed as universally obligatory, as mere parochial restrictions directed by the apostles to women within a specific sociocultural and historical setting. "All the advice given by the apostles to the women of their day," wrote Lucretia Mott, "is [not] applicable to our own intelligent age; nor is there any passage of Scripture making those texts binding upon us" (qtd. in Behnke, *Religious*, 129). Consequently, in reference to Paul's call for feminine silence in the church, Willard pointed out that "places of worship, in the age of the Apostles, were not built as they are with us, but that the women had a corner of their own, railed off by a close fence reaching above their heads. It was thus made difficult for them to hear, and in their eager, untutored state, wholly unaccustomed to public audiences, they 'chattered' and asked questions" (*Woman*, 30). For Willard, Paul's command for women "to remain in silence with all subjection" represented a sort of compromise; he was avoiding new grounds for opposition while at the same time allowing women to enter church life more actively than before. She explained: "Paul, who was 'all things to all men that by all means he might save the most,' deemed it expedient for the infant Church, among the many pitfalls in its way, to conform while it endeavored to reform; and that those fateful words 'It is not permitted' and the rest are simple statements of facts as to the customs of that day" ("How," 93). Hence, without compromising either the integrity of the Bible or of the apostle Paul, Willard refashioned biblical interpretations toward prowoman ends. In other words, rather than attempt to circumvent the power structure of patriarchal Christianity and the Scriptures, the Christian feminists opted to alter the biblical system within its own boundaries — to perform a similar feat to what Willard claims Paul did in Corinth — that is, "to conform while [they] endeavored to reform."

Thus, Willard and the other Christian feminists betrayed the conservatives' inconsistent hermeneutic not to denigrate the Bible's worthiness as a transmission of spiritual wisdom nor to demean orthodox clergy. Instead, they sought to open up a more diverse wealth of possible sources of divine truth. As opposed to the conservatives and their literal inclination, Christian feminists believed that self-revelation was mediated in and through the flow of experience; consequently, not just the words of the Bible but its overarching spirit and the whole human historical process were seen as revelatory. As Whitall Smith remarked, "The Bible is a book of principles, and not a book of disjointed aphorisms. Isolated texts may often be made to sanction things to which the principles of Scripture are totally opposed. I believe all fanaticism comes in this way. An isolated text is so impressed upon the mind that it seems a necessity to obey it, no matter into what wrong it may lead; and thus the principles of Scripture are violated, under the plea of obedience to the Scriptures" (*Christian's*, 58). Toward this end, these women counseled their readers to compare scripture with scripture to uncover the Bible's general truths and to use their own conscience and experience to determine which verses were still binding (Diaz, *Only*, 139). The Bible, then, was to be read in manifold ways — with historical knowledge, philological imagination, the guidance of one's individual conscience, as well as committed Christian faith.

Because historical criticism served to open more possibilities for discovering spiritual truths and for interpreting the Bible, women such as Ellen Battelle Dietrick saw it as beneficial to women's cause. She declared, "Now that every two-penny journal of Christendom has taken the Garden of Eden myth as a standing object of ridicule, the cornerstone of the ecclesiasticism built thereupon is, indeed, crumbling, and the subjection of woman to man maintains its tenure by a thread whose bitterness no sagacious person can fail to see" (*Women*, 70–71). Likewise, Mary Cook avouched, "God is shaking up the church—He is going to bring it up to something better, and that too, greatly through the work of women" (qtd. in Brooks, "Feminist," 37). Christian feminists generated an array of historical-critical tactics to help formulate a new woman-oriented hermeneutic.

In addition to using historical perspectives to critique traditional biblical translation and interpretation, Christian feminists utilized them more globally to refute traditional but nonbiblical notions of the past and present roles of women. For instance, in her 1883 book, *Woman's Place Today,* Blake overturned the conservative and evangelical belief in Christianity impelling the steady historical improvement in woman's social position. She underlined the point that with regard to their ability to inherit property, transact business, and contract honorable marriages, many ancient Roman women, for example, were better off than American Christian women today. Moreover, instead of gradually increasing women's rights, the Christian Church has done the opposite: "Let us then see what this man-made Church has done for women: In the early days of Christianity women and men labored together to teach the new religion. Women were preachers and deaconesses, St. Paul himself frequently speaking of their work in his epistles.... But, as the years passed on, the priesthood grew in arrogance and the desire for power" (14). For Blake and other Christian feminists, true Christianity differed from the "man-made" one that has kept woman in subordination. As B. T. Roberts emphasized, "Christianity...has not secured for [woman], even in the most enlightened nations, that equality which the Gospel inculcates" (*Ordaining,* 16).

Just as Christianity with its "virtues of love, charity, forbearance...has been perverted to many base purposes" (Blake, *Woman's,* 13), domesticity—according to this group—has been falsely promoted as historically and currently beneficial to women. Elizabeth Oakes Smith reported, "I have had the secret experience of many hundreds of women confided to my keeping, and have become cognizant in this way of a mass of petty oppression and domestic disorder most painful to a reflective or benevolent mind" ("Woman," 33). Rather than cast women's domestic duties as divinely ordained and a privilege as conservatives did, the Christian feminists went so far as to suggest that the wife is "the actual bondservant of her husband" (Roberts, *Ordaining,* 17); and they spent considerable time urging their women readers to reduce their labor responsibilities rather than to endure them cheerfully. Counseled Hannah Whitall Smith, "God's part is to work" (*Christian's,* 11); women, on the other hand, must fully trust in the Lord and "must lay off every burden—your health, your reputation, your Christian work, your houses, your children, your business, your servants; everything, in short, that concerns you, whether inward or outward" (18).

In addition to bucking traditional notions of domesticity, the Christian feminists, using logic coupled with a historical perspective, also contradicted the conservatives' contention that woman must repress her intelligence and public talents. To say that woman has no right to pursue public office or to vote is "to reproach the First Cause for having imparted to his creatures a superfluous intelligence" (Oakes Smith, "Woman," 14); or as another put it, "God gives no eyes to the fish of Mammoth Cave, that are never to see light, nor creates any organ incommensurate to its intended use. Woman has as large lungs as man, in proportion to her size; therefore, it was not meant for her to abide perpetually behind closed doors" (Woolson, *Woman,* 209). Thus, the Christian feminists reasoned that rather than suppress the endowments God "bestowed upon each one of us, . . . we might in some especial manner gladden and bless the world, by bestowing upon it our best" (Willard, "How," 24). Implicit in their call for women to cultivate their gifts and act upon their impulses and feelings was their view that woman is an inherently good being, "an heir of God through faith in Christ" (Whitall Smith, *Christian's,* 37). Because of this innate goodness, woman, they also reasoned, should enjoy all of the individual rights due citizens in a liberal democratic society: "Every human being has a right to life, liberty, and the pursuit of happiness—a God-guaranteed charter, which no created being may infringe" (Oakes Smith, "Woman," 36).

Relying upon history, logic, miming of conservative and evangelical principles and practices, and principles of liberalism, the Christian feminists amassed an array of heterogeneous strategies to unseat conservative gender norms. While the Christian feminists' practice of miming and appropriating conservative thought had the advantage of undermining the uniform authority of dominant thought, it also had a potential disadvantage. By inculcating a wide array of varying strategies, they ran the risk of incorporating deleterious and oppressive means of persuasion. For example, in a few instances, these writers expressed nativist, racist, and elitist sentiments. Arguing for women's right to vote, Dodge wrote: "Undoubtedly a very large number of women are by their education unfit to vote; but does the same standard of fitness apply to men? Are American women, as a class, more unfit to vote than Irishmen? Are they less capable of understanding issues involved, and of passing judgment upon measures proposed, than negroes who have been slaves for generations?" (*Woman's,* 87). Carolyn De Swarte Gifford reports that in the 1880s, the W.C.T.U. ran a suffrage advertisement with a similar insidious undertone. The image portrayed a prim, well-dressed, and lily-white Frances Willard encircled by ethnically- and class-coded representatives of three nonvoting groups: idiots, Native Americans, and insane males.[15] Many of the advertisements carried the ironic title, "American Woman and Her Peers," with the following caption:

> The incongruity of the company Miss Willard is represented as keeping is such as to attract and excite wonder, until it is explained that such is the relative political status of American women under the laws of many of our states.
>
> No one can fail to be impressed with the absurdity of such a statutory regulation that places women in the same legal category with the idiot, the Indian and the insane person. (qtd. in Gifford, "Home," 107)

The goal of this performance was obvious and, in one sense, laudable; it aimed to reverse the depiction of the politically active woman as the deviant Other, but regrettably the point was made at the expense of other disenfranchised groups and with a distinct nativist and classist tinge. Such an image divulges the potential harm of the Christian feminists' fluid performance: they could conciliate with opprobrious strains of dominant thought.

The Christian feminists' racism was particularly detrimental for the African-American women within their ranks. It prompts a curious question: Why is it that black women aligned themselves more frequently with this group rather than with secular feminists? Even more curiously, why did they seem to follow Protestantism so loyally and fully? As an example, at the beginning of her 1835 address, Maria W. Stewart made a highly self-effacing statement that neither white Christian feminists nor even nonwhite Christian men (such as William Apess or Olaudah Equiano) would utter: "I feel almost unable to address you; almost incompetent to perform the task; and, at times, I have felt ready to exclaim, O that my head were waters, and mine eyes a fountain of tears, that I might weep day and night, for the transgressions of the daughters of my people. Truly, my heart's desire and prayer is, that Ethiopia might stretch forth her hands unto God . . . and cultivate among ourselves the pure principles of piety, morality and virtue" ("Productions," 5–6). At first glance, Stewart's pronouncements seem curious. Not only is she highly self-deprecatory, but she also reproaches her fellow Africans and African-Americans for their lack of Christian "piety, morality and virtue." Why would Stewart — one of the most outspoken black abolitionists in early nineteenth-century New England — prostrate herself and others in the service of an institution that had worked to oppress her own people?

For African-American Christian feminists (all of whom were women), cultural performance or operating as the "domestic slave" was not only more imperative but also involved higher risks than it did for white Christian feminists. Hazel Carby contends that unlike white women, black women in the New World were not defined in human terms. Instead they were marked racially and sexually as "female (animal, sexualized, and without rights), but not as woman (human, potential wife, conduit for the name of the father) — in a specific institution, slavery, that excluded them from 'culture' defined as the circulation of signs through the system of marriage" (qtd. in Haraway, "Ecce," 93–94). At the time of Stewart's speech, white women may not have been legally or symbolically fully human; but black women had to confront the reality of not being considered legally or symbolically human at all. Hence, black women faced a form of social ostracism worse than shame; they routinely confronted utter contempt and disgust. As noted in earlier chapters, for shame to operate, a connection between two people or groups, or the possibility thereof, must exist. Judith Jordan writes, "shame is most importantly a felt sense of unworthiness to be in connection, . . . with the ongoing awareness of how very much one wants to connect with others" ("Relational," 6). Disgust, on the other hand, entails the complete renunciation of the other, the full repudiation of their humanness, their womanness. Thus, black women were compelled to operate in a world that refused them even the possibility of shame; and if shame (as Sedgwick and Frank contend) is the site wherein a sense of self most develops ("Shame," 6), then the social refusal of shame to black women and the willingness of some of them such as Maria Stewart to shame themselves takes on an unusual significance and may ironically mark a space of self-definition and empowerment.

In this section, I argue that like the white Christian feminists, African-American Christian feminists mimed conservative rhetoric or inculcated what Evelyn Brooks Higginbotham calls "a politics of respectability." But because they had the unique challenge of overcoming a popular antihuman and racist image, they had to perform to an even greater excess than did the white Christian feminists — that is, both to display more vehemently their own obedience to those Protestant principles and practices they could accept, while simultaneously either minimizing or otherwise compensating for those they could not follow. Thus they vacillated between assuming what at first may appear to be antithetical roles—that of the secret rebel and the shamed repentant. However, because the two roles assisted these women in locating a definable role of respectability in U.S. society, both strategies were mutually reinforcing and ultimately empowering. Indeed, I would contend that without having gained a socially recognizable identity that the shamed repentant role afforded them, these women would not have felt entitled to combat more directly the racism and sexism they encountered in their thoroughly Protestant world.

In her recent book, Brooks Higginbotham argues that late-nineteenth-century black Baptist women cultivated a politics of respectability that "demanded that every individual in the black community assume responsibility for behavioral self-regulation and self-improvement along moral, educational and economic lines" (*Righteous*, 196). In an attempt to distance themselves from racist stereotypes, these women advocated, with a hyper-vigilance, Victorian sexual morals, temperance, thrift, industriousness, refined manners, and piety. Brooks Higginbotham's findings also play out in the writings of other black evangelical women throughout the century. Sojourner Truth, for example, took her own sense of honesty to almost ridiculous proportions. Following her mother's instructions to be always honest, Truth

> had educated herself to such a sense of honesty, that, when she had become a mother, she would sometimes whip her child when it cried to her for bread, rather than give it a piece secretly, lest it should learn to take what was not its own! And the writer [Frances Gage, Truth's narrator] knows, from personal observation, that the slaveholders of the South feel it to be a religious duty to teach their slaves to be honest, and never to take what is not their own! Oh consistency, art thou not a jewel? Yet Isabella glories in the fact that she was faithful and true to her master; she says, "It made me true to my God"—meaning, that it helped to form in her a character that loved truth, and hated a lie, and had saved her from the bitter pains and fears that are sure to follow in the wake of insincerity and hypocrisy. (*Narrative*, 34)

The invocation of honesty in this passage not only affirms Truth's remarkable ability to express it even under extreme duress but also implicitly critiques the Christian slaveholders' warped conception of that virtue. Thus, the standard hierarchical dualism of honest white man and dishonest black slave is toppled, and honesty in white people is exposed as something to be demanded from others rather than from one's self. Virginia Broughton (referring to herself in third-person) deployed a similar move of reversal and affirmation in her description of her own capacity for self-sacrifice and submission: "Immediately after her graduation [from Fisk University in 1875], in answer to a telegram, she went to Memphis and there passed a creditable examination for a position in the public schools of that city. So brilliant was her success in the examination, her friends insisted that she take the principal's examination. This, however, she declined to do, as she did not wish to be a rival of her male classmate who was aspiring for that position" ("Twenty," 8). At the moment that Broughton asserts her own self-abnegation and humility in the service of a man, she also highlights the superiority of her sense of virtue and intelligence over the male in question. By morally outdoing others, Broughton and Truth underlined their self-professed right to membership in the Christian human community.

For similar reasons, many African-American Christian feminists also underscored their maternal impulses. Harriet Jacobs, for example, hid away in a cramped attic for years in order to watch over and rescue her children from bondage. After her son was suddenly snatched from her and sent South by her former master, Truth went to court to retrieve him. And years later, when reflecting on her successful legal case and her overriding love for her son, Truth commented, " 'Oh, my God! I know'd I'd have him agin. I was sure God would help me to get him. Why, I felt so tall within — I felt as if the power of a nation was with me!' " (*Narrative*, 45). Embedded within black Christian feminists' self-shaming is an implicit shaming of others. In short, if excessively virtuous women like Truth and Broughton were unworthy of praise, then neither was anyone else; and more significantly, those others (who typically initiate the rebuking and shaming) were deserving of more retribution than simple shame.

In another speech, Truth masterfully interwove the contrary impulses of shaming and being shamed so much that by the end of it the distinction between the object and the subject of shame is lost. Shortly after offering the self-shaming pronouncement, "Well if woman upset the world, do give her a chance to set it right side up again," Truth queried, "And how came Jesus into the world? Through God who created him and woman who bore him. Man, where is your part?" (xxxiii). In this passage, shame and the concomitant effects of defeat and alienation customarily turned against women are suddenly directed at men, the typical perpetrators of shame. Sedgwick and Frank note that "shame turns the attention of the self and others away from other objects to this most visible residence of self, increases its visibility, and thereby generates the torment of self-consciousness" ("Shame," 136). Thus, by shaming the shamers, Truth redirects the spotlight of humiliation from herself (and other women) to men, and by doing so, grants herself a new and recognizably respectable identity — that of the morally superior, shaming woman.

Excessive morality and shaming power, however, were not enough to secure African-American women's full membership into the middle-class world of humanity. Living in a Protestant world, they also needed to prove their exemplary piety and trust in God. As a measure of her trust in God's powers, Amanda Berry Smith forewent taking medicine for over a year (*Autobiography,* 99). Both Smith and Truth traveled around the country (and in Smith's case, the world) without a steady income or assured lodgings. Moreover, these women continually proved their remarkable spiritual powers in public, dramatic, and (owing to their lack of formal educational opportunities) often nonwritten ways. Between January and March 1871, Berry Smith — while operating as a full minister — was credited with 156 conversions and 112 rededications to the Mount Pisgah A.M.E. congregation. In an 1844 camp meeting led by a white woman preacher, Truth witnessed an uproar started by about 100 young men, angry at the presence of a woman evangelist. While at first she hid in fear, the spirit led Truth to approach the young men with song; and almost instantly the men's fury was quelled (*Narrative,* 115).

Along with commandeering dramatic spiritual responses in public, black Christian feminists had dramatic private spiritual experiences that they conveyed in writing and oral presentations. Amanda Berry Smith engaged in numerous conversations with Satan and at one point witnessed Jesus in "loose flowing purple robes [and] his hair and beard as white as wool" peering at her through the latticework of her window (*Autobiography,* 144). Truth heard God's voice on several occasions; and Julia A. J. Foote claimed that Christ "led me into the water and stripped me of my clothing, which at once vanished from sight. Christ then appeared to wash me, the water feeling quite warm" ("Brand," 203). The black Christian feminists' witnessing of visions, their dramatic ability to move others to Christ, and their capacity for enduring immense hardships in pursuit of the Lord all served to underscore their extraordinary piety and thereby to distinguish them from other white Christian believers.

As another means of proving their excess piety, black Christian feminists often accentuated the racist obstacles they confronted in their spiritual journeys. Black women evangelists and missionaries who took the road faced extraordinary hazards of racism. As Stetson and David note, "The strain of solitary travel was increased by the rigid segregation of transportation as they traveled on foot through the countryside and by steamer, canal boat, or coach" (*Glorying,* 93). Late in her life, Sojourner Truth once remarked to Elizabeth Cady Stanton that she had " 'been sent into the smoking-car so often she smoked in self-defense—she would rather swallow her own smoke than another's' " (qtd. in Stetson and David, *Glorying,* 94). Julia Foote, Amanda Berry Smith, and Maria Stewart also had to contend with abusive passengers and lack of adequate lodging, food, and seating.

In addition to difficult travel conditions, African-American Christian feminists were also criticized by family members for wanting to venture into the public world of ministry, evangelism, and missionary work. Julia Foote's husband threatened to commit her to an insane asylum. When Truth's children heard she had ventured away from New York to follow God's calling, her children's "imaginations painted her as a wandering maniac—and again, they feared she had been left to commit suicide" (*Narrative,* 109; also qtd. in Stetson and David, *Glorying,* 94). After deciding to give away holiness pamphlets, Amanda Berry Smith mused, "I knew I would be criticised, for I had become a speckled bird among my own people, on account of the profession of the blessing of holiness" (*Autobiography,* 108). As shown in the examples of Olaudah Equiano and William Apess in earlier chapters, nonwhite peoples often had to endure a highly isolating and sometimes humiliating series of ordeals to enter the Protestant community—ordeals not encountered by their white counterparts. As Berry Smith put it, "It is often said to me, 'How nicely you get on, Mrs. Smith'. . . . Then I said: 'But if you want to know and understand properly what Amanda Smith has to contend with, just turn black and go about as I do, and you will come to a different conclusion. And I think some people would understand the quintessence of sanctifying grace if they could be black about twenty-four hours. We need to be saved deep to make us thorough, all around, out and out, come up to the standard Christians, and not bring the standard down to us' " (116–17).

Although racism definitely had deleterious consequences on them, African-American Christian feminists learned to construct themselves within it. In *Bodies That Matter,* Judith Butler argues that rather than simply setting a limit on identity, constraint impels and sustains it: "an identification always takes place in relation to a law, or, more specifically, a prohibition that works through delivering a threat of punishment. The law, understood here as the demand and threat issued by and through the symbolic, compels the shape and direction of [identity] through the instillation of fear" (105). And indeed, prompted by the racist derision they encountered, African-American Christian feminists adopted a subservient position but not precisely the one their racist foes had in mind. Instead of being subservient to whites and to men, they retranslated the term to mean utter submission to God. Thus, they may have reiterated the degradatory label assigned to them, but by doing so, they deferred the dominant authority of the label and carved out a new measure of agency. In other words, "the force of repetition in language may be the paradoxical condition by which a certain agency — not linked to a fiction of the ego as master of circumstance — is derived from the impossibility of choice" (124). Not being granted any acceptable identity by dominant society, these women created one for themselves by reiterating or miming in excess that true womanhood role assigned to white Christian women. By miming in excess, they deferred the authority of both the denigrating label assigned to black women as sexualized "females" and the true womanhood role assigned to Christian women as "white, passive, pure, domestic, and pious."

Whereas the miming objective of white Christian feminists was to outdo white men, black Christian feminists — in order to gain entitlement to the true womanhood identity — had to outdo both white men and white women. This task, of course, was not only arduous; it was impossible — particularly for those women who had once been enslaved. Nell Irvin Painter notes, "With educated white women as woman and black men as the slave, free, articulate black women simply vanished. What little social category existed for black woman was reserved for the slave: if dark-skinned, as mother; if light-skinned, as sexual victim" ("Difference," 158). While free women had to construct an identity for themselves, formerly enslaved women had to combat a heinously sexualized one, making it particularly difficult for them to fulfill the "purity" requirement of the true womanhood ideal. Black Christian feminists attempted to compensate for this difficulty by accentuating their overachievement of the other true womanhood components and minimizing their consideration of women's role as sexual beings. For instance, although her narrative spans over four hundred pages, Berry Smith barely mentioned her encounters with men and two marriages. Similarly, Harriet Jacobs spent relatively little time discussing her relationship with the father of her children. In her sixteen-chapter spiritual narrative, Virginia Broughton devoted only one brief chapter to her "private life" and, even in that chapter, omitted any reference to romance. Although Truth may have been sexually abused, she refused to provide any details or evidence. In analyzing Truth's proclivity for this form of suppressed interiorization, Erlene Stetson and Linda David write: "With the tactical reversal that was her defining strategy, Truth anticipated her audience's fascination with the enslaved woman's life as a secret, enculted, gothic existence, compounded of torture and forced sex; then between herself and this audience she drew a homespun curtain, around which they could not peek because they were the 'uninitiated,'... as if they were themselves too simple, too naive, too unschooled to read the horrific book they had written themselves. Perhaps she ... decided that her life was not their fiction" (*Glorying*, 39).

By focusing on their lives as spiritual rather than racial or sexual beings, black Christian feminists could avoid focusing solely on the current historical and sexualized white-black drama and conceptualize instead a broader agenda, one that offered freedom from oppression as a result of one's gender, class, or race. Under the banner of Christianity, they could voice criticisms of the present society and envision a new society that they no doubt could not have done as simply black women. In an 1853 speech in New York, Sojourner Truth was reported to have characterized conservative preachers as

> big Greek-crammed, mouthing men, who, for many a long century, had been befogging the world, and getting its affairs into the most terrible snarl and confusion, and then when women came to their assistance, cried, "shame on women!" They liked the fat and easy work of preaching and entangling too well, not to feel alarmed when woman attempted to set matters aright. [Truth] conceived that women were peculiarly adapted to fill the talking professions, and men should no longer unsex themselves by leaving the plow and the plane, for the pulpit and the platform. She hoped all of her sex would set to work and drag the world right side up, disentangle it from the snarl which men have wilfully got it into, and set matters in general aright, and then keep them so. They could only do this by being united and resolutely putting their shoulders to the wheel. (qtd. in Stetson and David, *Glorying*, 211)

The African-American Christian feminists' excessive miming, then, served not only to overturn the negative sexualized popular image of the black female but also to put new power and agency in black women's hands, functioning as a means of linking their concerns with those of white women. Hand in hand, black Christian feminists envisioned themselves embarking with white Christian feminists in a radical social change.

Like Truth and the black Christian feminists, the white Christian feminists advanced a utopian vision of a new society founded upon full labor parity, mutuality, and free choice, a world with "natural" spheres rather than masculine-prescribed ones. Wrote Dodge, "we shall never know what woman's natural sphere is till she has an absolutely unrestricted power of choice" (*Woman's*, 85). Winnifred Harper Cooley included this poem, entitled "The New Paradise," in her book:

> *In the sweet reason of our larger day,*
> *Each must his work contribute to the whole,*
> *Knowing, together, we must rise or fall.*
> *Man will not look to God, and woman find*
> *"Her God in man," as sang the bigot-bard,*
> *But both will pray and toil in unison,*
> *Finding the sweetness of togetherness,*
> *United labor, heaven upon earth! (New, 33)*

And Abba Goold Woolson offered this image: "Side by side they will strive to build up a nobler, political state, with homes founded upon justice to each other and mutual respect, and make abodes of health, purity and intelligence. One sex will scorn to assume general control of the other as a right; but love, united interests, and the exercise of Christian virtues shall harmonize and bless their lives" (*Woman*, 86).

Although their vision of social harmony is laudable, Cooley and Woolson neglected to articulate specifically how it could be achieved. Indeed, most of the Christian feminists were content to imply that through a true devotion to God and Christ and a careful reading and study of the Bible, Americans would all miraculously consent to woman's full equality and entry into the realm of politics, government, and higher education. Moreover, little attention was given to the massive class and racial inequities that existed alongside of and impacted the sexism that concerned them most. None of the whites seemed aware that their new vision of equality required the eradication of deeply ingrained racial and class disparities. As will be shown in chapter 6, unfortunately, Elizabeth Cady Stanton and the secular feminists also succumbed to such prejudices.

Neither secular nor religious white feminists were willing to recognize the confluence of racism and classism with sexism; yet both entertained similar visions of a fully benevolent, equal society. If the two groups held the same objective and fell into similar errors, why have scholars differentiated and hierarchized the two feminist coalitions? The basic difference between the groups is that white and black Christian feminists, unlike their radical secular sisters,

124

were able to do battle against specific religious and social outrages without rejecting the doctrine and institution of Christianity altogether. As a result, not only did their calls seem less threatening to the general—still largely Protestant—public, but also they were able, because of their outward evangelical behavior, to thwart the standard conservative charges of unfemininity or heathenism that Ginzberg claims effectively served to undermine many of the radical feminist causes of nineteenth-century America (*Women*, 220). In addition, these women eschewed launching malevolent attacks on either conservatives or radicals, and instead they tended to accentuate the similarities among the three camps. For instance, despite her fundamental and public disagreement with the antisuffrage Reverend Morgan Dix (rector of New York City's Trinity Episcopal Church),[16] Blake nevertheless opened her book by praising him as "a man of great learning, of wide culture, and of much excellence of character, a man whose broad benevolence has made him a benefactor to many" (*Woman's*, 6). In his 1874 defense of Christian feminism, Leo Miller highlighted one crucial intersection among the three groups' viewpoints. After quoting a clergyman's comment that "'man is a giant of selfishness, passion and wrong,'" he remarked, "That is certainly severe; but as it does not come from Susan B. Anthony, or Anna E. Dickinson, but rather from a Doctor of Divinity who wars against Woman Suffrage, masculine opposers will doubtless accept the statement as orthodox" (*Woman*, 75–76). In short, by the late nineteenth century, all three groups could agree on the existence of pressing social ills as well as of men's moral turpitude. For the Christian feminists, the aim of assuaging these problems that so profoundly injure women was more important than the means. By pointing up the shared assumptions and intentions of the three camps, they attempted to redirect the focus to their larger common goals rather than to their differences and to forge alliances rather than divisions.

Thus, the Christian feminists may have been able to achieve a certain limited effectiveness not only through their conciliatory rhetoric and conservative demeanor, but also for a number of other reasons. First, despite the waning hegemony of Protestantism in the latter part of the century, Christianity was still woven into the very fabric of American life. Even turn-of-the-century secular newspapers (both in small towns and in urban areas) reported the content of sermons delivered from local pulpits in excessive detail and discussed at length the doctrinal, hermeneutical, and hierarchical issues and disputes among various ecclesiastical bodies. As revealed earlier, women formed the centerpieces of (particularly evangelical) Protestantism. Thus, a woman's rights agenda that recognized and at least partially reconciled itself with Christianity may have been more appealing to the large numbers of fin-de-siècle women still thoroughly ensconced in church life. Even Ellen Carol DuBois (a scholar generally unsympathetic to religious feminism) admits that because Willard and the W.C.T.U. "spoke to women in the language of their domestic realities, ... [women] joined [the movement] in the 1870s and 1880s in enormous numbers" ("Radicalism," 135). Ruth Bordin offers a possible explanation for this disparity between the public reception of the secular and the Christian feminists' natural rights contentions:

> Elizabeth Cady Stanton ... most often chose "confrontation and a high moral stance" over political maneuver and compromise. Unlike Willard, Stanton was an enthusiast, not a politician. She was always forthright in speaking her mind. Willard was an inveterate dissembler and a clever and effective insinuator. She played the role of sweet conciliator whereas Cady Stanton assumed the stance of militant radical. Stanton herself recognized Willard's talent for conciliation. When in March 1888 Willard appeared before a United States committee investigating suffrage as a representative of the International Council of Women, Cady Stanton, who was making the arrangements, scheduled Willard as the final speaker, believing she would leave the committee in a friendly mood. (*Willard,* 104–5)[17]

Hence, the form of Willard's and the Christian feminists' language may have been as significant as their content. Rather than making direct and strident criticisms, Willard and the others often delivered their prowoman ideas by utilizing what julia penelope has called the "COSMETIC UNIVERSE OF DISCOURSE" or "CUD" — that is, by asking leading questions, bypassing spiteful name-calling, and using "empty" or overly approbatory and melodramatic adjectives, modals, and intensifiers in their language (*Speaking,* 1–15). In other words, because of their conciliatory rhetoric, the late-nineteenth-century Christian feminists galvanized large groups of women into social and moral action.

Second, although the majority of Christian feminists were evangelical, white, and middle-class, Christian feminism did appeal to other groups of women. African-American educator and suffragist, Nannie Helen Burroughs once declared, "The Negro Church means the Negro woman" and insisted that the bulk of black women reformers were avidly religious (qtd. in Andolsen, "Daughters," 56). In addition, black and white women embraced an overtly ecumenical outlook. At the time of Willard's death (March 3, 1898), the *Chicago Tribune* noted that perhaps her major triumph had been "winning into heartiest fellowship and drawing into enthusiastic cooperation along the main lines of

Christian and humanitarian effort, persons of all grades of culture and religionists of every name, Protestant or Catholic" (Bordin, *Willard*, 167–68).

Third, the Christian feminists' ability to mime conservative Christianity enabled them to forge an alliance with prominent clergymen and to receive a relatively favorable hearing in the legislature. Both Willard and Dodge make reference to ministers as among the most amenable of male professionals to woman's enfranchisement (Willard, *Woman*, 9; Dodge, *Woman's*, 1–2), and contemporary historians Evelyn Brooks and Aileen Kraditor also cite the liberal clergy as being particularly loyal to the woman's rights cause (Brooks, "Feminist," 41; Kraditor, *Ideas*, 94). Furthermore, since these women often used bibliocentric arguments to bolster their feminist goals, they could more convincingly address and refute the religiously based contentions of the antisuffragists.[18]

According to several scholars, legislators also tended to be significantly more receptive to Christian feminists than to the secular feminists. Mary P. Ryan explains that "because [these] women did not convert the nineteenth-century political sphere into a feminist forum about sexuality does not mean that they were merely pawns in a male-dominated sexual politics. While clearly second-class citizens, women did batter away at the urban political system, winning concessions here and there, imprinting their ideas on public debates, and adding their perspectives to the array of conflicting interests that influenced policy decisions" (*Women*, 129). Elizabeth Pleck also points out that it was the more "conservative," religious feminists rather than the radicals (such as Stanton and Anthony) who could assault (in terms of initiating legislation) wife abuse and other crimes against women precisely because they did not openly support divorce ("Feminist," 462–64). In other words, in the late nineteenth century, feminists could either do battle against specific outrages against women without attacking the institution of Protestantism (as did the Christian feminists); or they could assail Christianity while remaining vague about the circumstances that required it (as did Stanton); they could not do both. Stanton could oppugn Protestant clergy and the Bible, but as a result, she was not able to push through much successful legislation and church reform. Conversely, the Christian feminists may have been able to effect some changes within the institutions of religion and politics, but at the expense of offering an expansive and revolutionary feminist vision.

Finally, although Stanton is definitely a household word in U.S. feminist circles today, in the late nineteenth century the fame of such Christian feminists as Frances Willard, Catherine Booth, Amanda Berry Smith, and Mary A. Livermore matched and perhaps surpassed hers (Bordin, *Willard*, 90). Because of their ability to maneuver comfortably in clerical circles, these women reached broad audiences. In November 1876, for example, Henry Ward Beecher asked Willard to speak at his world-famed Plymouth Church in Brooklyn, one of the nation's most sought-after forums. During the following year, she led prayers and spoke at some of Dwight Moody's revivals before groups numbering as many as nine thousand persons (86–89). Mary A. Livermore delivered portions of her advice book in lectures over eight hundred times and was fondly known as "the Queen of the Platform" (James, *Notable*, 2:413). And Hannah Whitall Smith's book, *The Christian's Secret of a Happy Life*, sold more than two million copies in the nineteenth century and is still considered a spiritual classic today (3:314). By contrast, although Stanton's *The Woman's Bible* received considerable press coverage upon its publication, it fell into relative obscurity shortly thereafter and remained there until academic feminist historians recently revived interest in it.

The fact that the Christian feminists (and their writings) were more favorably received by larger audiences in their own time than were the radicals does not necessarily indicate that they constitute a "better" model for feminists either then or now. Neither group was consistently superior. In fact, both feminist camps were in many ways mutually dependent. Indeed, one of the main reasons that the Christian feminists could position themselves in the strategically beneficial position of conciliator or synthesizer is that Stanton and her followers so publicly voiced their views and cleared a space in which mainstream feminists could more freely and "safely" play.

In her 1889 autobiography, Willard noted, "I am an eclectic in religious reading, friendship and inspiration. My wide relationships and constant journeyings would have made me so had I not had the natural hospitable mind that leads to this estate. But, like the bee that gathers from many fragrant gardens, but flies home with his varied gains to the same friendly and familiar hive, so I fly home to the sweetness and sanctity of the old faith that has been my shelter and solace so long" (*Glimpses*, 627–28). Like the bee Willard described "that gathers from many fragrant gardens," the Christian feminists culled from others' (in this case, the conservative Christians and radical feminists) flower beds to nurture their own and to cross-pollinate the others' gardens. Thus, they were unique not as much in their call for feminine equality or their devotion to Protestantism as in their utilization of an open, conciliatory, and insurgent method of cultural performance.

Chapter Five

Untangling the Biblical Knot

Reconsidering Elizabeth Cady Stanton and
The Woman's Bible

At the 1878 Woman's Suffrage Convention, Elizabeth Cady Stanton — the elder stateswoman of the feminist movement — introduced a resolution endorsing women's self-development and condemning their self-sacrifice. When Frederick Douglass, one of the reigning spokesmen for abolitionism and then for civil rights, attempted to speak in favor of self-sacrifice, Lucy Coleman retorted, "Well, Mr. Douglass, all you say may be true; but allow me to ask you why you did not remain a slave in Maryland, and sacrifice yourself like a Christian for your Master, instead of running off to Canada to secure your liberty" (qtd. in Welter, "Introduction," xxiii). Coleman's sentiment paralleled that of her friend and activist ally, Elizabeth Cady Stanton. In an 1888 article for the *North American Review,* Stanton wrote: "A consideration of woman's position before Christianity, under Christianity, and at the present time shows that she is not indebted to any form of religion for one step of progress, nor one new liberty; on the contrary, it has been through the perversion of her religious sentiments that she has been so long held in a condition of slavery" ("Has").

Stanton's (and her friend Coleman's) renunciation of Christianity's call for self-sacrifice was a sentiment not honored by the majority of late-nineteenth-century feminists (Gifford, "Politicizing," 54). As is evident in the individuals studied in this book, a large number of the most successful liberal and progressive activists of the nineteenth century not only openly identified as Christians and utilized Christian rhetorical forms, conventions, and codes, but also either accepted or at least paid lip-service to the Protestant domestic ideal of woman's self-abnegation. Historian Betty DeBerg goes so far as to argue that this inculcation of Protestant domestic, gendered rhetoric helped to make women's suffrage "more palatable to most Americans" and thus advanced the feminist cause (*Ungodly,* 33). Yet, Stanton chose a far different approach, believing that the "Church has done more to degrade woman than all other adverse influences put together" (*Bible,* 12). By doing so, Stanton lost favor among the younger feminists (most of whom were self-identified Christians) as well as some of her oldest friends and allies, including Susan B. Anthony (Fitzgerald, "Religious," xxiv). Moreover, in 1896, the National American Woman Suffrage Association (NAWSA) effectively ended Stanton's leadership role in the organization by formally censuring her ambitious project, *The Woman's Bible.*

Sparked by her frustration over the public's lack of interest in the feminist cause in the last decades of the nineteenth century, Stanton decided to combat directly what she saw as perhaps the most pervasive purveyor of antifeminism: the Holy Bible. Toward this end, she assembled a group of white, middle-class, educated, and mostly American women to produce a set of commentaries on scriptural passages they deemed of special interest to women. Although *The Woman's Bible* received mostly derision at the time of its publication, it has been extolled appreciably by contemporary feminist scholars. Indeed, in the past decade, Stanton's onetime censured project has been lauded in more than thirty articles and books. It has been praised as Stanton's "most audacious and outrageous act of independence," "a truly revolutionary deconstruction of patriarchy," and "a radical rejection of the Bible."[1] Maureen Fitzgerald dubs it "an extraordinary document, in part because the questions asked, the topics covered, and the sense of righteous indignation throughout its pages are still resonant today" ("Religious," xxix). While Carolyn De Swarte Gifford points out some of the significant difficulties with *The Woman's Bible,* she too eloquently states its merits: "As an impassioned call for women's dignity and self-development whose author steadfastly refused to countenance the notion of women's inferiority in the face of powerful institutions and sacred texts which seemed to justify that power, it can be an empowering text for women at all times who struggle for a similar sense of dignity and worth" ("Politicizing," 61).

On top of her project's commendation, Stanton herself has been romanti-
cally heroicized. Cynthia Wolff, for example, has recently portrayed her as an
isolated and misunderstood activist, "strain[ing] through the present, reaching toward the future to leave a heritage for her generation to follow" ("Dickinson, Stanton," 644). Similarly, Kathi L. Kern accentuates that following the
book's unfavorable reception, Stanton became "a virtual shut-in," "repudiated
by the very constituency she hoped to convert" ("Rereading," 371–72). The contrast between feminists' perceptions of *The Woman's Bible* today and one hundred years ago is startling; and it raises some interesting questions: Why did
Stanton choose to attack the Protestant Church, an institution that had served
in many ways as the vehicle for women's increasing public role and empowerment? Was it her rejection of the Bible and Christianity that caused her political power and influence among feminists to decline in the latter decades of
her life? If not, what factors contributed to her disenfranchisement during
her own time and then to her widespread acceptance among feminist scholars
today?

Scholars have rightly underscored that Susan B. Anthony as well as the
younger feminists (those born in the second half of the century, a generation
after Stanton and Anthony) focused their energies primarily on securing the
vote and (not wanting to repel believing feminists) downplayed their disapproval of Christianity's call for women's subservience. Wrote Anthony to Stanton in an 1896 letter, "Get political rights first and religious bigotry will melt
like dew before the morning sun; and each will continue still to believe in and
defend the other" (Harper, *Life*, 2:857). Stanton, by contrast, believed that, like
a cord in a tautly wound rope, orthodox Christianity was inextricably inter-
twined with all other major strains of power in U.S. culture. She wrote: "Here,
then, is a fourfold bondage [family, politics, society and religion], so many
cords tightly twisted together, strong for one purpose. To attempt to undo
one is to loosen all . . . To my mind, if we had at first bravely untwisted all the
strands of this fourfold cord which bound us, and demanded equality in the
whole round of the circle, while perhaps we should have had a harder battle
to fight, it would have been more effective and far shorter" (qtd. in Pellauer,
Toward, 23). Thus, for Stanton, without loosening the knotted cord of traditional Protestantism, women's political and social emancipation could not be
realized. Combating Protestantism and the Bible was a necessary first step in
untying society's misogynist knot.

Interestingly, despite Stanton's strong criticism of Protestantism and nine-teenth- and twentieth-century feminists' view that *The Woman's Bible* repre-sented a radical rejection of Christianity, the methods she used to untangle the knots of traditional Protestantism were drawn not so much from an athe-ist or secular sentiment as from the scholarship, doctrines, and rhetoric of Protestantism itself. Moreover, although she quite boldly and admirably jetti-soned the Christian domestic rhetoric of self-sacrifice in favor of a more free-thought version of self-development, because she was unable to extricate her-self fully from the binary thinking so endemic to conservative Protestantism, she ended up reinscribing a hierarchical gendered dualism of her own. Thus, rather than operate outside of the religious and dominant forces of her own time, Stanton and *The Woman's Bible* were deeply inflected by them. In other words, she actually culled from the very system contemporary and past femi-nists contend she repudiated.[2] Her unwitting reliance on traditional Protes-tant ways of thinking coupled with her ironic overt denunciation of that sys-tem may have contributed to her lack of favor by her contemporaries.

Despite her call for complete liberation from Protestantism, Stanton's think-ing was part of—while simultaneously resistant to—her religious context. And despite her reliance on outmoded forms of rhetoric and thought, her project, *The Woman's Bible,* also managed to offer new and progressive possi-bilities for women coping with the often tangled cords of Protestantism.

Stanton's biographers and critics have underlined the fact that during the fi-nal decades of her life (which encompass the time she spearheaded *The Woman's Bible* project), she joined the Free Religious Association and was heavily in-fluenced by such free-thought leaders as Robert G. Ingersoll (Fitzgerald, "Re-ligious," xi). Originating in England, free thought was adopted in select radi-cal American circles and popularized by the charismatic Ingersoll. Influenced by the English utilitarian philosophers (Bentham, Grote, J. S. Mill) and ad-vances made in geology (Lyell), biology (Darwin), anthropology (Robertson Smith), philosophy (Comte, Hegel) and higher biblical criticism (Colenso, Strauss, Renan), free-thought proponents denied the plenary inspiration of the Bible and disavowed any supernatural or nonrational articles of belief. For them, religion was not only a human construction designed to support those nations and groups in power, but it also deliberately precluded human happiness, individual effort, and the spirit of investigation, three hallmarks of a free, democratic society. According to Ingersoll, "[religious] superstition is the child of [mental] slavery. Freethought will give us truth. When all have the right to think and to express their thoughts, every brain will give to all the best that it has. The world will then be filled with intellectual wealth" (*Liberty*, 48). Thus, in place of theology and metaphysics, freethinkers endorsed intellectual liberty brought about through science and reason. Instead of focusing on the world hereafter, humans should turn their "entire attention to the affairs of this world, to the facts in nature.... And [they should] avoid waste— waste of energy, waste of wealth" (56). For them, the inequities of wealth, labor, and gender will be reconciled once "the passions are dominated by the intellect, when reason occupies the throne, and when the hot blood of passion no longer rises in successful revolt" (75).

The belief that reason and science can uplift the individual and by extension society is certainly evident in Stanton's commentary on the ten virgins parable (Matthew 25:1). In this parable, five wise virgins arrive at a wedding party equipped with extra oil for their lamps; the other five virgins, by contrast, neglect to bring any. When the bridegroom tarries, the women slumber; and at the midnight announcement that he approaches, the latter group of "unequipped" women must leave to refill their lamps, while the well-prepared ones triumphantly enter the marriage feast with the groom. When the others return from retrieving the needed oil, the door to the celebration is predictably shut.

As was the tendency of the freethinkers, Stanton shears her interpretation of any otherworldly or theological symbolism and applies the parable strictly to this material world and to humanity (or to be specific—to women alone): biblical women are equated specifically and solely with contemporary U.S. women. No other interpretations or allegorical signifiers are offered. The wise virgins are those women "who have improved every advantage for their education, secured a healthy, happy, complete development, and entered all the profitable avenues of labor, for self-support."[3] As opposed to Catharine Beecher, who publicly applauds the virtue of feminine self-sacrifice, Stanton boldly advocates self-development. In an 1884 article, Stanton advances three interrelated resolutions that (1) affirm self-development as women's first priority; (2) proclaim self-abnegation as detrimental to women and men; and (3) blame the Church for propagating the subservience of women (see Gifford, "Politicizing," 55). Self-developed women, for Stanton, are not simply financially self-sufficient:

These are the women who to-day are close upon the heels of man in the whole realm of thought, in art, in science, in literature and in government. With tele-scopic vision they explore the starry firmament, and bring back the history of the planetary world. With chart and compass they pilot ships across the mighty deep, and with skilful fingers send electric messages around the world. In galleries of art, the grandeur of nature and the greatness of humanity are immortalized by them on canvas... In music they speak again the language of Mendelssohn, of Beethoven, of Chopin, of Schumann, and are worthy interpreters of their great souls... They fill the editors' and the professors' chairs, plead at the bar of justice, walk the wards of the hospital, and speak from the pulpit and the platform. (2:126)

Whereas the wise virgins step into the lucrative realms of academia, pro-fessionalism, and high culture, the foolish virgins, "in their ignorance, ... sac-rifice themselves to educate men of their households, and to make of them-selves ladders by which their husbands, brothers and sons climb up into the kingdom of knowledge, while they themselves are shut out from all intellec-tual companionship" (2:125). Furthermore, these fatuous figures sadly miss the extravagant nuptial feast, with its "music, banners, lanterns, torches, guns and rockets" and its attendants "brilliant in jewels, gold and silver" (2:124). Beyond losing out on the sumptuous delicacies of the wedding dinner, the women are unable to light the way for the approaching "bridegroom," which, for Stanton, epitomizes the moment "when the philosopher, the scientist, the saint, the scholar, the great and the learned, all come together to celebrate the marriage feast of science and religion" (2:125).

Stanton's utopian vision in many ways parallels that of the freethinkers, who, according to J. B. Bury, held that "the ideal of progress, freedom of thought, and the decline of ecclesiastical power go together" (*History,* 231). For her, no profession, no secular field of knowledge, no region of the universe should be inaccessible to women, and once these avenues are fully open to women, they will soon be able to compete equally with men. Yet, despite the magnanimity of her vision, Stanton's scenario nonetheless presupposes a rather limited and dual notion of womanhood: middle-class women who remain at home nur-turing and supporting the intellectual and economic advancement of the men in their family (lower-class women, by contrast, would need to work and could not remain at home); or middle-class women who have the resources to pur-sue educations and professional careers of their own. The class-specificity of her perspective is somewhat surprising given her realization of the intercon-nection between various forms of oppression (as shown in the passage cited earlier) and her 1886 statement that Christianity serves as "a powerful police institution" to control and silence the impoverished and downtrodden (qtd. in Pellauer, *Toward,* 16). This class-conscious view was also advanced by the freethinkers who, says J. B. Bury, believed that "theology has been regarded as a good instrument for keeping the poor in order.... It is highly desirable to keep them superstitious in order to keep them contented, that they should be duly thankful for all the theological as well as social arrangements which may have been made for them by their betters" (*History,* 223). Yet, neither the freethinkers nor Stanton mapped out a specific, concrete means for the empowerment of the underclasses and the overturning of hegemony other than by calling for the cultivation of the intellect. In this parable exegesis, Stanton makes no provisions for working-class or poor women without access to the privileges of higher education and leisure.

Besides reinforcing a class elitism, the women in the parable ironically await the exultant return of a man who will assist them in reaching the higher realms of science, politics, philosophy, and academics and in abandoning a sacrificial lifestyle. Thus, the world Stanton has constructed may offer paths heretofore unnavigated by women and may recognize women's intelligence as potentially equivalent to men's; but it is also a polarized and thoroughly masculine-controlled realm where women are either economically dependent (as in the case of the foolish virgins) or intellectually dependent (as with the wise virgins) upon white, middle-class, and educated men. As Stanton says, the most praiseworthy women are those who follow "the heels of man in the whole realm of thought, in art, in science, in literature and in government" (2:126).

In addition to the class and gender coding of her interpretation of the parable is her unquestioning acquiescence with the good girl/bad girl dualism. Stanton segments womanhood into two sweeping camps, neglects to underline the women's lack of solidarity, and then proceeds to pronounce rather severe judgment upon the "guilty" party. Underpinning this good woman/bad woman split is the issue of public and private spheres. Literary critic Kathi Kern argues that in *The Woman's Bible,* Stanton undermines the concept of "separate spheres" in three principal ways:

> In the mode most familiar to women reformers, Stanton co-opted male activity—
> in this case, gender-bound biblical criticism—and claimed it as fair turf for women.
> More profoundly, Stanton asserted an analysis of the historical origins of "separate spheres." She argued in *The Woman's Bible* that "woman's divinely ordained sphere" was a creation of men who had manipulated the Bible to distort woman's

true equality with men. Finally, and most provocatively, Stanton critiqued "woman's sphere" by charging that woman's piety and supporting religious networks were naive and short-sighted in their subservience to a male-dominated clergy, religious hierarchy, and a masculine God. ("Rereading," 379)

While I agree that Stanton does coopt male activity, blame feminine confinement on biblical authority, and criticize women's present forms of spirituality, I do not see these acts as constituting a radical dismantling of the public-private opposition.[4] Stanton indeed does call for certain women (white, middle-class, educated, and not too pious) to enter freely into the masculine, elite, and public world of politics, academia, and the arts, but she nevertheless accepts that the (superior) public-masculine and (inferior) private-feminine distinction does exist. Moreover, if such a clear-cut gap was operating at that time (and recent scholars such as Linda Kerber seem to question that it was), Stanton remains unclear about who will tend to the so-called "private" responsibilities of domestic labor and child-rearing and who will assume all of the "lower"-level manual jobs that make the elite, intellectual, professional positions possible.

The fact that Stanton glosses over this public-private split is understandable and perhaps to be expected, given that it is endemic to liberal thinking. Notes Rebecca S. Chopp, "The public arena comes to represent not only individual rights and freedoms, but market exchange. This public, in order for the autonomous individual to exist, depends upon the private sphere in the form of women's place, not only to take care of procreation, but increasingly to absorb the private values that the bourgeoisie has to deny, things like friendship, tradition, religion, and kinship" (*Power*, 113–14). Thus, while Stanton's demand for women's equal right to full humanity is indeed admirable, her proposal rests upon a public-private split and the repression of the private, "feminine" realm. The autonomous individual must have certain domestic and labor needs met in a hidden or effaced manner.

While this hierarchical dualism is in keeping with the liberal thinking of Stanton's own time, it is also not that far afield from the public-private and good-bad woman binaries that form the foundation of Protestant domestic rhetoric. As in the traditional Protestant notion of true womanhood where all women are said to possess the same features and values (piety, purity, domesticity, and submissiveness), woman in Stanton's exegesis seems to possess no individuality. As Mary Pellauer notes, "even individuality was read by Stanton as the respect in which all human beings [are] alike, not different from one another" (96). Indeed, the underlying assumption of her parable interpretation is that the ten women wholly approve of the binary union of the feminine but absent bride of religion and the masculine and bodily present groom of scientific reason. Although the foolish virgins are excluded from the connubial celebration, their "difference" is portrayed as a character flaw or personal deficiency rather than as self-conscious resistance or legitimate political disgruntlement. While their lot is certainly preferable to that of the foolish women, Stanton's wise women are still not fully equal to the bridegroom; for he controls everything from their sleeping schedules to their intellectual capacity. The women, in turn, continue to pose as his adoring servants, and they display little subjectivity or self-reflection. Hence, the wise virgins are split subjects — simultaneously alienated from their own physicality and "private" selves and still unable to fit comfortably and equitably in the public political world. Therefore, what Stanton accomplishes in her vision is to forge an imaginary space for the bourgeois, white woman — one that is hierarchically superior to the "feminized" (ignorant, superstitious, and laboring) underclass but not quite on a par with educated, rational white males.

A similar hierarchical attitude surfaces at many other points in *The Woman's Bible*. For example, when explicating the injunction in Numbers 36 for the daughters of Zelophehad to marry only men within their own tribe, she observes that the command implied that "these noble women [were] destitute of the virtue of patriotism, of family pride, of all the tender sentiments of friendship, kindred and home, and so with their usual masculine arrogance [the tribal leaders] passed laws to compel the daughters of Zelophehad to do what they probably would have done had there been no law to that effect" (1:124). Surely, thinks Stanton, no rational woman would possibly desire miscegenation. Mapping her own fears and prejudices onto these women, Stanton ascribes to them a "natural" nativism.[5] Moreover, Stanton suggests in this example that, if given the chance to think for and monitor themselves, they would (at least on the issue of race and nationalism) agree with white, educated, middle-class men.

The problem, then, with Stanton's stance is not that her preferred notion of womanhood entails a repudiation of a certain aspect of the Protestant agenda: the self-sacrifice and subjugation of women. The problem is that Stanton attempted to maintain too coherent of a feminist subject position that did acknowledge some of the exclusions on which it was dependent (for example, the self-sacrificing Protestant woman) but that also neglected to recognize its convergences with dominant Protestant strains of thought. By doing so, Stanton maintained a false rhetorical unity that denied the plurality of her own and her fellow committee members' thought and thus may have discouraged certain women from following her women's rights cause. (It would have been difficult for sincerely believing Christian feminists to identify with a feminist identity that insulted their faith.) Indeed, despite Stanton's reliance on hierarchical binaries, an amazing diversity of thought did erupt at various points in the book.

Stanton's project worked best when Stanton and the other writers' openly identified their convergences with (usually liberal) Protestant and other more radical forms of spiritual thought, yet did not neglect to differentiate themselves from antifeminine aspects of Christianity. In short, *The Woman's Bible* was most progressive when it set up feminism (and by extension the feminist subject) as a site of struggle and interchange among a range of voices at the same time that it refused to lose its political impetus for equal rights and responsibilities for women. While Stanton's binary and absolute thinking may have repelled her feminist contemporaries and served to undermine her political power, when *The Woman's Bible* opens up rather than forecloses new forms of interpretation and feminist thought, her project is most appealing to feminist scholars today and warrants the praise it has received from so many contemporary critics.

One reason it was impossible (if not advisable) for *The Woman's Bible* writers to escape Protestant thinking entirely was that most of them had been thoroughly enmeshed in traditional Protestantism since birth. For example, Stanton was born into a rigid Calvinist-based Presbyterian home; Matilda Joslyn Gage, Phebe Hanaford, and Ursula Gestefeld were reared as Baptists, and Clara Bewick Colby and Lillie Devereux Blake had Congregationalist backgrounds. By the end of the century, when *The Woman's Bible* was published, many of these women had changed their affiliations to more liberal Protestant and radical spiritual movements, such as Universalism (Hanaford, Olympia Brown, Augusta Chapin — the three ministers on the committee), Unitarianism, New Thought and Theosophy (Gestefeld, Gage, Colby, Lucinda Chandler, Clara Neyman, Frances Ellen Burr). Thus, while these women were certainly not part of the mainstream or fundamentalist religious movements, they were definitely not wholly secular or antireligious. Religion, and especially Protestantism, formed a cornerstone in their adult and childhood lives.

Yet, because the religious backgrounds and allegiances of *The Woman's Bible* committee members were not uniform, their perspectives on how to interpret the Bible differed markedly. Indeed, while the message projected in *The Woman's Bible* was somewhat unified in its call for the revision of patriarchal Protestant doctrine and exegesis, its writers' solutions to the problems inherent in patriarchal Christianity and conservative biblical scholarship were multifarious. For example, Stanton, along with Josephine Henry[6] and Clara Bewick Colby, habitually called for (what she saw as) deplorable sections of the Bible to be expunged and was often hard-pressed to locate any beneficent scriptural parts. The New Thought proponents, by contrast, advocated esoteric readings of the Scriptures and hesitated to regard the Bible or any of its verses as wholly ineffectual. Other writers, such as Hanaford, Dietrick, and Blake, assumed what could best be described as a Christian feminist stance, arguing that, through historical-critical scholarship and a feminist sensibility, the Bible can be interpreted to empower women. By incorporating a diversity of writers and approaches in this project, *The Woman's Bible* subverted the fundamentalist Christian notion that there exists a uniform truth of the Bible or a singular religious mind-set of American women. No one interpretation is definitive or eternal, and truth must be ferreted out through the readers' interactions with the book's assorted passages. Hence, *The Woman's Bible* project was most successful when it positioned itself (and the Bible) as "a cacophony of interested historical voices and a field of rhetorical struggles in which questions of truth and meaning are being negotiated" rather than as a coherent, unified viewpoint in staunch opposition to Protestantism (Fiorenza, "Transforming," 8).

Not only was *The Woman's Bible,* then, progressive when it positioned biblical interpretation as a site of struggle, it was also admirable in that women alone composed the commentaries.[7] Although the desire for a woman-oriented biblical hermeneutic had been voiced in the United States since the 1830s (Gifford, "American"), there were almost no notable women in the world of biblical scholarship in the late nineteenth century. In the 1890s, for example, the renowned Society for Biblical Literature voted only one woman (Anna Ely Rhoads) into its membership (Bass, "Women's," 7–9). Consequently, *The Woman's Bible* project did not involve many accomplished biblical scholars (in fact, few of its contributors had studied theology or religion formally), but it was remarkable for the admirable audacity of its goals: to interrogate the rarely assailed authority of the Bible; and to make the androcentric and elitist field of biblical scholarship accessible both to women and to people unschooled in the accepted hermeneutical practices. As Stanton writes in the preface to the second part of *The Woman's Bible,* "other critics say that our comments do not display a profound knowledge of Biblical history or of the Greek and Hebrew languages . . . [We do] not need a knowledge of either Greek, Hebrew or the work of scholars to show that the Bible degrades the Mothers of the Race" (2:8). Elitist pretensions to scholarship serve more often to mask and preclude basic knowledge or awareness of heinous truths than to uncover divine or abstruse wisdom. In other words, intelligent women do not need masculine authority figures or traditions to decipher or (more often) to warp the meanings of important texts for them. Thus, by engaging in this project, *The Woman's Bible* writers were explicitly expanding the field of biblical scholarship.

In derailing conventional standards of biblical and interpretative authority, *The Woman's Bible* was drawing upon the liberal advances made in the historical and source criticism of the period. As discussed in the previous chapter, historical criticism was initially propagated in German universities in the latter part of the eighteenth century; but U.S. liberal Protestant ministers and theologians, such as William Robertson Smith, Edwards A. Park, and William Newton Clarke, did not adopt it until the early and mid-nineteenth century. This critical method perceived the Bible as a collection of historical writings that are, to varying degrees, true. For these scholars, the truth of biblical religion resided in those texts and traditions that were older or more historically verifiable. Thus, they established a canon within a canon of sorts that portrayed the more historically reliable texts as the more divinely inspired and sacred; historically suspect passages, by contrast, were considered to be a human (and thus a fallible) rather than a divine construction. While Stanton herself shied away from engaging in historical-critical methods, many of her cocontributors used and acknowledged them liberally. Beginning in her exegesis of the first book of Genesis, Ellen Battelle Dietrick cited the earliest known historical-biblical critic, Jean Astruc of France, and his discovery of the two versions of the creation story in order to validate that the first version (Genesis 1:26–28), which asserts that man and woman were created simultaneously and equally, is older and therefore more accurate than the second version (Genesis 2:21–24) which describes Eve as emanating from Adam's rib. Furthermore, she disclaimed Moses as the sole author of the Pentateuch and proposed that those five books may have been written by several different people (1:16, 101–102). Thus, in borrowing openly from the liberal Protestant higher critics, *The Woman's Bible* commentators destabilized the unity of the Bible's authorship (the notion that each book was written by a single, inspired male writer). By emphasizing history over doctrine, these women chipped steadily away at the simple but lofty authority of the Scriptures and traditional Christian faith and thereby opened up new possibilities for interpretation and by extension welcomed a greater diversity of voices within the feminist movement.[8]

In addition to interrogating the Bible's authorship, many of *The Woman's Bible* contributors (like the liberal exegetes of the period) acknowledged translation errors and made distinctions between doctrinal truths and historical happenings. Clara Bewick Colby, at one point, hypothesized that "portions of the Bible are only histories of events given as a chain of evidence to sustain the fact that the real revelations of the Godhead . . . are true" and also that "our translators were not inspired, and . . . prejudice of [their] education was in some instances stronger than the grammatical context, in translating . . . contested points" (1:37). Similarly, Dietrick underscored these points by submitting that the holy books were typically written "by uncritical copyists, who altered passages greatly, and did not always even pretend to understand what they were copying"; and she added, "great as were the liberties which the [copyists] took with Genesis, those of the English translators, however, greatly surpassed them" (1:16, 17).

While Colby and Dietrick willingly conceded the errancy of biblical copyists and translators without rejecting the divine inspiration of the "original" writers, Stanton readily jettisoned the plenary inspiration of the holy book altogether and thus dethroned it as grand arbiter of sacred truth (2:8). After explicating Numbers 31 where the Israelites wage war against the Midianites taking captive thirty-two thousand women along with many animals, Stanton penned, "Surely such records are enough to make the most obstinate believer doubt the divine origin of Jewish history and the claim of that people to have been under the special guidance of Jehovah" (1:119). This rejection of the Bible's inspiration was also advanced in the liberal Unitarian circles of the time. Theodore Parker, a well-known Boston minister and personal friend of Stanton, also doubted the divine inspiration of the Scriptures, since he "could not put [his] finger on any great moral or religious truth taught by revelation in the New Testament, which had not previously been set forth by men for whom no miraculous help was ever claimed" (*Experience,* 37). By including a range of interpretive possibilities — from the purely rational to the more historical to the more spiritual versions — *The Woman's Bible* undercut implicitly conservative Protestant orthodoxy.

Another means *The Woman's Bible* writers used to test the Bible's reputation as the perfect transmission of the one and only God and to open up women's spiritual and interpretive opportunities was to measure the Bible against other religious and ethical writings. Better communications and travel opportunities helped to popularize a comparative study of religions in the late-nineteenth-century United States. For instance, James Freeman Clarke's *Ten Great Religions: An Essay in Comparative Theology* (1871) (which was originally a series of articles in *Atlantic Monthly*) went through five editions in seventeen years. The Columbian Exposition of 1893 hosted a World's Parliament of Religions, which featured representatives from all the major faiths of the world. Following the paths forged by the World's Fair and theologians such as Clarke, Colby compared and contrasted the first creation story in Genesis with Mayan, Yucatan, North American Indian, and Norse creation tales (1:32) and revealed their striking similarities. Stanton likewise maintained that while the Bible contains some stories that promote the beneficial principles of "love, charity, liberty, justice and equality" as well as the golden rule, the holy books of all religions perform the same benevolent function (1:12).[9] For *The Woman's Bible* writers, the Bible did not assume an exalted status, and as a result, it should be treated as any other ancient text—that is, to be compared to other religious writings and to be subjected to historical and authorial verification and to contemporary moral valuation.[10] By doing so, they located truth in a variety of texts derived from a wealth of cultures and historical moments rather than from a single source.

Despite the fact that the Bible, for *The Woman's Bible* writers, may not always serve as a godly source of inspiration and ethical instruction, it did paradoxically provide a means of illuminating the situations and problems of their own historical and social context. First, it exposed the roots of modern patriarchy and sexism. According to Stanton, Eve did not instigate evil or sexist distinctions between men and women, as traditional Christians so often proclaim; rather the origin of sin can more accurately be attributed to "some wily [biblical] writer, [who] seeing the perfect equality of man and woman, felt it important for the dignity and dominion of man to effect woman's subordination in some way" (1:21). Consequently, noted Stanton, this writer inserted the second creation story that makes woman "a mere afterthought" (1:20) and that catalyzed men's misogynist impulse, which continues to pervade society today. Although Stanton's proffering of a single-cause theory of patriarchy may be reductive, some of the larger implications of her critique are intriguing. Unlike traditional Protestants, she did not raise the Bible to a grand and inaccessible height; instead, she blurred the formerly rigid binary categories of biblical and nonbiblical, sacred and secular, and she demonstrated that the Bible was as much a political as a religious document. In fact, she engaged in what feminist theologian Elisabeth Schüssler Fiorenza has termed the "hermeneutics of suspicion," which "invites readers to investigate biblical texts and traditions as one would 'search' the place and location where a crime has been committed. It approaches a canonical text as a 'cover-up' for patriarchal murder and oppression" ("Transforming," 11).

The Woman's Bible offered a heterogeneous array of liberal and radical Protestant elements at the same time that its main author, Stanton, at times reinforced dominant binary thought. At this point, such a vexed position is not surprising; all of the writers studied in this book found themselves in similar contradictory stances. What makes *The Woman's Bible* and Stanton somewhat different, however, from the other subjects of this study is that as a self-proclaimed radical activist, she aligned herself not only with liberal dominant thought but also with some of the most conservative or fundamentalist ways of thinking of her time. Such a juxtaposition is especially curious given the fact that each had a very different political agenda. While Stanton spent much of her life combating the prevailing notion of true womanhood, fundamentalists adhered to and propagated it. Indeed, Betty DeBerg argues that it was their focus on binary gender roles that made fundamentalism so popular in the final decades of the century among the urban middle class.

While akin in many ways to what I termed conservative Protestantism in chapter four, fundamentalism, which gained popularity in the last decades of the century, had specific and unique traits. Most scholars agree that this religious movement emerged as a conservative reaction to a variety of modernist happenings: historical biblical criticism, comparative religion, corporate capitalism, and immigration. According to Ernest Sandeen, fundamentalism was characterized in part by its reliance on premillennialism (an apocalyptic view that held that the world would deteriorate completely before Christ's second coming) and Princeton orthodoxy, two beliefs not held by the freethinking Stanton.

In addition to holding very different views on women and Christian orthodoxy, Stanton and the fundamentalists frequently engaged in defamatory attacks on the other. It was the fundamentalists, after all, who routinely castigated women's rights' activists, assigning them every imaginable invective from "Amazonian disputants" to "leprous dregs of corruption" (Wise, "Young,"

85; Burnap, *Sphere,* 204). Upon publication of *The Woman's Bible,* James H. Brookes (one of the founding fathers of American fundamentalism) decried it as "that miserable abortion...that is only the impudent utterance of infidelity" (qtd. in DeBerg, *Ungodly,* 1). When a disgruntled minister termed *The Woman's Bible* "the work of women, and the devil," Stanton dubbed him, "His Satanic Majesty" (2:7). Each side defined itself by what it deemed the other was not. Despite their differences and animosity, the fact that the two sides shared similar binary thinking may not be all that surprising. After all, the dichotomies of the public-private realm and the educated elite-laboring underclass formed the social fabric of nineteenth-century U.S. culture. But binary thinking does not form the only link between Stanton and the fundamentalists.

They shared more subtle and most likely unconscious rhetorical, philosophical, and methodological similarities, which may have caused Stanton's message to appear out-of-touch to her younger feminist counterparts. As Mary Pellauer points out, despite Stanton's disgruntlement with conservative clergy, she often incorporated Christian rhetoric into her speeches: "To Stanton the ballot box was a 'holy of holies'; voting was a religious duty to be exercised religiously in more than a debased sense of that word.... The suffrage cause was religious not because of St. Paul's injunctions or any biblical text, but intrinsically so, on its own grounds" (*Toward,* 39). Thus, Stanton turns religious authority on its head, measuring it according to her own external standard rather than the other way around. Her willingness to position theology rather than allow it to position her represents a significant trend in nineteenth-century biblical scholarship. Hans Frei argues that early exegetes viewed the Bible as the arbiter of all meaning; this attitude engendered an inclusive world to which extrabiblical history had to be accommodated. With the higher criticism of the nineteenth century, the frame of reference shifted from the world inside the Bible to a world outside, and the goal became one of repositioning the Bible to meet those external criteria (*Eclipse,* 1–16). Yet, Stanton's attitude was not one of collaboration or compromise; she had no desire to modulate her view to all of those views around her or to acknowledge any truth of the Bible. Like the fundamentalists, she believed she was spreading a gospel of her own, her conception of truth being "the only safe ground to stand upon" (1:11).

Although Stanton most likely did not self-consciously emulate her conservative foes, her self-righteousness does resemble that of the most prominent fundamentalist thinkers of the late nineteenth century, the Princeton seminarians. As Charles Hodge, the most well-known of the nineteenth-century Princeton theologians, contends, "we are certain... that our ideas of God, founded on the testimony of His Word, correspond to what He really is, and constitute true knowledge" (*Systematic,* 1:134). No trace of accommodation appears in Hodge's or Stanton's statements. One possible reason for these two thinkers' assertion for their own inerrancy is that both were under constant and formidable attack. Not only were popular ministers and legislators by the end of the century denouncing Stanton's proposals, but as stated earlier, rising younger and more mainstream feminists such as Carrie Chapman Catt and Anna Howard Shaw had also publicly repudiated her and *The Woman's Bible* project. Similarly, in the final decades of the century, Princeton theologians, clinging to what they saw as a sacred system of divine truths, were confronted with an onslaught of various "foes": German higher criticism, the theory of evolution, Catholic immigration, and a perceived decay of public virtue. Rather than invent new solutions, Stanton and the fundamentalists reverted to an apologetic stance that was dependent on older and in some ways outdated philosophical and methodological principles. They appropriated, for their own very different ends, the basic tenets of the school of Scottish Common Sense Realism as propagated by the students of Thomas Reid: Dugald Stewart, James Oswald, and James Beattie.

From 1790 to 1870, Common Sense thinking served as a shaping force for virtually all Protestants and for mainstream American culture (Gauvreau, "Empire," 226). It was comprised of three interrelated emphases: epistemological, ethical, and methodological, not all of which were fully accepted by every Protestant denomination (Noll, "Common," 220). Put simply, the epistemological and ethical components of Common Sense accepted the premise that truth is approximately the same for everybody everywhere and propagated the notion that everyone can understand the world, grasp facts directly (with a minimum of distortion), and perceive truth through sensory perceptions. Whereas eighteenth-century Protestants (following the tenets of Calvinism) held that the human mind and faculties had been utterly blinded by the Fall, nineteenth-century common-sense-based Protestants generally believed that humans came equipped with the innate ability to perceive truth and to make moral judgments (at least in part) through a dynamic interaction between the mind and the natural world. After the Civil War, however, this system of thought vanished both from intellectual life and from liberal Protestant circles as a result of new patterns of economic organization, the restructuring of American higher education, and the upsurge of Kantian idealism and Darwinianism. No longer were most Protestant thinkers able to enjoy such complete faith in the power of the individual to understand reality and truth so easily. Modernist forces served to complicate Americans' vision of the world and their belief in the individual's ability to grasp truth solely through the senses and to perceive it as fixed and universal. As a result, Common Sense thinking waned in liberal Protestant circles; in fact, the only Protestants to continue to cling to this philosophy were the fundamentalists (Noll, "Common," 232). Yet, curiously, in *The Woman's Bible* project, Stanton also utilizes it heavily. Repeatedly, she calls on her readers to "be guided by their own unassisted common sense" (2:159) and to read the "unvarnished texts" of the Scriptures "in plain English" (1:8) and "in harmony with science, common sense, and the experience of mankind in natural laws" (1:20).

Such an exegetical methodology (or antimethodology) is in keeping with the Common Sense school and with fundamentalist hermeneutical practices. Common Sense methodology asserts that truths about the world or religion must be gained from a strict induction from irreducible facts of experience. Scottish Realists assumed naively that error could not arise in the observation of facts or from the inductive method, and both Stanton and fundamentalists, like Reuben A. Torrey and Charles Hodge, apply this inductive method to the Bible. Hodge affirms that God "gives us in the Bible truths, which, properly understood and arranged, constitute the science of theology. As the facts of nature are all related and determined by physical laws, so the facts of the Bible are all related and determined by the nature of God and of his creatures" (*Systematic,* 1:3). In a like manner, Stanton contends that this inductive approach yields infallible and patent truth: "What seemed to me to be right I thought must be equally plain to all other beings" (qtd. in Welter, "Introduction," xxii). For her, no matter who the reader is, the Bible leads to one ultimate conclusion or truth: It "does not exalt and dignify woman . . . The spirit is the same in all languages, hostile to her as an equal" (1:12).

Stanton and the fundamentalists believe in the inviolability of their own cause and eschew any legitimate development of doctrine or methodology. The Bible for both of them should be read straightforwardly; neither culture nor context need to be taken into account. In fact, at the celebration of his fiftieth year as professor at Princeton, Hodge proudly proclaimed that "a new idea never originated in this seminary. . . . The Bible is the word of God. That is to be assumed or proved. If granted; then it follows, that what the Bible says, God says. That ends the matter" (qtd. in Hodge, *Life*, 521). Stanton corre-spondingly employs a absolutist methodology: "In my exegesis, thus far, not being versed in scriptural metaphors and symbols, I have...merely com-ment[ed] on the supposed facts as stated. As the Bible is placed in the hands of children and uneducated men and women to point them the way of salva-tion, the letter should have no doubtful meaning. What should we think of guide posts on our highways, if we needed a symbolic interpreter at every point to tell us which way to go?" (1:64).[11]

Stanton and the fundamentalists both contend that the more liberal his-torical or symbolic readings of the Bible are mere superstitions or specula-tions rather than plain facts. For them, Common Sense reason offers surer grounds of knowledge than hypothetical flights of fancy or personal emotion. Princeton theologian, B. B. Warfield, warns future theologians that an overre-liance on "intrinsic evidence" — that is, "the testimony [or emotional feeling] which each reading [of the Bible] delivers" — can open "the floodgates to the most abounding error" (*Introduction*, 85). Stanton also implores her women readers to reject their "sentimental" and "blind" feelings of reverence for God and the Bible and to face the literal or absolute truth (1:10,11).

In keeping with Stanton's endorsement of literalism is her bifurcation of the natural and supernatural orders. For Stanton and many of *The Woman's Bible* writers, "church doctrine based not upon reason or the facts of life, is-sued out of crude imaginings; phantasms obstructed from truth, held in check the wheel of progress" (2:22). Thus, "natural" happenings signify truth, and supernatural events are produced through either ignorance or an overac-tive imagination. For example, Stanton explains the raising of Elijah in a char-iot of fire as follows: "Much of the ascending and the descending of seers, of angels and of prophets which astonished the ignorant was accomplished in balloons — a lost art for many centuries. No doubt that the poor widow, when she saw Elijah ascend, thought that he went straight to heaven, though in all probability he landed at twilight in some retired corn field or olive grove" (2:72). While fundamentalists do not equate supernaturalism with superstition, they too exact a definite break between the natural and supernatural realms and tend to abandon the notion that supernatural forces are intervening dra-matically and miraculously in this world at every moment (Marsden, *Funda-mentalism*, 50). As with Stanton, fundamentalists tended to view "miracles" as more or less aligned with the laws of nature and Newtonian principles of sci-ence. Wrote Hodge,

> After all the suspension or violation of the laws of nature involved in miracles is nothing more than is constantly taking place around us.... When a man raises a weight from the ground, the law of gravity is neither suspended nor violated, but counteracted by a stronger force. The same is true of Christ on the water, and the swimming of the iron at the command of the prophet...The truth on the subject was beautifully expressed by Sir Isaac Newton, when he said,..."God is the author of nature: He has ordained its laws:... He governs all things by cooperating and using the laws which He has ordained." (*Systematic*, 1:621–22)

For both Stanton and the fundamentalists, the emphasis is placed on the external, not the internal, the objective rather than the subjective, the natural over the supernatural, and uniformity over diversity. Indeed, both groups strip their exegeses of the text's historical vicissitudes and multiple meanings in order to lay open, naturalize, and eternalize their own absolute but antithetical positions. Stanton's and the fundamentalists' rejection of symbolic, figurative, and mythical biblical interpretations flies squarely in the face of some of the most skilled liberal theologians of her time, such as Horace Bushnell, D. F. Strauss, Johann G. Herder, and J. G. Eichhorn. These thinkers, who sought to escape from Common Sense assumptions, suggested that the Bible was as much figurative poetry as objective truth and was to be read not just with faith but with historical, philological, and literary imagination. Although it might contain inaccuracies and inconsistencies, the Bible's ability to spawn strong religious sentiment and the prevailing spirit of its language compensated for any errors. Furthermore, many liberal ministers utilized these methods to support women's enfranchisement, arguing that if interpreted figuratively or historically, passages that seemed demeaning when taken literally could be salvaged.[12] Nevertheless, in her introduction, Stanton demeans "liberal translations, interpretations, allegories and symbols" as promoting the Bible's fetishization. Moreover, at several points, she goes so far as to reinforce the conservative exegete Adam Clarke by paraphrasing his denouncement of liberal hermeneutics: "if we begin by taking some parts of the Scriptures figuratively we shall soon figure it all away" (1:70). For both Stanton and the fundamentalists, single, fixed meanings are easier to contain and control. If it is once granted that multiple meanings possess more or less equal legitimacy, then individuals may be less willing to submit to the fixed notion of truth as defined by Stanton or the fundamentalist ministerial elite.

My reason for exposing this uncanny alliance between Stanton and the fundamentalists is neither to denigrate either side nor to uncover some unconscious hypocrisy on Stanton's part. Moreover, I do not want to minimize or ignore the very real differences in purpose between the two groups: one sought to remedy the gender inequities in this world, while the other was concerned with spreading the gospel, in part by maintaining a gendered hierarchical dualism. Instead, what I want to underline is that Stanton's stance in *The Woman's Bible* does not represent a complete rejection of or emancipation from Christian ways of thinking. Rather, it not only mirrors shifts and struggles that were already occurring within Protestantism in the last quarter of the nineteenth century but it also discloses the way in which Stanton was deeply entrenched in the varieties of religious thinking of her own time. Moreover, it signifies the myriad "voices" Stanton incorporated and combined to fight for women's rights. Scholars have argued that by the end of the nineteenth century, postmillennial/evangelical Protestantism was slowly giving way either to the more absolutist fundamentalist and dispensationalist movements or to the more secular-oriented social gospel and agnostic (free-thought) movements (Sandeen, *Roots*). Moreover, between 1870 and 1930, almost every mainline denomination dealt with an inner struggle centering on the authority of Scripture, its scientific accuracy, or the supernatural elements in Christ's work or person (Marsden, *Fundamentalism*, 103). The social gospel's and freethinkers' concern with ameliorating current-day inequities, the conservatives' emphasis on scientific exactitude, literalism, and facts, and the mainstream Protestant Church's internecine battles over scriptural authority are all present in one form or another in *The Woman's Bible*.

Indeed, despite Stanton's proclaimed aversion for Protestant clergy and contemporary critics' conviction that she was a "militant anticleric" (DuBois, "Limitations," 161), in actuality, she often found them receptive to her feminism:

> In 1874, during her speaking tour of Michigan on behalf of a woman suffrage referendum, she enthusiastically noted that ministers of all denominations invited her to speak on suffrage in place of their Sunday sermons. "Sitting Sunday after Sunday in the different pulpits with revered gentlemen. . . . I could not help thinking of the distance we had come since that period in civilization when Paul's word was law. . ." In 1883, after preaching in a London pulpit on the topic, "Has the Christian Religion Done Aught to Elevate Woman?" she admitted privately that, although her sermon had focused on the negative, a strong case could be made for a positive interpretation. (Banner, *Stanton*, 156–57)

What this passage discloses is that Stanton's real complaint was not so much with religion or Christianity per se, but with the slow progress of the feminist cause. In 1886, she wrote to Antoinette Brown Blackwell about her frustration with the stagnancy of the women's movement: "I feel like making an attack on some new quarter of the enemies [sic] domain. Our politicians are calm & complacent under our fire, but the clergy jump round the minute you aim a pop gun at them like parched peas on a hot shovel" (qtd. in Kern, "Rereading," 373). For rhetorical and political reasons, she chose to feature clerical resistance over accommodation and to totalize all of Protestantism as evil; but in actuality, her thinking was in line with much of late-nineteenth-century Protestantism.

My emphasis on Stanton's reliance (however unconscious) on Protestant thought does not negate her much more conscious alliance with freethinkers who also rejected supernatural phenomena and theology in favor of rationality, literalism, and science. But Stanton differed from the freethinkers and shared subtle linkages with the fundamentalists in some crucial ways. First, as Elisabeth Schüssler Fiorenza has underscored, unlike the freethinkers who wanted to jettison biblical authority entirely, "the discourses engendered by *The Woman's Bible* did not break through their canonical limitations and theological frameworks. Insofar as they restricted their attention to the women's passages of the Bible, they reinforced the discursive boundaries set by the canon. By contesting the authority claims of the women's passages, they reinscribed canonical authority" ("Transforming," 9). Second, unlike Stanton who enjoyed a certainty in her own position, the freethinkers honored the unrestricted freedom of discussion and diversity of opinion. Writes J. B. Bury, freethinkers believed in the following: "History shows that knowledge grew when speculation was perfectly free in Greece, and that in modern times, since restrictions on inquiry have been entirely removed, it has advanced with a velocity which would seem diabolical to the slaves of the mediaeval [sic] church. Then, it is obvious that in order to readjust social customs, institutions, and methods to new needs and circumstances, there must be unlimited freedom of canvassing and criticizing them, of expressing the most unpopular opinions, no matter how offensive to prevailing sentiment they may be" (*History,* 240). Rather than honor a variety of opinions and express a willingness to be transformed by them as the freethinkers recommended, Stanton more often adopted a fixed position. Moreover, unlike the freethinkers who tended to propagate scientific reason and intellectual inquiry, she more fully relied on Common Sense thinking.

Unfortunately, these departures from freethought—her reinscription of canonical authority and absolute truth and her adoption of Common Sense thought—may have proven detrimental to the appeal and effectiveness of her feminist agenda. First, the Scottish Common Sense philosophy is founded on a troubling contradiction. Its acceptance of free agency and an irrefragable moral intuition and its suspicion of hierarchy and expertise appear to empower the common person, but upon closer examination, this hope for the enfranchisement of the individual and the underclass proves illusory. Common Sense more accurately connotes the sense of the dominant group—whichever one that may be. For the fundamentalists, it meant accepting the literal truth of the Bible, a dispensationalist and premillennial view of history, and the divinity of Christ. For Stanton, it meant confronting the "rational" truth of the Bible's misogyny and the consequent subjugation of woman in society.

Second, beyond promoting each group's individual cause, Common Sense philosophy also induced its believers to merge their convictions with the values of the wider culture (Noll, "Common," 226). Clearly, it was a belief system congruent with the idea of majority rule, and as such it necessarily aligned itself with the larger forces of patriarchy, liberal individualism, and capitalism. In other words, by articulating a cultural order centered on the individual believer/citizen as the prime mover and on a work ethic that asserted that honest labor would be financially rewarded, Common Sense Realism undergirded the rules and identities of the expanding market, the status quo, male dominance, and the national polity. As Kathryn Kish Sklar notes, "Combining 'an exalted view of man's potential with a determination to preserve traditional values,' it fostered an energetic moral leadership, yet discouraged assertive, bold, or innovative behavior in the society as a whole" (*Beecher,* 82–83). Thus, Stanton's articulation of conservative Common Sense thinking may have served to discourage radical thinkers and ideas from impacting her cause.

Moreover, her rhetorical stand against liberal theology and methodology may have hampered the expansion and popularity of her fourfold feminist agenda. At the end of the nineteenth century, thousands of religious women were involved simultaneously in the suffrage movement as well as in every aspect of the U.S. Protestant Church—from serving as ordained, itinerant, and lay ministers to serving as board members, deaconesses, missionaries, and church members (Zikmund, "Biblical," 85). Yet, rather than openly acknowledge her own utilization of Protestant thinking or display understanding toward Christian suffragists, Stanton continually argues that Protestantism or "priestcraft" has molded women into gullible, uneducated beings: "Priestcraft did not end with the beginning of the reign of Protestantism. Woman has always been the greatest dupe, because the sentiments act blindly, and they alone have been educated in her. Her veneration, not guided by an enlightened intellect, leads her as readily to the worship of saints, pictures, holy days, and inspired men and books, as of the living god and the everlasting principles of Justice, Mercy, and Truth" (Stanton, Anthony, and Gage, *History,* 1:850). Ursula Gestefeld conveys the same argument later in the book: "unintentionally women have been and will continue to be bigoted until they allow a higher ideal to penetrate their minds; until they see with the eye of reason and logic" (1:144). Gestefeld's choice of the infinitive "to penetrate" is revealing; while Stanton's and Gestefeld's intentions are no doubt in many ways well-meaning and meritorious, these women imbibe and project a troubling hierarchized logic of their own. Rational women, who are well-versed in the male-authored theories of evolution, scientific reason, and higher biblical criticism, definitely rank above those religious women who are "always most ready to believe miracles and fables, however extravagant and though beyond all human comprehension" (2:143). Because of women's recalcitrance and bigotry, raising a more rational feminist consciousness is a baffling task. Stanton writes, "I have been deeply impressed with the difficulty of substituting reason for superstition in minds once perverted by a false faith . . . Not conversant with works on science and higher criticism, which point out its fabulous pretensions, they cling to [the Bible] with an unreasoning tenacity, like a savage to his fetich [sic]" (2:213). By labeling all Protestant women as savages, she ends up negating the validity of these women's religious practices, deauthorizing their role in fashioning a religion of their own, and invalidating their hard-earned accomplishments within the Church and society. Thus, she may have ended up cutting off the constituency she hoped to recruit.

Realizing that Stanton's philosophy joins in some uneasy ways with fundamentalist Christianity does not mean that scholars should scorn her. What it does indicate is that we should begin to consider her not so much as an alienated heroine misunderstood by everyone (including her fellow suffragists) in her own time, but as a figure embedded in the dynamic struggles and transformations of her particular historical, religious, and social context. Although the project contained its share of problems, in fairness to Stanton and her committee members, it is important to note that no one during her era — or even (I would venture to suggest) now — was or is able to hold an unadulterated feminist viewpoint, unencumbered by "opposing" patriarchal or religious ideologies. Ideologies, even putatively antipathetic ones, unexpectedly and continually collide and converge.

My purpose in writing this chapter represents something akin to what many of *The Woman's Bible* contributors attempted to do in creating their project: to untangle the thickly wound, seemingly unified knot of authorship and authority. Just as *The Woman's Bible* writers discovered that the Bible contains its share of laudable as well as dubious messages and figures influenced by the writers' historical situations and that the Pentateuch was not issued from the hands of a single author, I have striven to demonstrate that Stanton and her work also possess variegated impulses and agendas. In my view, Stanton's project was most interesting and radical when it strove to unwind the taut rope of the social hegemony and less intriguing when it constructed a power cord of its own. Undeniably, *The Woman's Bible* contains its share of linear, binding, and conservative (or, to use her image, ropelike) strategies: its racist and classist dimensions; its repression of the "private" sphere; its adoption of hierarchical ordering; its literalist, reductive readings; and its absolutist stance. While these strategies warrant acknowledgment and critical interrogation, they should not overshadow the book's more liberal and radical untangling and transgressive tactics: its welcoming of a diversity of interpretative methods; its opening of the previously male-dominated and elitist field of biblical scholarship; its willingness to redefine notions of biblical authority and authorship; its comparativist approach to religions; its reading of the Bible as a political as well as a religious text; and its tendering of a more woman-oriented hermeneutic. Not only do such tactics validate the creativity, intelligence, and agency of the project's producers, they also offer new, open-ended possibilities for readers coping with that traditional, patriarchy-ridden, and multicorded cultural icon: the Bible.

Conclusion

In 1819, while delivering a sermon based on God's declaration to Joshua that "there remaineth yet very much land to be possessed," Heman Humphrey, pastor of the Congregationalist church in Pittsfield, Massachusetts, spoke: "As the land of Canaan belonged to Israel, in virtue of a divine grant, so does the world belong to the church; and as God's chosen people still had much to do, before they could come into full and quiet possession of the land, so has the church a great work to accomplish, in subduing the world 'to the obedience of Christ.' "[1]

As the individuals studied in this book have illustrated, the quest to subdue "the world 'to the obedience of Christ' " entailed more than securing people's faith in the divinity of Jesus and the authority of the Bible; it also demanded their acceptance of Anglo-American cultural superiority, middle-class norms, and rigid dualistic gender roles. In short, the Protestant notion of manifest destiny asked its adherents to "dissolve" their old identities and to be reborn into a new, unified, fixed, culture- and gender-specific image, one supposedly in keeping with divine will.

The process of forming and maintaining a Christian identity was not an easy one for the subjects of this book. Indeed each faced various forms of opposition. During their processes of conversion and sanctification, they were

tempted by numerous worldly vices. Equiano, for example, continually bat-
tled with the temptation to swear and curse; Apess struggled with a desire to
drink and cavort. George Whitefield and Amanda Berry Smith fought the urge
for extreme asceticism, and Catharine Beecher and Harriet Beecher Stowe continually doubted their own conversions. In addition to dealing with self-doubt,
these individuals faced other psychological challenges. Whitefield, Berry Smith,
and Beecher faced charges of arrogance and self-aggrandizement. Equiano,
Apess, Truth, Whitall Smith, Berry Smith, and Stanton were sometimes called
incompetent or unfit to speak, preach, pray, or sing in public. Equiano, Truth,
and Berry Smith routinely confronted the threat of physical attacks, while
Whitefield regularly dealt with physical illness and occasionally with abusive
scoffers. Others, like Truth, Broughton, and Berry Smith, were deemed insane
by those around them. And finally, many (Equiano, Apess, Beecher, Truth,
Berry Smith, Stewart, Stanton) faced scorn because of their lack of "adequate"
formal education.

Opposition, for all of the individuals studied here, derived from both external and internal sources, a combination that inevitably led them to a sense
of shame. Unlike guilt, which is remorse for a single act of wrongdoing, shame
is "most importantly a felt sense of unworthiness to be in connection, a deep
sense of unlovability" brought about because one feels "defective or flawed in
some essential way" (Jordan, "Relational," 6). Although shame contributes to
a sense of personal defectiveness, it does not necessarily engender a sense of
complete abjection from society or humanity. As Judith Jordan notes, "while
shame involves extreme self-consciousness, it also signals powerful relational
longings and awareness of the other's response" ("Relational," 6). Thus, for
shame to emerge, the shamed subject must already identify with the shamer
or the shaming community (in this case, Protestantism).

Although shame has the potential to contain and control the subject and is
often associated with prohibition and opposition, it is, more important, "a
form of communication ... a desire to reconstitute the interpersonal bridge"
(Sedgwick, "Shame," 211–12). Shame, then, is not so much "an enforcer of proper
behavior" as "the place where the question of identity arises most originarily
and most relationally" (213, 212). Or as Judith Butler puts it, repression oper-
ates as "a modality of productive power" (*Bodies*, 22). Thus, for these individuals,
identity is not attached to some inner essence or divinely ordained inheritance
but rather is constructed through interactions with others. The identities of
individuals like Equiano, Apess, Stowe, Truth, and Stanton are informed by

their interactions with both evangelical Protestants and those of other denominations, faiths, or beliefs; and they are constituted by their relations with whites as well as with other ethnicities and races. Hence, because he was connected to various groups and peoples, Equiano can be as much West African as Anglo-Protestant, just as Apess can be both Pequot and Methodist. Stowe can be a devotee of Calvinism and Arminian-based evangelicalism, and Stanton can simultaneously be informed by both fundamentalism and women's rights because she was in dialogue with members of both groups.

In addition to their identities being constituted in multiple ways through relations with others, these individuals demonstrate that although interaction and shaming can "make identity," the identity created is neither ready-made, fixed, contained, separate, nor fully reified. The self for these individuals is marked by a "capacity for flexibility, responsiveness, adaptation, receptivity, creativity, activity and change through connection" (Surrey, "Empathy," 3). Thus, not only is the self open, ever-changing, and in continual dynamic interaction with others but it also has the power to produce change. Each of the individuals studied did not accept unequivocally the identity offered or (in the case of Native Americans and blacks) not offered to them through the Protestant rhetorics of manifest destiny and domesticity. Instead they found creative and empowering ways to displace these rhetorics as normative and universal and thereby to alter the identities projected by the rhetorics.

Early Anglican versions of manifest destiny did not accord either George Whitefield, a poor, unskilled, and fatherless boy, or Olaudah Equiano, an enslaved West African, acceptable social roles. Rather than attempt to escape their projected identities (an impossibility anyway) or to accept them wholesale, these members of the eighteenth-century class-stratified, slave-based society of Anglo-America displaced their abject or denigrated status by undergoing extreme self-abnegation through Christian conversion. Ironically, by dissolving the self under the framework of Calvinist-evangelical Protestantism, the men were able to create a more exalted and (in the case of Whitefield) a transcendent subject position. Whitefield, in fact, took on such self-aggrandizing proportions that he literally came to impersonate God. Butler argues that "when material positivities appear outside discourse and power . . . , that is precisely the moment in which the power discourse regime is most fully dissimulated and most insidiously effective" (*Bodies,* 35). By assuming a transcendent position, Whitefield was projecting a new hierarchy of his own, one that placed him (as the deity) in full control of all others.

Although none of the other individuals utilized as extreme (and albeit insidiously effective) a strategy as did Whitefield, all sought to overturn their abject status by shaming — and thereby creating — a new group of outsiders. William Apess, Harriet Beecher Stowe, Mary Livermore, Frances Willard, and Elizabeth Cady Stanton boosted their sense of selves by reiterating racialized stereotypes of blacks. By revisioning Africa as a Christian commercial utopia, Equiano conveyed the dominant Anglo-American ideology of colonialism and repudiated Africa as he knew it. Catharine Beecher inflated the sense of her own identity and power by denigrating woman's rights activists, and Stanton did the same by rejecting self-sacrificing, believing Christian women. While it "is doubtless true that certain disavowals are fundamentally enabling, and that no subject can proceed, can act, without disavowing certain possibilities and avowing others" (Butler, *Bodies,* 116), it also is troubling that identification in these cases was based on the denigration and exclusion of other groups.

While the two strategies of impersonating God and shaming others entail a reinscription of power *over* others, other strategies these individuals used involved a different notion of power. In a recent book, Jean Baker Miller proposed a new use of the word *power* as "the capacity to produce change, to replace the notion of power as domination, control, mastery" (qtd. in Surrey, "Relationship," 163). Rather than strive toward self-determination in the image of the highly individuated self-actualizer, these individuals, for the most part, preferred to work within a framework of relational empowerment. They sought to increase the potential for mutually affirming relationships with those different from themselves.

Toward that end, both Equiano and Apess employed a culturally relativistic strategy known as "bifocality," or the ability to see ourselves against a background of others and others against a background of ourselves. They took advantage of their liminal cultural positions to make Anglo-Americans aware of the worth and plights of African or Native American people and of their (whites') complicity in exacerbating those plights; and conversely, they used their entrance into the white Protestant world to attempt (although sometimes in misguided ways) to better the situations of their native peoples. By vacillating between two cultural milieux, these two men unseated the certainty or superiority of any one ethnicity, race, or culture. Their ability to shift identifications was not necessarily a sign of a lack of integrity or conviction on the part of the subject, nor did it "mean that one identification [wa]s repudiated for another"; rather, "shifting may well be one sign of hope for the possibility of avowing an expansive set of connections" (Butler, *Bodies,* 118). Bifocality, then, opened up new possible identifications, new ways of constituting the self through simultaneously differing relationships.

In addition to bifocality, the individuals in this study deployed another strategy to displace normative Protestant rhetorics — that of miming. For them, miming did not represent an enslavement to or simple repetition of the original but "an insubordination that appear[ed] to take place within the very terms of the original, and which call[ed] into question the power of origination" (Butler, *Bodies*, 45). Both the Christian feminists and Stanton reiterated Protestant assumptions, methods of interpretation, and practices — drawing from evangelical perfectionism and liberal historical criticism to Scottish Common Sense thinking and Princeton orthodoxy — to displace, not to affirm, conservative and fundamentalist suppositions about women and religion. For the most part, these women used miming to bypass the logic of repudiation and exclusion in order to create new identification possibilities for themselves and other women.

For most of the individuals of this study, the goal of bifocality and miming was greater empathy or mutuality. Engaging in empathic, mutually satisfying relationships did not mean that the self-other differentiation was "lost, opening the way for uncontained merging or the use of the other as a narcissistic extension of self" (Jordan, "Empathy and the Mother," 3). As Alexandra Kaplan writes, "empathy can more clearly be recognized as a complex, refined, and highly developed process that simultaneously encompasses knowledge and affect, self and other, action and receptivity, inner and outer experiences, and mutual growth toward empowerment. Empathy, then, requires awareness of one's own cultural milieu and the experiences of the other in her own context and in her own words" ("Empathy," 8–9).

The mutually empathic self does not seek to eradicate difference, opposition, or conflict. As opposed to merging or fusion, which entails one self being enveloped by another, the relational, mutually empathic being works toward developing "a more articulated and differentiated image of the other and hence responds in a more accurate and specific way" (Jordan, "Empathy and the Self," 73). Moreover, as demonstrated in the analyses of these individuals, the subject itself is the site of conflicting and converging relations of power that are not univocal. Indeed, identity formation occurs amidst contradiction, conflict, opposition, and prohibition; thus, the subject represents an amalgam of converging and conflicting relations of power. While negative conflict seeks the loss and degradation of connection, productive conflict leads to a more self-conscious understanding of ourselves and others and to greater possibilities of connection. Although not immune from falling into patterns of exclusion and abjection, the individuals in this study, at their best, struggled within the existing regime of Protestantism to create a new destiny for themselves, one that moved toward the kinds of contestatory and empowering connections that exemplify a democratic community.

Although the struggles examined in this book occurred over a century ago, they do not seem unfamiliar or irrelevant today. Within fundamentalist and mainline Protestant circles, women and nonwhite men — as ministers, church leaders, religious scholars, and theologians — have still not achieved full parity with their white male counterparts, nor has a feminist Christian theology been integrated fully into church doctrine and practice. Too often, women still function — like Katy and Mary Scudder — in Stowe's 1859 novel — as the invisible galvanizing and coalescing forces of the Christian Church, the silent "seamstresses" stitching together the diverse patches of their communities, while male leaders reap the glory and benefit of women's erased labor. Although the exact phrases and vocabulary may have altered, antifeminist rhetoric and shaming tactics remain common and recurring themes in many American churches today. In response, enterprising feminist and antiracist Christians have had to continue the legacy of radical obedience begun by their nineteenth-century ancestors: Olaudah Equiano, William Apess, Harriet Beecher Stowe, Frances Willard, Amanda Berry Smith, Hannah Whitall Smith, Virginia Broughton, Sojourner Truth, and Elizabeth Cady Stanton. On the one hand, these people's efforts seem to have paid off: women and people of color have gained greater power in the Church, and ministers' criticisms of feminists and nonwhites has become somewhat less vitriolic. Yet, on the other hand, ministers' greater acceptance of public women and nonwhite leaders may not necessarily indicate an increased empathic desire to confront all difference and enhance all forms of connection. For, in the past decade, a new abject other — the homosexual — has emerged to replace these two groups and thus to make women and nonwhite men's place in Protestantism somewhat more palatable. An exchange almost identical to that explored in this study has recently surfaced between conservative and mainline church leaders and gay and lesbian Christians. My hope in writing this book is not only to offer insight into the history of nondominant Protestant identity and identity formation but also to provide glimpses into how present and future nondominant identities can be formed and welcomed in Protestant churches and American society without repudiation and exclusion.

Notes

INTRODUCTION

1. Qtd. in Merk, *Manifest,* 31; he cites: *Congressional Globe,* 29 Cong., 1 Sess., 342 (Feb. 9, 1846).
2. Qtd. in Berkhofer, *Salvation,* 8; from *Minutes of the Baptist Board,* Apr. 26, 1822, deposited at Treasury Department, American Baptist Foreign Mission Society, New York City.
3. Qtd. in Wood, *Arrogance,* 213; from Josiah Strong, *The New Era; or, The Coming Kingdom* (New York, 1893), 79–80.
4. See Wood, who argues that scholars have greatly exaggerated the percentage of blacks who converted to Christianity prior to the Civil War (*Arrogance,* 137–62).

CHAPTER ONE

1. Fortes writes that the African social structure is based on spiritual associations with ancestors, especially with authoritative fathers who in death possess mystical powers over the living sons (*Oedipus,* 30). Thus, Equiano's West African upbringing may also have influenced his respect for his masters.
2. See J. Wesley Bready, *England: Before and After Wesley* (London: Hodden and Stoughton, 1939), 228–29.
3. For an example of Whitefield being hit with a cudgel, see his *Journals,* 306.
4. George Whitefield, *Three Letters from the Reverend Mr. G. Whitefield* (Philadelphia, 1740). Previous quotations from Letter 3, pages 1, 13, 14.

5. Rather than argue (as I do) that Equiano and New Light Calvinists perceived piety and profit as mutually reinforcing, Houston Baker argues the opposite. He claims that Equiano struggles between his entrepreneurship and his spirituality and eventually supplants his spiritual focus with his desire for profit. Baker writes, "The narrator...realizes, in effect, that only the acquisition of property will enable him to alter his designated status as property" (*Blues*, 35).

6. Whitefield apparently helped to convert numerous blacks. The black poets Jupiter Hammon and Phillis Wheatley were deeply influenced by Whitefield. Wheatley was so impressed with him that she praised his preaching talents in a poem, "On the Death of the Rev. George Whitefield" (Costanzo, *Surprizing*, 11). John Marrant, a black freeman, was converted by Whitefield as a teenager. He became an itinerant preacher in Nova Scotia. See Marrant, *Narrative*.

7. See Saillant ("Slavery") who argues that Jonathan Edwards and Samuel Hopkins, two other prominent American Calvinist evangelicals, held a view on slavery and divine providence similar to that of Whitefield. He also notes that Lemuel Haynes, a black New Divinity minister, put forward a counterview (not unlike that of Equiano) around 1800. Saillant interprets Haynes's view as radical, a "black protest."

CHAPTER TWO

1. Material from this chapter comes from my article of the same title in *Early American Literature* 31:1 (1996): 25–44.

2. The spelling of Apess's name is not definitive. As is evident from Krupat's quotation, the spelling "Apes" has been used by some scholars and was used by Apess himself for part of his life. I use the name "Apess" because evidence suggests that he came to prefer it and because he was using it when he published his conversion narrative, which is the topic of this chapter.

3. For more information on Apess's involvement in the Mashpee Revolt, see Kim McQuaid, "William Apes, Pequot: An Indian Reformer in the Jackson Era," *New England Quarterly* 50 (1977): 605–25. For a more focused and recent discussion, see Donald M. Nielsen, "The Mashpee Indian Revolt of 1833," *New England Quarterly* 58 (1985): 400–20.

4. See also Barbara Epstein, *Politics of Domesticity*, who argues a similar point (45–65). According to her, women's conversion is propelled by a personal resistance to divine authority, while men's regeneration is prompted by social pressure from loved ones. Susan Juster takes issue with Epstein's point that gendered differences in conversion led to greater sexual differentiation and antagonism. She argues that while "evangelical men and women reached the pinnacle of grace through different paths, the final destination is the same for both sexes: a mature union with God" (36–37). Thus, for Juster, there may exist gender-specific processes of conversion, but the regeneration itself is "androgynous."

5. For examples, see the Appendix to *A Son of the Forest* and *Eulogy on King Philip, as Pronounced at the Odeon, in Federal Street, Boston,* in Apess, *On Our Own Ground.*

6. The Pequots lost vast portions of their land following the 1637 war. The government issued the tribe small land grants in the 1650s, which caused the establishment of four small Indian towns, supervised by two Pequot "governors." During the early eighteenth century, the heirs of John Winthrop illegally took more of their land, including the entire town of Groton, Massachusetts. Within the next several decades, local farmers and government officials illegally appropriated more land so that by 1761, the Pequot land holdings had been reduced to a mere 989 acres. For more information on the history of the New England Pequots, see Hauptman and Wherry, "Pequots," and Salisbury, *Manitou.*

CHAPTER THREE

1. Edwards is integrated into the story not only because he was the actual maternal grandfather of Aaron Burr but also because he serves as a significant influence on Hopkins. As a symbol of his devotion to Edwards, Hopkins, we learn, holds an original copy of Edwards's famous "Resolutions" (271). Moreover, on several occasions, the narrator herself even invokes Edwards and his theology directly (337). Bellamy enters into the characters' conversation at one point when they identify him as Burr's former teacher and Hopkins's friend (226).

2. According to Ann Douglas, Bellamy focused on and popularized Edwards's concept of Atonement and wrote in a more direct, accessible manner; Hopkins stressed a more pragmatic version of Edwards's true virtue (the concept of Disinterested Benevolence) and was well-known for his prayer circles for women and his abolitionist stance (Douglas, *Feminization,* 101).

3. Foster (*Rungless Ladder,* 105) and Caskey (*Chariot,* 188) affirm Stowe's ambivalence toward Calvinism. For a counterposition, see Kimball, *Religious.*

4. This is Charles Foster's expression.

5. Douglas (*Feminization*), Mead (*Nation*), and others have written extensively about the powerful assaults on U.S. Protestantism launched by the disestablishment of religion and the rise of deistic rationalism in the late eighteenth century. As a result of these threats, ministers were confronted with the real possibility of reduced church membership and a diminution of their own prestige.

6. In 1822, Catharine Beecher's fiancé, Alexander Fisher, died suddenly in a shipwreck with a soul in questionable condition. Similar to Hopkins, Lyman Beecher used the "mourning process as an exercise in right thinking" (Hedrick, *Stowe,* 40) by interrogating Catharine repeatedly on her own redemptive status. Hedrick argues that Harriet was personally troubled by this heated exchange between Lyman and Catharine (41).

7. According to Sklar, the classic description of conversion and the one followed by Lyman Beecher was Philip Doddridge's *The Rise and Progress of Religion in the Soul* (31).

8. The doctrine of Arminianism, postulated by the Dutch Protestant theologian, Jacobus Arminius (1560–1609), holds that Christ died for all people and not only for the elect.

9. William McLoughlin declares that this trend toward Arminianism was so pronounced in U.S. Protestantism that by 1835 the distinction between Calvinism and Arminianism was negligible (*American*, 5).

10. An alternative interpretation of the exchange of foreign market items (and one worth exploring in another context) is that Stowe is supporting a colonial economy where artifacts are brought back from foreign countries and exoticized.

11. Adams and Foster write that as a young girl, Stowe was enchanted with "a sea-faring uncle, Captain Foote, [who] spun his fabulous yarns, and, in a spirit of mischief, asserted that Catholics were well-intentioned folk on the whole, and that some Turks were as honest as some Christians" (*Heroines*, 91).

12. In her book, *Gossip*, Patricia Spacks has done interesting research on the way in which gossip functions—particularly for women—as a sophisticated means of communication and storytelling.

13. Stowe's letter to Charles E. Stowe is dated Feb. 16, 1881.

14. On the other hand, as Crozier asserts, Burr's rigid system of thought might have been influenced more by his strict Edwardsean upbringing than by his atheism (*Novels*, 128).

15. See Stowe's 1832 letter to Elizabeth Bates where she expresses the same sentiments that Candace does to Ellen (qtd. in Hedrick, "'Peaceable'" 315).

CHAPTER FOUR

1. For scholars who view Christian feminism as ultimately inferior to "secular" feminism and disempowering for women, see DuBois, *Feminism;* O'Neill, *Everyone;* Hewitt, *Women's*.

2. For scholars who see some benefit in women's place and influence in the Protestant church, see Ryan, *Women in Public;* Ginzberg (who views Christianity as being empowering only in the early part of the century), *Women;* and Epstein, *Politics*.

3. The original passage comes from the 1881 Woman's Christian Temperance Union (W.C.T.U.) Minutes, page 1.

4. The W.C.T.U. did become more narrow in its legislative goals after Willard's death in 1897—a fact that testifies to her tremendous persuasive powers.

5. As noted in the previous chapter, Harriet Beecher Stowe argues a parallel gendered view of religion in *The Minister's Wooing*.

6. In fact, Dayton points out that American evangelicals continually experimented with worshiping practices such as "field preaching," setting hymns to popular tunes, and playing folk instruments that George Whitefield had used effectively a hundred years earlier (*Discovering*, 87).

7. For more information, see Brereton, "Preparing," 178–99.

8. It was first adumbrated in Johann Gottfried Herder's *Another Philosophy of History* in 1774, where he posited all reality as a historical stream in which social institutions, intellectual constructing, and even logical categories are immersed.

9. See also Szasz, who asserts that "evolution and the comparative study of religion — which might have been as disruptive [as historical criticism] — were absorbed with relative ease and seemed only mildly threatening to most fin-de-siècle churchgoers" (*Divided*, 1).

10. This passage was written by Catherine Booth, the founder of the Salvation Army.

11. In 1891, B. T. Roberts, a Free Methodist minister, produced one of the few pamphlets written by a clergyman that, through biblical exegesis, advocates woman's equality with man.

12. In 1919, Katharine Bushnell published *God's Word to Women — One Hundred Bible Stories on Woman's Place in the Divine Economy*, which included three chapters devoted to the sex-bias influences on translations.

13. The two passages to which Cobbe is referring can be found in Philemon 1:11–12 (where Paul sends the slave Onesimus back to his owner, Philemon) and in Ephesians 5:22 (where Paul counsels wives to obey their husbands).

14. The scriptural references in Willard's example are 1 Timothy 2:11 (in which Paul exhorts women to learn in silence) and 1 Timothy 2:9 (in which he tells women to dress modestly and simply).

15. The illustration was designed by Henrietta Briggs-Wall of Hutchinson, Kansas — a W.C.T.U. member and suffrage advocate (Gifford, "Home," 107).

16. In fact, Blake composed her best-selling book, *Woman's Place Today*, as a direct result of her personal outrage over a series of lectures given by Dix on the nature of woman in 1883.

17. Gifford concurs with Bordin; she writes that "radical women's rights reformers, such as Elizabeth Cady Stanton and Susan B. Anthony, failed to evoke images of woman that appealed to the majority of mainstream Evangelical Protestant women, who were more timid and loath to challenge the status quo than Stanton and Anthony" ("Home," 97).

18. For scholars who confirm that the Bible reference was the most frequently used argumentative tactic by nineteenth-century antifeminists, see Solomon, *Voice*, 58; and Behnke, *Religious*, 250.

CHAPTER FIVE

1. The three quoted passages are respectively derived from Griffith, *In Her Own Right*, 210; Caraway, *Segregated*, 156; Kraditor, *Ideas*, 77.

2. The exception is Fiorenza; see her "Transforming."

3. Elizabeth Cady Stanton, *The Woman's Bible: Parts I and II* (New York: Arno, 1972), 2:126. Page references for subsequent citations will be noted parenthetically in the text.

4. For a more detailed discussion of this issue, see Eisenstein, "Stanton," 77–102.

5. A few scholars have documented Stanton's hierarchical (racist and classist) attitude. For example, shortly after African-American men were awarded the vote, Stanton spoke out: "If American women find it hard to bear the oppressions of their own Saxon fathers, the best orders of manhood, what may they not be called to endure when all the lower orders of foreigners now crowding our shores legislate for them and their daughters. Think of Patrick and Sambo and Hans and Yung Tung, who do not know the difference between a monarchy and a republic, who can not read the Declaration of Independence or Webster's spelling-book, making laws for Lucretia Mott, Ernestine L. Rose, and Anna E. Dickinson" (Stanton, Anthony, and Gage, *History,* 2:353). Caraway writes that Stanton also supported the call for a literacy test for "unfit" voters to ensure white, native-born control over legislation and government (*Segregated,* 141).

6. Henry did not contribute any commentary entries, but she did compose two lengthy and supportive letters to Stanton that were appended to the book.

7. While thirty-four women were listed as Revising Committee members, only twelve actually contributed biblical commentaries. Out of the roughly 200 entries, more than 150 were produced by Stanton herself.

8. Historian Mark Noll confirms that conservative Christian scholars firmly believed in the singularity and unity of the Pentateuch's and the Pauline epistles' authorship (*Between,* 1–38).

9. Stanton more often makes the more pessimistic claim that all world religions are equally detrimental to women: "You may go over the world, and you will find that every form of religion which has breathed upon this earth has degraded woman. There is not one which has not made her subject to man" (qtd. in Pellauer, *Toward,* 44).

10. Beginning in the 1880s, a prominent Unitarian school led by Reverend Joseph Henry Allen also demanded that the Bible be judged by the same standards used in evaluating any other historical record (Hopkins, *Rise,* 56).

11. In the appendix to the first part of *The Woman's Bible,* Stanton also praises Julia Smith's "exact literal translation" of the Bible (published in 1876), which supposedly served as the primary source for her revising committee.

12. Henry Ward Beecher serves as one notable example of such a minister. For verification that many liberal ministers were allies of the women's movement, see Kraditor, *Ideas,* 94. Janette Hassey writes that Ellen Battelle Dietrick (one of the contributors to *The Woman's Bible* and a respected theologian) named the liberal denominations as those that opened doors for women (*No Time,* 2).

CONCLUSION

1. Joshua 13:1; Humphrey, *Promised,* 5–6, 9–10. See also Hudson, *Nationalism.*

Works Cited

Accardo, Annalucia, and Alessandro Portelli. "A Spy in the Enemy's Country: Domestic Slaves as Internal Foes." In *The Black Columbiad: Defining Moments in African-American Literature and Culture*, edited by Werner Sollors and Maria Diedrich. Cambridge and London: Harvard University Press, 1994.

Acholonu, Catherine Obianju. "The Home of Olaudah Equiano — A Linguistic and Anthropological Search." *Journal of Commonwealth Literature* 22, no. 1 (1987): 5–16.

Adams, Elmer C., and Warren D. Foster. *Heroines of Modern Progress*. New York: Sturgis and Walton, 1913.

Ammons, Elizabeth, ed. *Critical Essays on Harriet Beecher Stowe*. Boston: G. K. Hall, 1980.

Andolsen, Barbara Hilkert. *"Daughters of Jefferson, Daughters of Bootblacks": Racism and American Feminism*. Macon: Mercer University Press, 1986.

Andrews, William L., ed. *Sisters of the Spirit: Three Black Women's Autobiographies of the Nineteenth Century*. Bloomington: Indiana University Press, 1986.

———. *To Tell a Free Story: The First Century of Afro-American Autobiography, 1760–1865*. Urbana and Chicago: University of Illinois Press, 1986.

Apess, William. *On Our Own Ground: The Complete Writings of William Apess, a Pequot*. Edited by Barry O'Connell. Amherst: University of Massachusetts Press, 1992.

Ashmore, Ruth. *Side Talks With Girls*. New York: Charles Scribner's Sons, 1896.

Baker, Houston A., Jr. *Blues, Ideology, and Afro-American Literature: A Vernacular Theory*. Chicago: University of Chicago Press, 1984.

Banks, William L. *The Black Church in the U.S.: Its Origin, Growth, Contributions and Outlook*. Chicago: Moody Press, 1972.

Banner, Lois W. *Elizabeth Cady Stanton: A Radical for Woman's Rights*. Boston and Toronto: Little, Brown, 1988.

Bass, Dorothy C. "Women's Studies and Biblical Studies, An Historical Perspective." *Journal for the Study of the Old Testament* 22 (1982): 3–72.

Beecher, Catharine. *Letters on the Difficulties of Religion*. Hartford: Belknap and Hamersley, 1836.

———. *A Treatise on Domestic Economy*. Boston: Source Book Press, 1841.

———. *Woman's Suffrage and Woman's Profession*. Hartford: Brown and Gross, 1871.

Behnke, Donna A. *Religious Issues in Nineteenth-Century Feminism*. Troy, N.Y.: Whitson, 1982.

Bercovitch, Sacvan. *The American Jeremiad*. Madison: University of Wisconsin Press, 1978.

Berk, Stephen E. *Calvinism Versus Democracy: Timothy Dwight and the Origins of American Evangelical Orthodoxy*. Hamden, Conn.: Archon, 1974.

Berkhofer, Robert F. *Salvation and the Savage: An Analysis of Protestant Missions and American Indian Response, 1787–1862*. Lexington: University of Kentucky Press, 1965.

Berkson, Dorothy. "Millennial Politics and the Feminine Fiction of Harriet Beecher Stowe." In *Critical Essays on Harriet Beecher Stowe*. Edited by Elizabeth Ammons. Boston: G. K. Hall, 1980.

Blake, Lillie Devereux. *Woman's Place Today*. New York: J. W. Lowell, 1883.

Booth, Catherine Mumford. "Female Ministry: Or Woman's Right to Preach the Gospel." n.d. In *Holiness Tracts Defending the Ministry of Women*. Edited by Donald Dayton. New York: Garland, 1984.

Bordin, Ruth. *Frances Willard*. Chapel Hill: University of North Carolina Press, 1986.

Bourdieu, Pierre. *Distinction: A Social Critique of the Judgement of Taste*. Translated by Richard Nice. Cambridge: Harvard University Press, 1984.

Boydston, Jeanne. *The Limits of Sisterhood: The Beecher Sisters on Women's Rights and Women's Sphere*. Chapel Hill: University of North Carolina Press, 1988.

Bozeman, Theodore Dwight. *Protestants in an Age of Science: The Baconian Ideal and Antebellum American Religious Thought*. Chapel Hill: University of North Carolina Press, 1978.

Bready, J. Wesley. *England: Before and After Wesley*. London: Hodden and Stoughton, 1939.

Brereton, Virginia Lieson. *From Sin to Salvation: Stories of Women's Conversions, 1800 to the Present*. Bloomington and Indianapolis: Indiana University Press, 1991.

———. "Preparing for the Lord's Work." In *Women in New Worlds: Historical Perspectives on the Weslayan Tradition*. Edited by Hilah F. Thomas and Rosemary Skinner Keller. Nashville: Abingdon Press, 1981–82.

Brereton, Virginia Lieson, and Christa Ressmeyer Klein. "American Women in Ministry: A History of Protestant Beginning Points." In *Women in American Religion.* Edited by Janet James. Philadelphia: University of Pennsylvania Press, 1980.

Brooks, Evelyn. "Feminist Theology of the Black Baptist Church, 1880–1900." In *Class, Race and Sex: The Dynamics of Control.* Edited by Amy Swerdlow and Hanna Lesinger. Boston: G. K. Hall, 1983.

Brooks Higginbotham, Evelyn. *Righteous Discontent: The Women's Movement in the Black Baptist Church, 1880–1920.* Cambridge and London: Harvard University Press, 1993.

Broughton, Virginia. "Twenty Years' Experience of A Missionary." 1907. In *Spiritual Narratives.* Edited by Henry Louis Gates Jr. Introduction by Sue E. Houchins. New York and Oxford: Oxford University Press, 1988.

Brown, Gillian. *Domestic Individualism: Imagining Self in Nineteenth-Century America.* Berkeley and Los Angeles: University of California Press, 1990.

Brown, Jerry Wayne. *The Rise of Biblical Criticism in America, 1800–1870.* Middletown: Wesleyan University Press, 1969.

Buell, Lawrence. "Calvinism Romanticized: Harriet Beecher Stowe, Samuel Hopkins and *The Minister's Wooing.*" In *Critical Essays on Harriet Beecher Stowe.* Edited by Elizabeth Ammons. Boston: G. K. Hall, 1980.

Burnap, George W. *The Sphere and Duties of Woman: A Course of Lectures.* Baltimore: John Murphy, 1848.

Bury, J. B. *A History of Freedom of Thought.* New York: Henry Holt, 1913.

Bushnell, Horace. *Barbarism the First Danger: A Discourse for Home Missions.* New York: William Osborn, 1847.

Bushnell, Katharine. *God's Word to Women — One Hundred Bible Stories on Woman's Place in the Divine Economy.* 1919. Oakland: The Author, 1923.

Butler, Judith. *Bodies That Matter: On the Discursive Limits of "Sex."* New York and London: Routledge, 1993.

Butler, Judith, and Joan W. Scott, eds. *Feminists Theorize the Political.* New York: Routledge, 1991.

Byrne, Donald E. *No Foot of Land: Folklore of American Methodist Itinerants.* Metuchen, N.J.: Scarecrow Press and American Theological Library Association, 1975.

Campbell, Karlyn Kohrs. *Man Cannot Speak for Her: A Critical Study of Early Feminist Rhetoric.* Vol. 2. New York: Praeger, 1989.

Campisi, Jack. "The Emergence of the Mashantucket Pequot Tribe, 1637–1975." In *The Pequots in Southern New England: The Fall and Rise of an American Indian Nation.* Edited by Laurence M. Hauptman and James D. Wherry. Norman and London: University of Oklahoma Press, 1990.

Caraway, Nancie. *Segregated Sisterhood: Racism and the Politics of American Feminism.* Knoxville: University of Tennessee Press, 1991.

Carby, Hazel. *Reconstructing Womanhood: The Emergence of the Afro-American Woman Novelist.* New York: Oxford University Press, 1987.

Caskey, Marie. *Chariot of Fire: Religion and the Beecher Family.* New Haven and London: Yale University Press, 1978.

Chauncy, Charles. *A Letter to the Reverend Mr. George Whitefield.* Boston: n.p., 1745.

Chinosole, "Tryin' to Get Over: Narrative Posture in Equiano's Autobiography." In *The Art of Slave Narrative: Original Essays in Criticism and Theory.* Edited by John Sekora and Darwin T. Turner. Macomb: Western Illinois University Press, 1982.

Chopp, Rebecca S. *The Power to Speak: Feminism, Language, God.* New York: Crossroads, 1989.

Clarke, Adam. *The Holy Bible Containing the Old and New Testaments, the Text Carefully Printed from the Most Correct Copies of the Present Authorized Translation including the Marginal Readings and Parallel Texts with a Commentary and Critical Notes Designed as a Help to a Better Understanding of the Sacred Writings.* London: Joseph Butterworth and Son, 1825.

Clarke, James Freeman. *Ten Great Religions: An Essay in Comparative Theology.* Boston: James R. Osgood, 1872.

Clifford, James. "Identity in Mashpee." *The Predicament of Culture: Twentieth-Century Ethnography, Literature and Art.* Cambridge: Harvard University Press, 1988.

Cmiel, Kenneth. *Democratic Eloquence: The Fight Over Popular Speech in Nineteenth-Century America.* New York: William Morrow, 1990.

Cobbe, Frances Power. *Duties of Women.* 8th American ed. Boston: George Ellis, 1881.

Cogan, Frances B. *All-American Girl: The Ideal of Real Womanhood in Mid-Nineteenth-Century America.* Athens: University of Georgia Press, 1989.

Collins, Adela Yarbro, ed. *Feminist Perspectives on Biblical Scholarship.* Chico, Calif.: Scholars Press, 1985.

Cooley, Winnifred H. *The New Womanhood.* New York: Broadway, 1904.

Costanzo, Angelo. *Surprizing Narrative: Olaudah Equiano and the Beginnings of Black Autobiography.* New York: Greenwood Press, 1987.

Cott, Nancy F. *The Bonds of Womanhood: "Woman's Sphere" in New England, 1780–1835.* New Haven and London: Yale University Press, 1977.

Crozier, Alice C. *The Novels of Harriet Beecher Stowe.* New York: Oxford University Press, 1969.

Dana, Stephen W., D.D. *Woman's Possibilities and Limitations: A Message to the Young Women of To-day.* New York: Fleming H. Revell, 1899.

Dayton, Donald. *Discovering An Evangelical Heritage.* New York: Harper and Row, 1976.

Dayton, Donald, ed. *Holiness Tracts Defending the Ministry of Women.* New York: Garland, 1984.

DeBerg, Betty A. *Ungodly Women: Gender and the First Wave of American Fundamentalism.* Minneapolis: Fortress Press, 1990.

Diaz, Abby Morton. *Only a Flock of Women*. Boston: D. Lothrop Co., 1893.

Dietrick, Ellen Battelle. *Women in the Early Christian Ministry*. Philadelphia: Alfred J. Ferris, 1897.

Dix, Morgan. *Lectures on the Calling of a Christian Woman, and Her Training to Fulfill It*. New York: D. Appleton, 1883.

Doddridge, Philip. *The Rise and Progress of Religion in the Soul*. Philadelphia: T. Seldon, 1788.

Dodge, Mary [Gail Hamilton]. *Woman's Wrongs: A Counter-Irritant*. 1868. New York: Arno Press, 1972.

Dodson, Jualynne E. Introduction to *An Autobiography: The Story of the Lord's Dealings with Mrs. Amanda Smith, the Colored Evangelist*, by Amanda Berry Smith. Edited by Henry Louis Gates Jr. 1893. New York and Oxford: Oxford University Press, 1988.

Douglas, Ann. *The Feminization of American Culture*. New York: Knopf, 1977.

DuBois, Ellen Carol, ed. *Elizabeth Cady Stanton, Susan B. Anthony, Correspondence, Writings, Speeches*. New York: Schocken, 1981.

DuBois, Ellen Carol. *Feminism and Suffrage: The Emergence of An Independent Women's Movement in America, 1848–1869*. Ithaca: Cornell University Press, 1978.

————. "The Limitations of Sisterhood: Elizabeth Cady Stanton and Division in the American Suffrage Movement, 1875–1902." *Women and the Structure of Society: Selected Research from the Fifth Berkshire Conference on the History of Women*. Durham: Duke University Press, 1984.

————. "The Radicalism of the Woman Suffrage Movement: Notes Toward the Reconstruction of Nineteenth-Century Feminism." In *Feminism and Equality*. Edited by Anne Phillips. New York: New York University Press, 1987.

Duren, Charles. "Place of Women in the Church, in Religious Meetings." *Congregational Review* 8, no. 39 (Jan. 1868): 22–29.

Eddy, Daniel Clark. *The Young Woman's Friend: Or, The Duties, Trials, Loves, and Hopes of Woman*. Boston: Wentworth, Hewes, 1859.

Edwards, Jonathan. *Representative Selections*. Edited by Clarence H. Faust and Thomas H. Johnson. New York: Hill and Wang, 1962.

Eisenstein, Zillah. "Elizabeth Cady Stanton: Radical Feminist Analysis and Liberal-Feminist Strategy." *Feminism and Equality*. Edited by Anne Phillips. Oxford: Basil Blackwell, 1987.

Ellis, Mrs. Sarah Stickney. "Daughters and Women." *The Young Lady's Guide*. New York: American Tract Society, 1870.

Epstein, Barbara L. *The Politics of Domesticity: Women, Evangelism and Temperance in Nineteenth-Century America*. Middletown: Weslayan University Press, 1981.

Equiano, Olaudah. "The Interesting Narrative of the Life of Olaudah Equiano or Gustavus Vassa, the African." In *The Classic Slave Narratives*. Edited by Henry Louis Gates Jr. New York: Mentor, 1987.

Fichtelberg, Joseph. "Word Between Worlds: The Economy of Equiano's Narrative." *American Literary History* 5, no. 3 (Fall 1993): 459–80.

Fiorenza, Elisabeth Schüssler. "Transforming the Legacy of *The Woman's Bible.*" *Searching the Scriptures,* Vol. 1, *A Feminist Introduction.* Edited by Elisabeth Schüssler Fiorenza. New York: Crossroads, 1993.

Fischer, Michael M. J. "Ethnicity and the Post-Modern Art of Memory." *Writing Culture: The Poetics and Politics of Ethnography.* Edited by James Clifford and George E. Marcus. Berkeley and Los Angeles: University of California Press, 1986.

Fitzgerald, Maureen. "The Religious Is Personal Is Political: Foreword to the 1993 Edition of *The Woman's Bible.*" *The Woman's Bible by Elizabeth Cady Stanton.* Boston: Northeastern University Press, 1993.

Foote, Julia A. J. "A Brand Plucked From the Fire: An Autobiographical Sketch." 1879. In *Sisters of the Spirit: Three Black Women's Autobiographies of the Nineteenth Century.* Edited by William L. Andrews. Bloomington: Indiana University Press, 1986.

Fortes, Meyer. *Oedipus and Job in West African Religion.* Cambridge: Cambridge University Press, 1959.

Foster, Charles H. *The Rungless Ladder: Harriet Beecher Stowe and New England Puritanism.* Durham: Duke University Press, 1954.

Foucault, Michel. "The Subject and Power." In *Michel Foucault: Beyond Structuralism and Hermeneutics.* Edited by Hubert L. Dreyfus and Paul Rabinow. Chicago: University of Chicago Press, 1982.

Frederic, Harold. *The Damnation of Theron Ware.* 1896. Cambridge: Harvard University Press, 1960.

Frei, Hans. *The Eclipse of Biblical Narrative: A Study in Eighteenth- and Nineteenth-Century Hermeneutics.* New Haven: Yale University Press, 1974.

Gage, Matilda Joslyn. *Woman, Church, and State: A Historical Account of the Status of Woman Through the Christian Ages.* Chicago: C. H. Kerr, 1893.

Gallay, Alan. "The Origins of Slaveholders' Paternalism: George Whitefield, the Bryan Family, and the Great Awakening in the South." *Journal of Southern History* 53, no. 3 (Aug. 1987): 369–94.

Gauvreau, Michael. "The Empire of Evangelicalism: Varieties of Common Sense in Scotland, Canada and the United States." In *Evangelicalism: Comparative Studies of Popular Protestantism in North America, the British Isles, and Beyond, 1700–1990.* Edited by Mark A. Noll, David Bebbington, and George A. Rawlyk. New York: Oxford University Press, 1994.

German, James D. "The Social Utility of Wicked Self-Love: Calvinism, Capitalism, and Public Policy in Revolutionary New England." *Journal of American History* 82 (Dec. 1995): 965–98.

Gifford, Carolyn DeSwarte. "American Women and the Bible: The Nature of Woman As A Hermeneutical Issue." In *Feminist Perspectives on Biblical Scholarship*. Edited by Adela Yarbro Collins. Chico, Calif.: Scholars Press, 1985.

———. "Home Protection: The WCTU's Conversion to Woman Suffrage." In *Gender, Ideology, and Action: HIstorical Perspectives on Women's Public Lives*. Edited by Janet Sharistanian. New York: Greenwood Press, 1986.

———. "Politicizing the Sacred Texts: Elizabeth Cady Stanton and *The Woman's Bible*." In *Searching the Scriptures*, Vol. 1, *A Feminist Introduction*. Edited by Elisabeth Schüssler Fiorenza. New York: Crossroads, 1993.

———. "Sisterhoods of Service and Reform: Organized Methodist Women in Late Nineteenth Century." *Methodist History* 24 (Oct. 1985): 15–30.

Gillies, Rev. John, ed. *Memoirs of the Life of George Whitefield, M. A.* 1772. New Haven: n.p, 1834.

Gilroy, Paul. *The Black Atlantic: Modernity and Double Consciousness*. Cambridge: Harvard University Press, 1993.

Ginzberg, Lori D. *Women and the Work of Benevolence: Morality, Politics and Class in the Nineteenth-Century United States*. New Haven: Yale University Press, 1990.

Gould, Sarah. *A Golden Legacy to Daughters, Or, Advice to Young Ladies*. Boston: Higgins, Bradley and Dayton, 1857.

Gramsci, Antonio. *Prison Notebooks*. New York: Columbia University Press, 1991.

Grant, Robert M. *A Short History of the Interpretation of the Bible*. New York: Macmillan, 1963.

Graves, Albert Phelps. *Twenty-Five Letters to A Young Lady*. Philadelphia: American Baptist Publication Society, 1879.

Griffith, Elisabeth. *In Her Own Right: The Life of Elizabeth Cady Stanton*. New York and Oxford: Oxford University Press, 1984.

Gura, Philip F. *The Wisdom of Words: Language, Theology and Literature in the New England Renaissance*. Middletown: Wesleyan University Press, 1981.

Hanaford, Phebe A. *Daughters of America, Or Women of the Century*. Augusta: True, 1882.

Handy, Robert T. *A Christian America: Protestant Hopes and Historical Realities*. 2nd ed. New York and Oxford: Oxford University Press, 1984.

Haraway, Donna. "Ecce Homo, Ain't (Ar'n't) I a Woman, and Inappropriate/d Others: The Human in a Post-Humanist Landscape." In *Feminists Theorize the Political*. Edited by Judith Butler and Joan W. Scott. New York: Routledge, 1991.

———. "Situated Knowledges: The Science Question in Feminism and the Privilege of Partial Perspective." *Simians, Cyborgs, and Women: The Reinvention of Nature*. New York: Routledge, 1991.

Hardesty, Nancy A. "Minister As Prophet? Or As Mother?" In *Women in New Worlds:*

Historical Perspectives on the Weslayan Tradition. 2 vols. Edited by Hilah F. Thomas and Rosemary Skinner Keller. Nashville: Abingdon Press, 1981–82.

———. *Women Called to Witness: Evangelical Feminism in the Nineteenth Century.* Nashville: Abingdon Press, 1984.

Hardesty, Nancy, Lucille Sider Dayton, and Donald W. Dayton. "Women in the Holiness Movement: Feminism in the Evangelical Tradition." In *Women of Spirit: Female Leadership in the Jewish and Christian Traditions.* Edited by Rosemary Ruether and Eleanor McLaughlin. New York: Simon and Schuster, 1979.

Harper, Ida Husted. *Life and Work of Susan B. Anthony.* 3 vols. Salem, N.H.: Ayer, 1983.

Hassey, Janette. *No Time for Silence: Evangelical Women in Public Ministry Around the Turn of the Century.* Grand Rapids: Academie, 1986.

Hauptman, Laurence M., and James D. Wherry, eds. *The Pequots in Southern New England: The Fall and Rise of an American Indian Nation.* Norman and London: University of Oklahoma Press, 1990.

Hedrick, Joan D. "From Perfection to Suffering: The Religious Experience of Harriet Beecher Stowe." *Women's Studies* 19, nos. 3–4 (1991): 341–56.

———. *Harriet Beecher Stowe: A Life.* New York and Oxford: Oxford University Press, 1994.

———. " 'Peaceable Fruits': The Ministry of Harriet Beecher Stowe." *American Quarterly* 40 (Sept. 1988): 307–32.

Herberg, Will. "Religion and Education" In *Religious Perspectives in American Culture.* Edited by James Ward Smith and A. Leland Jamison. Princeton: Princeton University Press, 1961.

Hewitt, Nancy A. *Women's Activism and Social Change: Rochester, New York, 1822–1872.* Ithaca: Cornell University Press, 1984.

Hietala, Thomas R. *Manifest Design: Anxious Aggrandizement in Late Jacksonian America.* Ithaca and London: Cornell University Press, 1985.

Hill, Suzan E. "*Woman's Bible:* Reformulating Tradition." *Radical Religion* 3, no. 2 (1977): 23–30.

Hodge, A. A. *The Life of Charles Hodge.* New York: Scribner's, 1880.

Hodge, Charles. *Systematic Theology.* 2 vols. New York: Charles Scribner's, 1871.

The Holy Bible: The Authorized or King James Version of 1611. 3 vols. London: Nonesuch, 1963.

Hopkins, Charles Howard. *The Rise of Social Gospel in American Protestantism, 1865–1915.* New Haven: Yale University Press, 1967.

Horsman, Reginald. *Race and Manifest Destiny: The Origins of American Racial Anglo-Saxonism.* Cambridge: Harvard University Press, 1981.

Howe, Daniel W. "American Victorianism as a Culture." *Victorian America.* Edited by Daniel W. Howe. Philadelphia: University of Pennsylvania Press, 1976.

Hudson, Winthrop S. *The Great Tradition of American Churches.* New York: Harper, 1953.

Hudson, Winthrop, ed. *Nationalism and Religion in America: Concepts of Identity and Mission.* New York: Harper and Row, 1970.

Humphrey, Heman. *The Promised Land: A Sermon, Delivered at Goshen, (Conn.) at the Ordination of the Rev. Messrs. Hiram Bingham and Asa Thurston, as Missionaries to the Sandwich Islands, Sept. 29, 1819.* Boston: Samuel T. Armstrong, 1819.

Ingersoll, Robert S. *The Liberty of Man and Other Essays.* London: Watts and Co., 1941.

Jacobs, Harriet. *Incidents in the Life of a Slave Girl.* 1861. Introduction by Valerie Smith. New York: Oxford University Press, 1988.

James, Edward T., ed. *Notable American Women, 1607–1950.* 3 vols. Cambridge: Belknap Press, 1973.

James, Janet, ed. *Women in American Religion.* Philadelphia: University of Pennsylvania Press, 1980.

James, Rev. John Angell. "From 'The Young Woman's Friend.'" *The Young Lady's Guide.* New York: American Tract Society, 1870.

Johnson, Allen, ed. *Dictionary of American Biography.* 15 vols. New York: Scribner, 1929.

Johnson, Ellwood. *The Pursuit of Power: Studies in the Vocabulary of Puritanism.* New York: Peter Lang, 1995.

Johnson, Paul E. *A Shopkeeper's Millennium: Society and Revivals in Rochester, New York, 1815–1837.* New York: Hill and Wang, 1978.

Jordan, Judith. "Courage in Connection: Conflict, Compassion, Creativity." Work in Progress, No. 45. Wellesley: Stone Center Working Paper Series, 1990.

———. "Empathy and the Mother-Daughter Relationship." Colloquium: Women and Enpathy — Implications for Psychological Development and Psychotherapy — Work in Progress, No. 82–02. Wellesley: Stone Center Working Paper Series, 1983.

———. "Empathy and Self-Boundaries." In *Women's Growth in Connection: Writings from the Stone Center.* Edited by Judith Jordan, et al. New York and London: Guilford Press, 1991.

———. "The Meaning of Mutuality." In *Women's Growth in Connection: Writings from the Stone Center.* Edited by Judith Jordan, et al. New York and London: Guilford Press, 1991.

———. "Relational Development: Therapeutic Implications of Empathy and Shame." Work in Progress, No. 39. Wellesley: Stone Center Working Paper Series, 1989.

Jordan, Judith, et al., eds. *Women's Growth in Connection: Writings from the Stone Center.* New York and London: Guilford Press, 1991.

Juster, Susan. "'In A Different Voice': Male and Female Narratives of Religious Conversion in Post-Revolutionary America." *American Quarterly* 41 (Mar. 1989): 40–48.

Kaplan, Alexandra. "Empathy and Its Vicissitudes." Empathy Revisited: Work in Progress, No. 40. Edited by Janet Surrey, Alexandra Kaplan, and Judith Jordan. Wellesley: Stone Center Working Paper Series, 1990.

Kerber, Linda K. "Separate Spheres, Female Worlds, Woman's Place: The Rhetoric of Women's History." *Journal of American History* 75 (June 1988): 9–39.

Kern, Kathi L. "Rereading Eve: Elizabeth Cady Stanton and the 'Woman's Bible.'" *Women's Studies* 19, nos. 3–4 (1990): 371–83.

Kimball, Gayle. *The Religious Ideas of Harriet Beecher Stowe: Her Gospel of Womanhood.* New York: Mellen Press, 1982.

Kleppner, Paul. *The Third Electoral System, 1853–1892: Parties, Voters, and Political Cultures.* Chapel Hill: University of North Carolina Press, 1979.

Kraditor, Aileen. *The Ideas of the Woman Suffrage Movement, 1890–1920.* New York and London: Columbia University Press, 1965.

Kraditor, Aileen, ed. *Up From the Pedestal: Selected Writings in the History of American Feminism.* Chicago: Quadrangle, 1968.

Krupat, Arnold. *The Voice in the Margin: Native American Literature and the Canon.* Berkeley and Los Angeles: University of California Press, 1989.

Lambert, Frank. *"Pedlar in Divinity": George Whitefield and the Transatlantic Revivals, 1737–1770.* Princeton: Princeton University Press, 1994.

Lee, Rev. Luther. "Woman's Right to Preach the Gospel. A Sermon, Preached at the Ordination of the Reverend Miss Antoinette L. Brown." 1853. In *Holiness Tracts Defending the Ministry of Women.* Edited by Donald Dayton. New York: Garland, 1984.

Livermore, Mary A. *What Shall We Do With Our Daughters?* New York: Charles T. Dillingham, 1883; New York and London: Garland, 1987.

Loeffelholz, Mary. "Posing the Woman Citizen: The Contradictions in Stanton's Feminism." *Genders* 7 (Mar. 1990): 87–98.

Lutz, Alma. *Created Equal: A Biography of Elizabeth Cady Stanton.* New York: John Day, 1940.

Lystra, Karen. *Searching the Heart: Women, Men, and Romantic Love in Nineteenth-Century America.* New York: Oxford University Press, 1989.

Marrant, John. *A Narrative of the Lord's Wonderful Dealings with John Marrant.* 1785. New York: Garland, 1978.

Marren, Susan. "Between Slavery and Freedom: The Transgressive Self in Olaudah Equiano's Autobiography." *PMLA* 108 (Jan. 1993): 94–105.

Marsden, George. *Fundamentalism and American Culture: The Shaping of Twentieth-Century Evangelicalism, 1870–1925.* New York: Oxford University Press, 1980.

Massa, Mark Stephen. *Charles Augusta Briggs and the Crisis of Historical Criticism.* Minneapolis: Fortress Press, 1990.

Mavor, James W., Jr., and Byron E. Dix. *Manitou: The Sacred Landscape of New England's Native Civilization.* Rochester: Inner Traditions International, 1989.

McCray, Florine T. *The Life-Work of the Author of Uncle Tom's Cabin.* New York: Funk and Wagnalls, 1889.

McLoughlin, William, ed. *The American Evangelicals, 1800–1900.* New York: Harper and Row, 1968.

————. *The Meaning of Henry Ward Beecher: An Essay on the Shifting Values of Mid-Victorian America.* New York: Knopf, 1970.

McQuaid, Kim. "William Apess, Pequot: An Indian Reformer in the Jackson Era." *New England Quarterly* 50 (1977): 605–25.

Mead, Sidney. *The Nation With the Soul of a Church.* Macon: Mercer University Press, 1985.

Merk, Frederick. *Manifest Destiny and Mission in American History: A Reinterpretation.* New York: Knopf, 1963.

Meyer, D. H. *The Instructed Conscience: The Shaping of the American National Ethic.* Philadelphia: University of Pennsylvania Press, 1972.

Miller, Jean Baker. "The Development of Women's Sense of Self." In *Women's Growth in Connection: Writings from the Stone Center.* Edited by Judith Jordan, et al. New York and London: Guilford Press, 1991.

Miller, Leo. *Woman and the Divine Republic.* Buffalo: Haas and Nauert, 1874.

Miller, Samuel. *Letters on Clerical Manners and Habits: Addressed to a Student in the Theological Seminary at Princeton, N.J.* New York: G. & C. Carvill, 1827.

More, Mrs. Hannah. "Excerpt." *The Young Lady's Guide.* New York: American Tract Society, 1870.

Murphy, Geraldine. "Olaudah Equiano, Accidental Tourist." *Eighteenth-Century Studies* 27 (Summer 1994): 551–68.

Newcomb, Harvey. *Christian Character: A Book for Young Ladies.* London and New York: T. Nelson, 1856.

Nielsen, Donald M. "The Mashpee Indian Revolt of 1833." *New England Quarterly* 58 (1985): 400–420.

Noll, Mark A. *Between Faith and Criticism: Evangelicals, Scholarship and the Bible in America.* San Francisco: Harper and Row, 1986.

————. "Common Sense Traditions and American Evangelical Thought." *American Quarterly* 37 (1985): 218–35.

Noll, Mark A., ed. *Religion and American Politics: From the Colonial Period to the 1980s.* New York and Oxford: Oxford University Press, 1990.

Noll, Mark A., David Bebbington, and George A. Rawlyk, eds. *Evangelicalism: Comparative Studies of Popular Protestantism in North America, the British Isles, and Beyond, 1700–1990.* New York: Oxford University Press, 1994.

Noll, Mark A., and Nathan O. Hatch, eds. *The Bible in America: Essays in Cultural History.* New York: Oxford University Press, 1982.

Nuttall, Geoffrey. "The Influence of Arminianism in England." *The Puritan Spirit: Essays and Addresses.* London: Epworth Press, 1967.

O'Connell, Barry. Introduction to *On Our Own Ground: The Complete Writings of*

William Apess, a Pequot. Edited by Barry O'Connell. Amherst: University of Massachusetts Press, 1992.

O'Neill, William L. *Everyone Was Brave: A History of American Feminism in America.* Chicago: Quadrangle, 1969.

Orban, Katalin. "Dominant and Submerged Discourses in The Life of Olaudah Equiano (or Gustavus Vassa?)." *African American Review* 27, no. 4 (Winter 1993): 655–64.

O'Reilly, Bernard. *The Mirror of True Womanhood: A Book of Instruction for Women in the World.* New York: Peter F. Collier, 1881.

Painter, Nell Irvin. "Difference, Slavery, and Memory: Sojourner Truth in Feminist Abolitionism." In *The Abolitionist Sisterhood: Women's Political Culture in Antebellum America.* Edited by Jean Fagan Yellin and John C. Van Horne. Ithaca and London: Cornell University Press, 1994.

Parker, Theodore. *Theodore Parker's Experience as a Minister.* Boston: Leighton, 1860.

Peck, Jesse T., D.D. *The True Woman; Or, Life and Happiness At Home and Abroad.* New York: Carlton and Porter, 1857.

Pellauer, Mary D. *Toward a Tradition of Feminist Theology: The Religious Thought of Elizabeth Cady Stanton, Susan B. Anthony, and Anna Howard Shaw.* Brooklyn: Carlson, 1991.

penelope, julia. *Speaking Freely: Unlearning the Lies of Fathers' Tongues.* New York: Pergamon Press, 1990.

Peters, Charles, ed. *The Girl's Own Indoor Book.* Philadelphia: J. B. Lippincott, 1892.

Phillips, Anne, ed. *Feminism and Equality.* New York: New York University Press, 1987.

Pleck, Elizabeth. "Feminist Responses to 'Crimes Against Women,' 1868–1896." *Signs* 8 (Spring 1983): 451–470.

Potkay, Adam. "Olaudah Equiano and the Art of Spiritual Autobiography." *Eighteenth-Century Studies* 27, no. 4 (Summer 1994): 677–92.

Richey, Russell E. *Early American Methodism.* Bloomington and Indianapolis: Indiana University Press, 1991.

Roberts, B[enjamin] T[itus]. *Ordaining Women.* Rochester: "The Earnest Christian" Publication House, 1891.

Rogers, Jack B., and Donald D. McKim. *The Authority and Interpretation of the Bible.* New York: Harper and Row, 1979.

Rothenberg, Albert. *The Emerging Goddess: The Creative Process in Art, Science and Other Fields.* Chicago: University of Chicago Press, 1979.

Ruether, Rosemary, and Eleanor McLaughlin, eds. *Women of Spirit: Female Leadership in the Jewish and Christian Traditions.* New York: Simon and Schuster, 1979.

Ruttenberg, Nancy. "George Whitefield, Spectacular Conversion, and the Rise of Democratic Personality." *American Literary History* 5, no. 3 (Fall 1993): 429–58.

Ryan, Mary P. "A Women's Awakening: Evangelical Religion and the Families of Utica, New York, 1800–1840." In *Women in American Religion.* Edited by Janet James. Philadelphia: University of Pennsylvania Press, 1980.

————. *Women in Public: Between Banners and Ballots, 1825–1880.* Baltimore and London: Johns Hopkins University Press, 1990.

Saillant, John. "Slavery and Divine Providence in New England Calvinism: The New Divinity and a Black Protest, 1775–1805." *New England Quarterly* 68, no. 4 (Dec. 1995): 584–608.

Sale, Maggie. "Antebellum Projects of Protest." *American Literature* 64, no. 4 (Dec. 1992): 695–718.

Salisbury, Neal. *Manitou and Providence: Indians, Europeans, and the Making of New England, 1500–1643.* New York: Oxford University Press, 1982.

Samuels, Wilfred. D. "Disguised Voice in The Interesting Narrative of Olaudah Equiano, or Gustavus Vassa, the African." *Black American Literature Forum* 19 (Summer 1985): 64–69.

Sandeen, Ernest R. *The Roots of Fundamentalism: British and American Millenarianism, 1800–1930.* Chicago and London: University of Chicago Press, 1970.

Sandiford, Keith. *Measuring the Moment: Strategies of Protest in Eighteenth-Century Afro-English Writing.* Selinsgrove: Susquehanna University Press, 1988.

Schmidt, Jean Miller. "Reexamining the Public-Private Split: Reforming the Continent and Spreading Scriptural Holiness." In *Rethinking Methodist History.* Edited by Russell Richey and Kenneth Rowe. Nashville: Kingswood Books, 1985.

Schneider, A. Gregory. *The Way of the Cross Leads Home: The Domestication of American Methodism.* Bloomington and Indianapolis: Indiana University Press, 1993.

Scofield Reference Bible. The Holy Bible, Containing the Old and New Testaments. New York: Oxford University Press, 1917.

Sedgwick, Eve Kosofsky. "Shame and Performativity: Henry James's New York Edition Prefaces." In *Henry James's New York Editions: The Construction of Authorship.* Edited by David McWhirter. Stanford: Stanford University Press, 1995.

Sedgwick, Eve Kosofsky, and Adam Frank. "Shame in the Cybernetic Fold: Reading Silvan Tomkins." In *Shame and Its Sisters: A Silvan Tomkins Reader,* by Silvan Tomkins. Edited by Eve Kosofsky Sedgwick and Adam Frank. Durham and London: Duke University Press, 1995.

Shaw, Susan Jean. "A Religious History of Julia Evelina Smith's 1876 Translation of the Holy Bible." Ph.D. diss., Drew University, 1991.

Simmons, William S. "The Mystic Voice: Pequot Folklore from the Seventeenth Century to the Present." In *The Pequots in Southern New England: The Fall and Rise of an American Indian Nation.* Edited by Laurence M. Hauptman and James D. Wherry. Norman and London: University of Oklahoma Press, 1990.

Sizer, Sandra S. *Gospel Hymns and Social Religion: The Rhetoric of Nineteenth-Century Revivalism.* Philadelphia: Temple University Press, 1978.

Sklar, Kathryn Kish. *Catharine Beecher: A Study in American Domesticity.* New Haven and London: Yale University Press, 1973.

Smith, Amanda Berry. *An Autobiography: The Story of the Lord's Dealings with Mrs. Amanda Smith, the Colored Evangelist.* 1893. Edited by Henry Louis Gates Jr. Introduction by Jualynne E. Dodson. New York and Oxford: Oxford University Press, 1988.

Smith, Elizabeth Oakes. "Woman and Her Needs." 1851. In *Women in America: From Colonial Times to the Twentieth Century.* Edited by Leon Stein and Annette K. Baxter. New York: Arno Press, 1974.

Smith, Hannah Whitall. *A Christian's Secret of a Happy Life.* 1870. Westwood: Barbour, 1985.

Smith, James Ward, and A. Leland Jamison, eds. *Religious Perspectives in American Culture.* Princeton: Princeton University Press, 1961.

Sollors, Werner, and Maria Diedrich, eds. *The Black Columbiad: Defining Moments in African-American Literature and Culture.* Cambridge and London: Harvard University Press, 1994.

Solomon, Martha M., ed. *A Voice of Their Own: The Woman Suffrage Press, 1840–1910.* Tuscaloosa and London: University of Alabama Press, 1991.

Spacks, Patricia. *Gossip.* New York: Knopf, 1985.

Stachniewski, John. *The Persecutory Imagination: English Puritanism and the Literature of Religious Despair.* Oxford: Clarendon Press, 1991.

Stansell, Christine. *City of Women: Sex and Class in New York, 1789–1860.* New York: Knopf, 1986.

Stanton, Elizabeth Cady. *Bible and Church Degrade Women.* Chicago: H. L. Green, 1894.

———. *Elizabeth Cady Stanton as revealed in her letters, diary and reminiscences.* Edited by Theodore Stanton and Harriot Stanton Blatch. New York: Harper, 1922.

———. "Has Christianity Benefitted Woman?" *North American Review* 14 (May 1885): n. pag.

———. *The Original Feminist Attack on the Bible: (The Woman's Bible).* Introduction by Barbara Welter. New York: Arno Press, 1974.

Stanton, Elizabeth Cady, Susan B. Anthony, and Matilda Joslyn Gage, eds. *History of Woman Suffrage.* 6 vols. New York: Fowler and Wells, 1881–1922.

Starna, William A. "The Pequots in Early Seventeenth Century." In *The Pequots in Southern New England: The Fall and Rise of an American Indian Nation.* Edited by Laurence M. Hauptman and James D. Wherry. Norman and London: University of Oklahoma Press, 1990.

Stearns, Peter. *Be a Man! Males in Modern Society.* New York: Holmes and Meier, 1979.

Stetson, Erlene, and Linda David. *Glorying in Tribulation: The Lifework of Sojourner Truth.* East Lansing: Michigan State University Press, 1994.

Stewart, Charles J., Craig Allen Smith, and Robert E. Denton Jr. *Persuasion and Social Movements.* 2nd ed. 1984. Prospect Heights: Waveland Press, 1989.

Stewart, Maria. "Productions of Mrs. Maria W. Stewart." 1835. *Spiritual Narratives.* Edited by Henry Louis Gates Jr. Introduction by Sue E. Houchins. New York and Oxford: Oxford University Press, 1988.

Stout, Harry S. *The Divine Dramatist: George Whitefield and the Rise of Modern Evangelicalism.* Grand Rapids: William B. Eerdmans, 1991.

Stowe, Harriet Beecher. *The Minister's Wooing.* New York: Derby and Jackson, 1859.

———. *Uncle Tom's Cabin.* 1851–52. New York: Bantam, 1981.

Sundquist, Eric J., ed. *New Essays on Uncle Tom's Cabin.* Cambridge: Cambridge University Press, 1986.

Surrey, Janet. "Empathy: Evolving Theoretical Perspectives." Empathy Revisited: Work in Progress, No. 40. Edited by Janet Surrey, Alexandra Kaplan and Judith Jordan. Wellesley: Stone Center Working Paper Series, 1990.

———. "Relationship and Empowerment." In *Women's Growth in Connection: Writings from the Stone Center.* Edited by Judith Jordan, et al. New York and London: Guilford Press, 1991.

Szasz, Ferenc Morton. *The Divided Mind of Protestant America, 1880–1930.* University: University of Alabama Press, 1982.

Thayer, William M. *The Good Girl and True Woman; Or, Elements of Success.* 1858. Boston: Gould and Lincoln, 1866.

Thomas, George M. *Revivalism and Cultural Change: Christianity, Nation Building, and the Market in the Nineteenth-Century United States.* Chicago: University of Chicago Press, 1989.

Thomas, Hilah F., and Rosemary Skinner Keller, eds. *Women in New Worlds: Historical Perspectives on the Weslayan Tradition.* 2 vols. Nashville: Abingdon Press, 1981–82.

Tomkins, Silvan. *Shame and Its Sisters: A Silvan Tomkins Reader.* Edited by Eve Kosofsky Sedgwick and Adam Frank. Durham and London: Duke University Press, 1995.

Tompkins, Jane. *Sensational Designs: The Cultural Work of American Fiction, 1790–1860.* New York: Oxford University Press, 1986.

Tonkovich, Nicole. "Advice Books." *Oxford Companion to Women's Writing in the United States.* Edited by Cathy Davidson and Linda Wagner-Martin. New York: Oxford University Press, 1995.

Truth, Sojourner. *Narrative of Sojourner Truth; A Bondswoman of Olden Time, With a History of Her Labors and Correspondence Drawn from Her "Book of Life."* Edited by Henry Louis Gates Jr. Introduction by Jeffrey C. Stewart. New York and Oxford: Oxford University Press, 1991.

Tyler, Sarah. "Papers for Thoughtful Girls." *The Young Lady's Guide.* New York: American Tract Society, 1870.

Vineyard, H. K. *Woman Neglected in Education and the Causes and Effects.* Knoxville: Ogden Brothers, 1886.

Wacker, Grant. "The Demise of Biblical Civilization" In *The Bible in America: Essays in Cultural History.* Edited by Mark A. Noll and Nathan O. Hatch. New York: Oxford University Press, 1982.

Warfield, Benjamin B. *An Introduction to the Textual Criticism of the New Testament.* New York: Thomas Whittaker, 1887.

Weber, Timothy P. "The Two-Edged Sword: The Fundamentalist Use of the Bible." In *The Bible in America: Essays in Cultural History.* Edited by Mark A. Noll and Nathan O. Hatch. New York: Oxford University Press, 1982.

Weisenfeld, Judith. "We Have Been Believers: Patterns of African- American Women's Religiosity." In *This Far By Faith: Readings in African-American Women's Religious Biography.* Edited by Judith Weisenfeld and Richard Newman. New York and London: Routledge, 1996.

Weisenfeld, Judith, and Richard Newman, eds. *This Far By Faith: Readings in African-American Women's Religious Biography.* New York and London: Routledge, 1996.

Weiss, Ellen. *City in the Woods: The Life and Design of an American Camp Meeting on Martha's Vineyard.* New York and Oxford: Oxford University Press, 1987.

Welter, Barbara. *Dimity Convictions: The American Woman in the Nineteenth Century.* Athens: Ohio University Press, 1976.

———. "Introduction." In *The Original Feminist Attack on the Bible: (The Woman's Bible),* by Elizabeth Cady Stanton. New York: Arno Press, 1974.

———. "She Hath Done What She Could: Protestant Women's Missionary Careers in Nineteenth-Century America." In *Women in American Religion.* Edited by Janet James. Philadelphia: University of Pennsylvania Press, 1980.

Whitefield, George. *George Whitefield's Journals (1737–1741).* Introduction by William V. Davis. Gainesville: Scholars' Facsimiles and Reprints, 1969.

———. *Three Letters from the Reverend Mr. G. Whitefield.* Philadelphia: n.p., 1740.

Wilcox, Ella Wheeler. *Men, Women and Emotions.* Chicago: W. B. Conkey, 1893.

Wilde, Oscar. *The Rise of Historical Criticism.* 1905. Folcroft: Folcroft Press, 1969.

Willard, Frances E. *Glimpses of Fifty Years: The Autobiography of An American Woman.* Introduction by Hannah Whitall Smith. Boston: G. M. Smith, 1889.

———. "How to Win: A Book for Girls." 1886. In *Women in American Protestant Religion.* Vol. 5. Edited by Carolyn De Swarte Gifford. New York and London: Garland, 1987.

———. *Woman in the Pulpit.* 1889. Washington D.C.: Zenger, 1978.

Willard, Frances, and Mary Livermore, eds. *A Woman of the Century.* 1893. Detroit: Gale, 1967.

Winslow, Hubbard, and Mrs. John Sanford. *The Benison: The Lady's Manual of Moral and Intellectual Culture.* New York: Leavitt and Allen, 1854.

Wise, Daniel. "Bridal Greetings: A Marriage Gift In Which the Mutual Duties of Husband and Wife Are Familiarly Illustrated and Enforced." 1851. In *The American Ideal of the "True Woman": Women in American Protestant Religion.* Edited by Carolyn De Swarte Gifford. New York: Garland, 1987.

————. "The Young Lady's Counsellor, Or, Outlines and Illustrations of the Sphere, the Duties, and the Dangers of Young Women." 1855. In *The American Ideal of the "True Woman": Women in American Protestant Religion.* Edited by Carolyn De Swarte Gifford. New York: Garland, 1987.

Wolff, Cynthia G. "Emily Dickinson, Elizabeth Cady Stanton and the Task of Discovering a Usable Past." *Massachusetts Review* 30 (Winter 1989): 629–44.

Wood, Forrest G. *The Arrogance of Faith: Christianity and Race in American from the Colonial Era to the Twentieth Century.* New York: Knopf, 1990.

Woolson, Abba Gould. *Woman in American Society.* Boston: Roberts Brothers, 1873.

Yellin, Jean Fagan, and John C. Van Horne, eds. *The Abolitionist Sisterhood: Women's Political Culture in Antebellum America.* Ithaca and London: Cornell University Press, 1994.

The Young Lady's Guide. New York: American Tract Society, 1870.

Zikmund, Barbara B. "Biblical Arguments and Women's Place in the Church." In *The Bible and Social Reform.* Edited by Ernest R. Sandeen. Philadelphia: Fortress Press, 1982.

Index